PRAISE FOR *HOW TO BEHAVE BADLY IN RENAISSANCE BRITAIN*

'Impeccable ... [Goodman's] research is as comprehensive as the advice she metes out to those wishing to emulate the bad behaviour of their ancestors.'

Tracy Borman, *BBC History Magazine*

'This is a masterclass of bad behaviour ... a lively romp through early modern British social history.'

Who Do You Think You Are? magazine

'Entertaining.'

History Revealed magazine

PRAISE FOR *HOW TO BE A TUDOR*

'This book is packed with delicious kernels of knowledge ... all served up by the most delightfully eccentric author I've ever encountered.'

The Times

'Always entertaining, and her narrative is often lifted by the fact that she has taken the trouble to experience many of the alien aspects of Tudor life.'

Observer

'Goodman's latest foray into immersive history is a revelation ... It's the next best thing to being there.'

New York Times Book Review

'A deeply researched and endlessly fascinating account of what it was like to live as a Tudor. The narrative is rich in period detail and based upon a thorough review of the contemporary sources, but what makes it unique is the fact that Goodman has put it all into practice – sleeping, eating, washing and dressing like a Tudor. [It] is one of very few books which can justifiably claim to bring every aspect of this enduringly popular period dazzlingly to life.'

Tracy Borman

'[Goodman's] enthusiasm is exhilarating and contagious.'
Kate Tuttle, *Boston Globe*

'Riveting. This is a real "people's history" that takes us straight into the sensate feelings of ordinary life – the feel, touch, smells and labour of people living five centuries ago, giving an earthy reality to our enduring fascination with the Tudors.'
Juliet Gardiner

PRAISE FOR *HOW TO BE A VICTORIAN*

'I absolutely love this book. Exuberant, absorbing.'
A. N. Wilson, *Mail on Sunday*

'Ruth – a woman who possesses so much elbow grease that she could probably can the overflow to sell on the side.'
Independent

'Written with such passion that one cannot help but be carried along ... Will fascinate and inform anyone who is in any way interested in Victorian ways of life.'
Ian Mortimer

'Makes you feel as if you could pass as a native.'
New Yorker

'If the past is a foreign country because they do things differently there, we're lucky to have such a knowledgeable cicerone as Ruth Goodman.'
Wall Street Journal

THE DOMESTIC REVOLUTION

How the Introduction of Coal into
Our Homes Changed Everything

RUTH GOODMAN

Michael O'Mara Books Limited

First published in Great Britain in 2020 by
Michael O'Mara Books Limited
9 Lion Yard
Tremadoc Road
London SW4 7NQ

A CIP catalogue record for this book is available from the British Library.

Papers used by Michael O'Mara Books Limited are natural, recyclable products
made from wood grown in sustainable forests. The manufacturing processes
conform to the environmental regulations of the country of origin.

ISBN: 978-1-782438-50-2 in hardback print format
ISBN: 978-1-782438-53-3 in ebook format

Every reasonable effort has been made to trace copyright holders.
Any errors or omissions that may have occurred are inadvertent, and anyone
with any copyright queries is invited to write to the publisher, so that full
acknowledgement may be included in subsequent editions of this work.

Printed and bound by CPI Group (UK) Ltd, Croydon, CR0 4YY

MIX
Paper from
responsible sources
FSC® C020471

To all those who have ever swept
the ashes from a hearth

CONTENTS

FOREWORD

Lived History

About ten years ago, for the purpose of making a TV programme, I found myself standing in front of a newly refitted coal-fired iron range. It was part of a semi-derelict cottage into which we'd already put a huge amount of work – rebuilding a staircase, replastering walls, renewing windows and doors, and re-laying a floor. We then inserted a salvaged range, giving it a thorough overhaul before gently easing it into its new home. Brickwork was adjusted around it, then all the gaps were sealed. We gathered round as the first fire was lit and became a tad overexcited when smoke began issuing from the chimney, with barely a wisp visible in the kitchen.

The programme we were making required me and my two colleagues to run a small farm for a year in the manner typical of British people in the second half of the nineteenth century. As the woman on the team, and following on from Victorian practice, this black metal box and its dirty black fuel were to be my responsibility. I had never cooked on coal before. I did, however, have a great deal of experience working with wood fires, including for a previous TV series that had run for a year, as well as twenty years' worth of weekends and short breaks in various structures and open spaces. I felt fairly confident that a coal range would be well within my capabilities. Well, I managed it – but the encounter was much more challenging and interesting than I had anticipated. And it was one that encompassed much more than cooking.

The radically different practices involved in running a coal-fired home in comparison to running a wood-fired one took me completely by surprise. So many things that I had taken for granted suddenly became immediate and pressing issues. The challenges that I was facing, and the adjustments I was having to make as I learnt to deal with coal, were wide-reaching. When I considered the impact such changes must have had, when multiplied by the number of households that had made these changes in the past, it was mind-boggling. I began to realize that the usual narratives about the development of the home, the countryside and the modern industrial world were missing something: the big switch to domestic coal in the late sixteenth and early seventeenth centuries.

In many ways I was in a highly unusual position. Most people experimenting with the use of coal as a fuel are approaching the problem from a modern perspective, making comparisons with gas and electricity. Our attitudes and assumptions are necessarily backwards-looking. But much of my experience came from older technologies; I have probably cooked more meals over a wood fire than I have over gas or electric cookers. I have certainly cleaned more houses heated by open wood fires than those with central heating, and long ago adapted my laundry regime to something inspired by earlier methods. My engagement with the great outdoors was almost entirely framed by historical experiment and experience, with weekends spent felling trees with axes and cross-cut saws, coppicing patches of woodland, building period styles of fencing and growing heirloom plants. Looking at the world through wood-burning eyes was second nature to me. From this vantage, it was obvious to me that the switch to coal would have had a huge impact on the daily routines of people from all walks of life.

I first became aware that some of the practical skills I was learning could genuinely form a useful addition to the scholarly understanding of this history when I was invited to help out some twenty years ago at the Mary Rose Trust. This charity is charged with caring for the archaeological remains of Henry VIII's flagship, which sank as he watched from the shore in the strait between the Isle of Wight and the English mainland on 19 July 1545. The excavation of the flagship's remains had revealed two brick structures sitting upon some loose gravel ballast at the ship's bottom, on either side of the central keel beam. These were assumed to be the galleys. However, when the ship reached the seabed upon that fateful day nearly five hundred years ago, it had tipped over onto one side, sending one of the two galley structures crashing over on top of the other. The excavations had thus mostly uncovered a mass of rubble. The trust had launched a project to reconstruct the cooking facilities and provide a better picture of life on board a mid-Tudor warship.

A great deal of thought and effort went into the work. Bricks, mortar, iron bars, flashings and metal pots were sampled and analysed. Reconstructions were made using techniques and materials that were as close to those available in the original period as possible. Wherever the original form had survived the passage of time, it was closely copied. The structures were square in plan, with an open firebox door on one side, and each held a single large metal pot supported in part by two iron bars. When I saw them I thought they resembled the laundry coppers common in outhouses in Edwardian days, although they did not have the iron grate and iron door usually found in these more recent domestic conveniences.

When all of the building work was completed, I was invited to reconstruct how the cooking structure might have been used.

I had at that point about ten years' experience with sixteenth-century kitchen equipment, utilizing both wood and charcoal, and I had been researching and practising the techniques and recipes of the era. I couldn't wait to get cooking.

My first meeting with the project's lead archaeologist was exciting. I learnt that not only had the two galley structures survived, albeit in fragmentary form, but so too had an array of cooking vessels and equipment: barrels with the remains of butchered meat and fish, a scattering of grains, various other plant materials including whole peppercorns and, perhaps most remarkable of all, the firewood to cook it upon. I was extremely eager to see this mass of physical evidence. But to begin, I was handed the team's drawings of the reconstructed galley.

'Oh, it's got a flue!' I exclaimed. I was quite surprised by this development. All of my previous work had indicated that flues and chimneys were rarely introduced into ovens, kilns, furnaces and other enclosed fireboxes when wood was burnt. Practical experience had shown me flues and chimneys were, in most cases, not only unnecessary but actively counterproductive as, along with the smoke, they channelled all of the heat up and away from where it was wanted. I wanted to see the photos of the underwater excavation site to get a sense for the dimensions and shape of these remarkable survivals. What was special about shipboard conditions, I wondered, that made a flue desirable?

The answer, it turned out, was *nothing*. The reconstruction team had simply assumed there must have been a flue. Since there was no sign of any metal or brick cowling or chimney, they guessed a vent had been situated at the top of each cooking structure's brickwork and had not survived the wreck. It was not such a preposterous assumption. Many old ovens and kilns had flues – but these ovens and kilns dated to the nineteenth and twentieth centuries, and they had burnt coal, not wood.

Over a series of visits, I was able to demonstrate how the fuel, fire and structure worked, both with the contentious flue in place and with it sealed up. When we filled a cauldron with water and lit a fire within the furnace with the flue in place, the experience was dismal. Four and a half hours of vigorous flame barely brought the pot of water to a simmer. Meanwhile, the air temperature around the vent was scorchingly hot – too hot in fact for our thermometer to register; we were past the top of the scale after fifteen minutes. When we blocked up the flue, the same volume of water was brought to the boil very much faster – in just forty-five minutes in one run-through, where the wood was well dried-out and we covered the pot with a wooden lid. When the flue was blocked, the fire's smoke and heat had to exit the cooking structure through the opening at the front. Here temperatures hovered around 200° to 250° C, but the heat was centred in a small sphere of about 6 inches (15 cm) in diameter. The air rapidly cooled to 150° C within 12 inches (30 cm) of the opening, and to about 80° C at ceiling height.

The physics is fairly straightforward. A flue creates a through-draught, which draws a large percentage of the heat up. Keeping that heat contained within a narrow channel maintains the high temperature of the exhaust gases. An oven-shaped space in which gases enter and exit by a single opening at the side has a much slower flow of air and smoke. More of the heat generated by combustion is trapped within the chamber, and the exhaust gases, when they do exit, having a wider escape route, dissipate their heat much more quickly. Flues of any sort were rare before coal became our preferred fuel.

Putting the *Mary Rose*'s galley to use allowed us to make other, unexpected discoveries. During one public demonstration, a member of the archaeological team approached to ask about a pell – a sort of flat wooden shovel – that I and some friends were using to pop a loaf of bread into the ship's reconstructed firebox. Though the galley was not primarily designed for baking, we were explaining how it could have been pressed into action to fulfil this function on a small scale, perhaps when the ship was at anchor and the captain was entertaining. 'I've just catalogued something very like that as an oar,' confessed the archaeologist. 'I wondered what it was doing at the bottom of the ship, next to the galley.' There is of course no way of being sure 'something very like that' was used as either an oar or a pell (or perhaps pressed into service for both purposes, depending on the demands of any given day). But such practical experience helps to open up the way we look at what the past has left behind for us.

Whether by putting the *Mary Rose*'s galley to use or by stoking a Victorian-era oven or popping a loaf of bread into a Tudor warship's firebox, I have gathered a great deal of practical experience in history as it was lived, and so I come to the subject of coal in the home from a very different angle to those who have studied the history of coal mining and production, or the history of the home in Britain. I started with a different set of questions and found beguiling new answers.

What I stumbled across is a quiet change in the way life was lived, a change that has had a profound effect upon history and continues to have relevance to this day. When we look more deeply and carefully, we can see the many traces and scars of the momentous change to burning coal in the home.

INTRODUCTION

The Big Switch

When Queen Elizabeth came to the throne in 1558, England and Wales were wood-burning nations. Scotland and Ireland used considerably more peat – the compacted, partly decayed plant matter collected across the bogs – but wood fuel also prevailed in both places. And fuel consumption followed much the same pattern around the rest of the globe. To keep warm and cook our food, people burnt wood.

By 1603, London's air had acquired a sulphurous tang – coal's calling card. Coal smoke and fumes were already caught in the basin of the River Thames, hanging over the city in the smog which has distinguished the metropolis for much of its recorded history. This gathering smog signified the start of something completely new and unexpected: the big switch in people's fuel consumption.

For millennia, the vast majority of the energy people harnessed was derived from short-term, renewable plant-based sources such as trees, bushes and scrubs, with reeds and grasses, or dung from plant-eating animals, being pressed into service here and there. These were occasionally supplemented, on a much smaller scale, by the medium-term stored energy of peat. It was a way of living that the historical demographer Edward Anthony Wrigley called an 'organic economy'. People were reliant upon the vegetation that grew around them for their fuel, just as they were reliant upon it to feed them and their livestock. If you wanted more fuel, you needed more land for plants to grow upon, or you needed to increase the efficiency of the system, focusing more intensively upon those species that suited your needs most closely.

When Elizabeth died in 1603 that way of living largely held, except for in her capital. London had changed. Alone among population concentrations outside of Asia, this city of just over 200,000 people had chosen to be fired by coal, becoming the first in the Western world to make the big switch. London was making use of a long-term stored energy, an energy source that was not produced on the earth's surface, competing with growing space for food, but instead stored mostly underground. More coal did not require more land be given over to fuel production. And the coal reserves were vast, at least to the eyes of Elizabethan Londoners, for whom coal quickly morphed from a novel, cheap fuel option into a daily necessity, taken for granted.

That coal began its takeover bid in London rather than the industrial centres of the day is significant and often overlooked. At the turn of the seventeenth century there were several cities worldwide with bigger populations and many places with more advanced technology. London did have some manufacturing, but Britain's major industry and export earner was then cloth, which, although it was often traded through the port of London, was made elsewhere. The country's iron industry was concentrated around the Weald in southern England, but coal and iron would not form their powerful partnership for another century. The great northern industrial powerhouses that came to dominate the eighteenth century were notably absent. London's brewing industry was the largest in Europe, but the demand for beer alone was not enough to explain the large-scale adoption of coal that was happening.

Indeed, London and Britain in general were considered by many to be a rather backward place. Much of the country's iron was imported from Sweden and blast furnace technology had only recently arrived from Europe. When it came to metallurgy of any sort, Britons lacked the knowledge and the skills abundant in other parts of the world. Their reputation was not much better in other areas. Glassmaking was stalled in medieval practice until a group of artisans from Lorraine brought modern methods to Britain. It took an influx of weavers from the Low Countries to revitalize a stagnating cloth industry. William M. Cavert, having studied the city's use of coal in *The Smoke of London*, came to the conclusion that, in 1600, 'it is unlikely that manufacturing industries exceeded 25 per cent of London's coal demand'.

The early rise of coal is not a story about industry; it is a tale of domestic needs and comforts, of individual, private choices. London had become a city of small home coal fires sending up thin plumes of smoke to join the communal smog. Household after household had shifted from wood to coal, outstripping commercial usage three times over. And the change came fast. In 1570 there was still little sign of any major divergence from the traditional use of wood as fuel. Less than forty years later, in 1607, a case brought by the Crown in the Star Chamber stated as fact that 'sea coal' – a name for the coal that arrived in London by ship from Newcastle – was 'the ordinary and usual fuel ... almost everywhere in every man's house'. A single generation had made the switch.

This shift from heating homes and cooking food with wood to doing so with coal was pivotal in the beginnings of the great transformation that is known as the Industrial Revolution. The leading experts on the history of the coal industry, John Ulric Nef and John Hatcher, were convinced that the domestic expansion of coal use in the Elizabethan period helped spur the country's mining industry and the later adoption of coal as the fuel of manufacturing, which transformed first Britain and then the world. Yet most of the academic focus has remained on industrial coal use in the seventeenth and eighteenth centuries. There are plenty of excellent and interesting publications documenting the switch to coal in the early salt industry, glassmaking and commercial beer breweries, or describing the experiments with coal in the nascent iron industry. The domestic switch, despite its much greater size, greater spread and earlier date, is practically skipped over in the eager rush to get to the (perhaps more manly) industrial stuff. But it is in the home that change really first took hold.

Traditionally, we have looked for the great tides of history within the worlds of military conflict, political manoeuvrings and industrial progress. The home and changes within it have been viewed as matters primarily of interest to women, and as being only of the most mundane interest even to them. When the change from wood to coal was occurring, the chroniclers of the day wrote primarily about battles and speeches and inventions. And in the main they wrote from a very masculine point of view, for their 'fellows'. To comment on domestic matters elicited much less, if any, social cachet, so fewer people did it, and when they did venture into the subjects of hearth and home, they did so in far less detail.

Further, coal within the home was handled primarily by decidedly non-elite women. Those who carried the buckets and coal scuttles, cleared out the ashes, scrubbed away the smuts, cooked the meals and boiled the water for the laundry were wives, mothers and daughters who did not have the resources to call on outside help, or they were the maids and servant girls working in someone else's house. These women commanded the smallest of financial purses, so rarely purchased published texts and provided scant market for the printed word. Of all groups within society they were also the least likely to receive a formal education, and were very rarely given the opportunity to publish writing themselves. The male elite of the day generally gave little weight to the experiences, opinions or insights of working-class wives and servants. Changes within these women's worlds, no matter how dramatic, passed almost unnoticed by those writing for posterity.

Very ordinary people, perhaps primarily poor people, in the later years of Elizabeth's reign, made the big switch and set the path for our future. The choices they made set off a chain reaction that encouraged their children and grandchildren to follow the same path, for neighbours to join them and for Londoners' habits to spread across the country and eventually beyond Britain's shores. Their choices remade the countryside, as fens were drained and woodlands reduced in favour of cropland, and they gave birth to a full-fledged coal trade, establishing new transport networks and fuelling generations of commercial and industrial pioneers in the process. And these ordinary Londoners' use of coal developed markets for new products specifically tailored to a life fired by coal.

Within the home, coal came to shape a new way of life, with new ways of doing things. Having personally experienced the running of domestic spaces using wood following the old practices and using coal with its newfound solutions, I can attest to the fundamental differences between the two ways of coping with everyday situations. The world of the home and hearth was forced to undergo a complete transformation between 1600 and 1800 as the demands of coal were bowed to.

Cooking techniques had to change, and so too did cooking tools and utensils. Coal encouraged the rise of certain styles of food and discouraged others, influencing the foods that are eaten as well as how they are prepared. But it was not just in the kitchen that coal had a powerful influence. As coal took over from wood,

THE LEAMINGTON STOVE, OR KITCHENER.

The result of centuries of experimentation and innovation, this 'Improved Leamington Kitchener' cast-iron range won a first-class prize at the Great Exhibition in 1851 and was singled out by Mrs Beeton as an archetype of the modern stove.

it forced a change in housework and laundry. Coal fires robbed people of their traditional cleaning agents and introduced a tricky new form of filth. Together these created a powerful demand for a soap 'industry'. Novel methods of cleaning-up were then exported around the globe with Britain's colonial incursions. So complete and thorough was the transformation in British household management practice that even where coal was not the dominant fuel, domestic coal methods, standards and thinking were often imposed – including in wood-burning households from South Africa to the Indian subcontinent.

A seemingly mundane domestic decision about how people heated their homes and cooked their food had profound consequences. It became the foundation of the modern economy, altering the landscape, promoting the rise of global industries and shaping cultures. It was clearly one of the factors that made the Industrial Revolution possible.

Why did these people at this time choose to make a big switch, and why did it prove to be such a permanent and influential move? What impacts did the switch have upon daily life, and how did these impacts ensure the change from wood to coal was more than just a passing phase? Was this domestic matter really all that important?

LIVING OFF
THE LAND

The green and pleasant landscape of modern Britain has been crafted, moulded and sculpted by successive generations seeking to make a living. And for millennia a significant part of the pressure upon the land has been people's need for fuel. Competing with the need for the arable land on which crops are grown and the pastureland by which livestock are fed, was the need for combustible plant material with which to cook food, brew beer and stave off the winter chill. People had to make choices: harvest peat or firewood or harvest food. Over time they found a variety of ways to combine land uses to maximize the yields of each of these essential components of life.

Britain has long been an extensively populated set of islands. The degree of population pressure on the land has fluctuated as different peoples have arrived, moved around and departed; famine, plague and war have each taken their toll, but these were followed by periods of quiet prosperity, when numbers have risen again. When Britain's population fell, fields that had been left to revert to scrub grew into woodland. When there were more mouths to feed, areas of marsh were drained to create needed pasture. Sometimes fuel was abundant and gathered rather casually; at other times it was scarce and carefully managed. These changing needs have been etched onto the landscape. The big shift in how Britain's homes were fuelled also played out in the surrounding woods, fields, moors, fens and heaths.

So what was the old order? What fuel was used to cook porridge, roast beef, bake pies, dry out sodden socks and warm toes before the advent of coal?

Choosing what to burn

It helps to begin with an understanding of how to make a fire. Different fuels burn in different ways, producing not just varying levels of heat, but a range of forms and shapes of it. Some fires release their energy in short, concentrated bursts, others do so over a longer, slower period. Flames from a coal fire tend to be small and uniform, peat rarely produces any recognizable flame, instead burning with a hot, smouldering glow, while a bundle of dry twigs can generate long, lazy tongues of wavering flame. But much depends on exactly what you're burning. Turves, which are cut from the very top layer of a peat deposit where plants are still growing, can behave quite unlike each other if they have been harvested from different areas, even when they were taken from the same moorland. Rye straw and barley straw have their own idiosyncrasies, quite distinct from those of wheat. Oak and pine are as different to burn as chalk and cheese. A hard black Welsh anthracite or 'stone coal' from Pembrokeshire combusts in a markedly different way from a softer, tarry, more bituminous sample extracted from the rocks around Newcastle.

Fuel can be treated in a number of ways to alter its nature and behaviour within the fire. Unit size is of particular importance: small chopped sticks burn differently to whole logs; coal dust and large lump coal are poles apart. For some fuels, orientation is crucial. A bundle of neatly aligned straw bound a couple of times along its length can sustain a concentrated flame where a similar amount of loose jumbled material would flash and dissipate into ash and dust and unburnt residue in no time.

Drying is particularly important for peat, which can easily contain 75 per cent water when first cut. But even anthracite coal burns better if it has had time out of the rain. And there are a whole host of controlled heating and burning processes that can turn fuels into more efficient versions of themselves. Wood can be transformed into 'white coal', or kiln-dried wood, or – continuing the metamorphosis – into charcoal, where the wood has been charred in an oxygen-depleted environment, driving out all moisture and impurities. Coal too can be cooked, or 'coked', into coke, where once again controlled burning removes unwanted matter, leaving behind a purer, hotter-burning fuel.

The permutations are almost endless, a fact that allows us humans to use fire in a myriad of ways to achieve a large range of effects. The blacksmith's forge offers an ideal demonstration of the possibilities. Working with coal, for example, you can create a fairly shallow fire, packed down flat on top, which is suitable for tempering, or hardening, a blade. In contrast, welding, or joining two pieces of metal together, demands a deep and narrow fire. For the highest heats, you can pack the right sort of coal – a rock that is bituminous but low in sulphur and phosphorus – into such a shape that it becomes a virtual oven; the fire can be practically contained within this globe of unburnt fuel, which retains most of the heat rather than allowing it to escape upwards with waste gases (otherwise known as smoke). Sometimes, and rather counterintuitively, mixing a little water with small pieces of coal can help to produce this globe of intense heat, by allowing the coal to bind together and form a 'shell' around the fire. This is one way in which coal is coked. By gradually moving the coked material towards the centre of the fire and replacing it with new coal, you increase the efficiency and heat at the centre and open up space around the periphery to turn more coal into coke.

We can see this knowledge about forging with coal being committed to print as early as 1677, in Joseph Moxon's *Mechanick Exercises*. Moxon finished his opening piece on smithing by declaring that he won't bother to describe lighting and using a smith's fire as the technique is too basic to bother with. He does, however, provide a few tips:

> you must with the Slice, clap the Coals upon the outside close together to keep the heat in the body of the Fire; and as oft as you find the Fire begin to break out, clap them close again, and with the Washer dipt in Water, wet the out-side of the Fire to damp the outside, as well to save Coals, as to strike the force of the Fire to the inside, that your work may heat the sooner.

Undoubtedly, smiths had been employing these techniques long before Moxon set them down for publication.

Fire management is not just about producing a particular temperature. The size of the physical space held at that temperature is also important – and adjustable. If a smith is working on a nail, then a single, small point of high heat is sufficient. Some work, however, requires heat to be diffused across a much larger area, and although iron will conduct heat along its length, raising the temperature of an entire area rather than overheating a single point is generally preferable. Gradations of heat within the same fire can also be useful in allowing a smith to move swiftly from one operation to another, from large to small work and back again. With skill and knowledge, a fire can be used to shape and bend metal; temper and adjust its hardness, brittleness or spring; divide it; or unite disparate pieces.

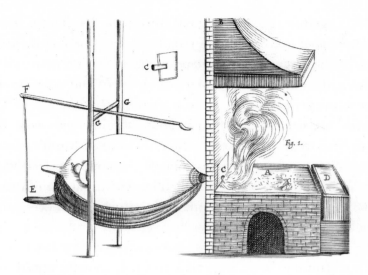

'Smithing' forge from Joseph Moxon's *Mechanick Exercises* (1677).

When we turn our attention from the forge to the kitchen we can see a similar range of options and subtleties at play. Managing the fire in your hearth gave you the power to render foodstuffs digestible, transform liquids into bacteria-free drink, conjure cleanliness out of filth and drive away the chill of northern climes. And just as with the blacksmith's work, different fuels could be brought into service to perform different functions by dint of the techniques and equipment particular to them. It is possible to boil a kettle upon wood, peat, heather, ling, gorse, dried dung and various types of straw if you are in possession of the right know-how. But each of these materials are just better suited to some jobs than to others.

For instance, dry thistle stalk combusts well, because the seed heads – if they have not blown away in the wind – are packed with oil. They are an excellent form of kindling, and many people in England, Wales, Scotland and Ireland have collected them for this purpose. Yet when Humphrey O'Sullivan watched the women of Callan, in County Kilkenny, Ireland, cut old thistle stalks at the end of 1828 for use as winter fuel, he was struck by the unusual

5

scale of their endeavour, with 'a bundle or load of them on a poor woman as big as a pig's sty'. He was witnessing an activity born of desperation and resourcefulness, not of preference. That's because, as a fuel to boil a kettle or cook a potato, thistle stalks have many drawbacks.

Like all the straws they burn very fast. Hollow stems direct air to the centre of the conflagration, the long, thin proportions producing a rapid draught, not only encouraging impressive flames but blowing ash, burning fragments, and loose, unburnt material up and away from the fire. Naturally this process goes even faster if the stems are standing vertically or placed at a rising angle. Capturing heat from this quick energy release can be tricky, but both fuel and hearth can be adapted to fit this purpose.

If the stalks are first formed into a set of straight, uniform bundles and securely bound, they can then be stacked and placed under a weight. This crushes the hollow stems flat, thus reducing the air flow capacity through them and slowing down the rate of their burn. It also makes the fire easier to handle and reduces the stoking rate. Ideally, you would burn material like thistle inside a firebox where the volatile mixture of gases, ash, cinders and unburnt material can be contained (and, hopefully, burnt again later, unlocking more of the thistles' energy).

If you didn't have a purpose-built firebox, and it is highly unlikely any of those women in Callan did, a crude version could be rigged up with a horseshoe-shaped arrangement of stones upon a flat hearth with a cooking pot balanced on top to form a lid. However, you can't leave the thistles for a moment, they burn quite quickly and continuous stoking is required. Indeed, a huge pile of prepared stalks would be needed to bring just one small pot of water to the boil. Anyone reliant upon thistle fuel will eat only the occasional hot meal and live in an almost completely unheated home – which is why the women of Callan must have been very desperate.

The commoners' fuel

Dung, particularly cattle dung, was pressed into service in parts of Britain where other sources of fuel were scarce, right up until the widespread adoption of coal for domestic use. It was often used by poorer members of rural communities who had commoners' rights upon areas of rough grazing.

Common land was (and is) not public land, nor was it 'free' land for anyone to use as they wished. It was an area held in common by a specific group of people who were permitted to use it in carefully specified ways. In most cases, commoners were the people who rented parcels of land fringing the common. They held the right to graze an agreed number of animals upon the common as well as the right to collect dead vegetation and other resources, including cow pats, from the land.

To be used as a fuel, the dung first had to be dried out. Celia Fiennes (1662–1741), the traveller and memoirist, recorded seeing this in action in 1698 outside the town of Peterborough, where she noticed cow dung 'upon the walls of the ordinary people's houses and walls of their outhouses'. She noted that the dung had been 'plastered up to dry in cakes which they use for firing'. Her visit to Leicestershire revealed the practice in operation there too. She didn't approve in either location. Around the same time, George Meriton published *A York-Shire Dialogue*, which contained a short scene where a mother asks her daughter to fetch some dried cow dung fuel: 'clawt some cassons out o' th' hurne', the mother said, 'cassons' being one of the many regional names for this form of fuel. In Buckinghamshire they were traditionally called 'clatts' and in Cornwall 'glaws'.

The custom of burning cassons in this part of the country was captured in the probate inventories of the parish of North Cave in the East Riding of Yorkshire from the mid-sixteenth to the mid-seventeenth centuries. (This period is not particularly special; it is just that the surviving inventories are from this time, and there is no reason to believe things changed quickly before then or after.) In a scattering of the inventories of both the poorer parishioners and the better off, the stocks of cassons 'on hand' when the head of household died were recorded. For example, Richard Brigham, who died in 1626, was neither wealthy nor destitute. He called himself a 'husbandman', a title which indicated he was farming on a modest scale. He lived in a house with three rooms – many of his neighbours had only one – and among a mix of livestock he had five mares, two colts, two foals and 'an old nag', a few cows and fifty pigs plus a similar number of sheep. His will was written in October, a time of year when most people would have been laying up fuel stores for the winter, and included 'helme baulks' – meaning 'bog oak', or old stumps and logs preserved within peat – as well as 'other old wood and turfes and cazons'. Thomas Clarke, who died in 1607, had a two-room house and a slightly smaller accumulation of livestock. His 'backer end', or outbuildings, contained 'casens, turves and certain old wood'. Thomas Pinder was just a touch less prosperous than these men, though he still had a two-room house, which he too kept stocked with 'turves and casons'. None of these men would have been designated as one of 'the poor' by their contemporaries. They were almost certainly commoners, fitting Celia Fiennes's description of the 'ordinary people'. Their use of cow dung as a fuel may have represented a mixture of tradition and thrift.

Other inventories in the same collection – forty-three in total – referred to 'the dung' and 'manure'. These words described the same resource, cattle dung, but indicated a different use. Cassons were individually dried out for fuel, while manure was left wet and gathered into heaps where it could break down, ready for use as a fertilizer. Rather surprisingly, the local vicar, Thomas Brabes, headed one of the eight households in 1638 that had cassons in their inventory. He was most assuredly one of the better-off members of his community. Among his wealth in the probate records, six rooms were mentioned, as well as such refinements as 'his library'. He also had a load of manure, a rare example of cassons and manure listed side-by-side.

Most people used the dung of their cattle for either fuel or fertilizer. Few had enough of this material to use it for both. The people of the parish of North Cave were exercising a choice as to whether to use the dung of their livestock as fertilizer or fuel – and, in at least one sacred case, a bit of both.

Dung is a rather curious fuel, in part because it is now a fuel we generally see only among traditional rural populations in hot and remote places. It is also a fuel that can initially be hard for people today to understand because much of the dung produced by modern farming methods is rather unsuitable for stoking a fire. We are accustomed to dung that is wetter, darker-coloured and much more smelly than the dung Richard Brigham and the other residents of the parish of North Cave would have encountered back in 1620. Modern cattle feed is designed to pack in nutrients, in order to produce high milk yields in dairy cows and rapid muscle growth in beef cattle. This super-rich diet has an effect upon the animals' digestive processes. It is, in the twenty-first century, a common sight to see cows with their own dung splashing down their legs. They live their lives with something akin to permanent diarrhoea.

Brigham's cows, and those of his neighbours, had to make do with a high-fibre diet rather than a high-nutrient one. Winter feed in particular was poor. Hay – comprised of dried grass and meadow plants, including their nutrient-packed seed heads – was largely reserved for draught animals who needed energy to work; the rest of the livestock typically ate straw, which was much less nutritious, consisting of the dried stems left over from a wheat, barley or rye crop after the grain had been harvested. In some areas where straw was in short supply, overwintering cattle were reliant upon holly branches cut especially as fodder. Their dung was much drier, more fibrous, paler and far more solid than that of a modern cow. A pat could be picked up after a day or two in the field and would hold together. Judging the right moment for gathering one before sticking it to the wall of an outbuilding to dry probably took a little experience, as a pat would need to be dry enough to handle but sticky enough to adhere to the wall. Leaving pats out in the field too long risked getting them trampled on, reduced to mush and crumble. Once properly dry, the dung could be stacked fairly easily until needed.

Personally, I don't have a great deal of experience burning dung. I have never tried to burn cow dung, though I have idly messed about with dried sheep dung (I was bored when camping). In my very limited experience, it catches easily and smoulders along with little difficulty in a rather hot fashion, but it is often smothered by its own ash, which clings around the burning core and has a distinctly pungent and acidic aroma. You could definitely rustle up a supper on it if you needed to, although I would advise keeping a firm lid on any pot to stop the smell infecting the flavour of your meal.

In nineteenth-century America, a similar resource – the dried dung of wild buffalo herds, also known as 'buffalo chips' – was an essential fuel for those heading out across the Great Plains. Frederick Piercy, an artist from Liverpool who accompanied a group of pioneers heading to the West, said the chips were 'composed of grass, masticated and digested, and dried in the sun'. In his illustrated travelogue *The Route from Liverpool to Great Salt Lake Valley*, published in parts between 1853 and 1855, he observed: 'It is a common joke on the plains that a steak cooked on these chips needs no pepper.'

According to Derek E. Earl in his book *Forest Energy and Economic Development*, dried dung releases about the same amount of energy as peat – a little more than wood does, and more than half of the energy produced by a similar weight of bituminous coal. And, of course, it is typically there for the taking.

Of peat and turves

If some of the good people of North Cave knew much more than me about the use of cassons in the home, far more were expert in the use of peat and turves. (Rather confusingly, 'peat' and 'turf' are sometimes used interchangeably, especially in Ireland.) There are more than four times the number of listings of turves than of cassons in the North Cave probate inventories, plus another handful of households that mention turf spades but no turves. This parish included a section of the Wallingfen, a wet and boggy area of thin peat, moss and patches of reed and thin grasses, for which many parishioners had commoners' rights.

These commons, as we have noted, were not a free-for-all, and turf-cutting was highly regulated. On St Helen's Eve – the third of May – each attested commoner was permitted to stake a claim for the coming turf-cutting season so long as he (or she, if she were a widow) did so before noon. Once claimed, the turf was permitted to be cut only during the hours of daylight and only until Midsummer's Day, towards the end of June. No fuel obtained from the fen was to be sold to anyone outside the jurisdiction of the 'liberties', which included all of the parishes that had a share of the land. The season's cutting was further restricted, in an attempt to preserve supplies for the future, to a single turf spade's deep – in this region, about 12 inches (30 cm) deep.

No one knows when people started cutting peat for fuel. We are equally in the dark about when people began to manage this resource in such an orderly manner. Besides extracting peat, the fens could be used in a variety of ways: as grazing for all sorts of livestock, for hay-making, for fishing and fowling or for the gathering of sedge and reeds for thatch, and of sallows for basket-making. Since digging the place up to get the peat out destroys the potential for most of these other uses, peat-cutting was restricted. The best known of the old peat-cutting areas in England today are the Norfolk Broads. Leases for areas of 'turbary' – the local name for fenland set aside for peat-cutting – indicate that people were cutting peat in the Broads in a regulated fashion by 1140.

Between the Norman Conquest in 1066 and the arrival of the Black Death in 1348, the population of the British Isles had risen from under 2 million people to around 4.5 million. Pressure on basic resources was acute. Marginal areas of land were brought into cultivation despite dreadfully poor yields. Peat-digging was confined to small, linear plots, so the cuttings were pushed deeper and deeper to extract much-needed fuel. Modern practice, continuing commercially right up until the Second World War, and a few walls of earth surviving from the medieval 'broads' – the open areas of fresh water created by peat diggings – suggest that each small pit was the result of a single season's campaign by a single digger, perhaps with the help of his family. Looking at the accounts of those involved in the last days of commercial hand-cut peat, we can piece together an understanding of the methods that left behind these traces in the shape of the earth and water bodies.

'Mad Jack' Darnell was a peat cutter. In the late spring of 1892, he was kind enough to demonstrate his traditional method of turf-cutting for the photographer P. J. Deakin, and these images, along with memories of people who knew Mad Jack or themselves worked in the peat business, were collected in 1999 by Anthony Day, the nephew of the last commercial peat cutter in the area of Wicken Fen, in Cambridgeshire, in his book *Fuel from the Fens*. During winter, Wicken Fen is very wet. The water table sits not far below the surface, and the waterlogged peat can freeze solid in the cold weather. Mad Jack's work therefore began in March, when the peat slowly began to thaw and dry, and finished in late August. With a piece of string stretched between two pegs thrust into the ground, he'd mark out a straight line parallel to pits he or others had worked in previous seasons. This new work area was not directly on the side of the old digging, because these diggings had filled with water over the winter. Instead, a strip was left untouched to act as a 'baulk', or wall, between the old, now flooded pit, and the new. This had the advantage of leaving Mad Jack room to stack drying turves along the edge of the pit on one side and still have space to run a barrow up and down the length of his workings.

'Mad Jack' Darnell demonstrating the procedure for cutting peat for photographer P. J. Deakin in 1892.

The surface vegetation was stripped off, leaving a bare and flat surface, into which the new season's hole was dug. First an edge was cut into the peat with a turf knife and then the real work began. Cutting into peat requires strength and perseverance. Water slowly seeps from the surrounding bog through the top section of peat, forcing diggers to stop and bail out water on occasion. Peat cutters tried to maintain a relatively standard block size, since this helped in monitoring how the blocks were drying. Extraordinarily straight and even, and about the size of a modern breeze block when first dug, each block of peat was stacked one atop another at the edge of the digging so that it could begin drying as soon as possible. The peat blocks had to be moved and restacked in different formations several times as they dried to permit the sun and wind to do their work. In an essay published by the Highland Society of Scotland in 1803, the Revd Dr John Walker noted: 'the "flaw" or surface peat affords but a very weak fire, like a parcel of dry sticks or straws, and leaves as few ashes behind … The heather peat, and the springy brown peat, formed by the decay of herbaceous plants, are somewhat better, being a little more lasting. But the solid black peat, formed from wood, and which lies deep, is much preferable to these, and makes the best fuel.' While his understandings of the origins of the different types of peat would today be refuted scientifically, Professor Walker's observations about the burning characteristics of peat taken from different depths is sound.

Deep, highly compressed peat burns much more steadily and for a longer period. The processes by which vegetation turns into peat have simply had longer to act, so the peat has a much more even texture and is less likely to contain intact stems or roots. The other reason to dig deep is a desire to maximize upon one's investment. Given how much better it performed, it is quite likely that deeper peat fetched a higher price at market. Some areas of the fen were subject to common rights but some areas could be leased, with fewer restrictions on where the peat was sold. Regardless, the surface areas claimed for cutting could be quite small. The deeper you dug, the more peat – and potentially profit – you could extract from your section.

Such diggings left behind a landscape of multiple small deep pools divided by walls of untouched peat. From the early fifteenth century onwards, we have evidence of some secondary rounds of peat extraction, conducted by cutting into these walls some time after the initial digging. The method did not survive in England, but something rather like it did continue in the Netherlands into the nineteenth century, when it attracted antiquarian and folklorist interest, and in Ireland in areas where the bog is especially wet. Evidence of the practice in England comes in the main from a set of accounts kept by the owners of Bartonbury Hall in Norfolk. In 1451, for example, a profit of '10*s* [shillings] 0*d* [pence] for 12 lasts of fen taken in the several pond-waters of the Lord with laggying' was recorded. Another entry mentioned the peat had been retrieved 'with a dyday', a tool identified through the writings of farmer-poet Thomas Tusser more than a century later, when he advised using one to clear out ditches in winter. Several of Bartonbury's accounting entries also make it clear that the estate's peat had not been cut in nice organized blocks, as it was 'sufficient for *making* 4000 turves' (my emphasis). Instead, it is likely some baulks were hacked away, with the loose peat being dredged out of the water with the dyday. This wet, broken peaty mass then had to be dried out and pressed into 'turves'. In Ireland, Humphrey O'Sullivan described similar 'peat pulp' which, he said, had 'been kneaded by human feet … and then made into brickettes by women's hands'. And lo, bit by bit, the 'several pond-waters' became a 'broad', as all the little peat divisions were removed.

A fire of smoke and spirit

Using peat as a fuel is a varied business. As Professor Walker pointed out at the beginning of the nineteenth century, its burning quality can vary quite a lot, depending on where it comes from. In addition, the structure of the peat block or turf was determined by the method of extraction.

Turves cut with a spade or other hand tool have a 'grain' representing the horizontal layers of year after year of material deposition. The grain is most obvious in mid-level peat, where the plant material has had time to begin to break up and been subject to a fair amount of pressure squeezing down upon it. Surface peat, which has not been subject to so much decomposition or pressure, retains more of the chaotic texture of intertwined stems and roots. Peat dug from deep layers has a grain that is finer, more densely packed and harder to discern; it becomes more obvious during combustion, when the ash maintains the structure of the block until it is disturbed and falls away into a soft, fine powder. Peat that has been dredged up out of the bog water and re-formed into briquettes has no structure whatsoever.

If there is a grain in the peat, the blocks tend to burn along it. Since peat is what might be called a 'contact burner' – fire spreads through direct contact – the grain makes a difference. Re-formed briquettes create a sphere or hemisphere of fire, since the initial spark catches on the outside surface and works its way steadily inwards. The fire in its early stages therefore remains largely within the block, with the surrounding, unburnt peat serving as something of an insulation. Hand-cut peat, with its grain running across the original deposit lines of plant fibres, helps to direct the spread of your fire, as it is more likely to ignite the peat within the same deposit layer rather than the peat in the layers above and below. A 'plate' of fire is formed. This fire tends to burn to the edges of the block, where it is exposed to the air, releasing heat in a usable fashion.

Once your fire has a good hold – which can take a considerable time with this slow-burning fuel – the burning peat starts to resemble charcoal. It is at this stage that it can successfully be used for cooking or heating water. You will not see any flames, and the heat dissipates very quickly if you move your pot away from direct contact with the fire. So while a pot can be suspended above a peat fire, it needs to be close. Actual boiling is best done with the pot's sides touching burning turves. If it is moved just a couple of centimetres further away, bringing a pot to the boil is almost impossible; maintaining a simmer is generally the best you might do. The high heat required for baking can be achieved by laying food upon some hot stone or iron surface in the centre of a peat fire, upturning a pot over the food and heaping burning turves around and on top of the pot. However, the need for such close contact places a significant limit on how many cooking vessels can be put into use at any one time.

A pot put to boil over a peat fire – note how the pot
is nestled by the turves.

There are two things that people particularly like about peat as a fuel: the smell and the staying power. Peat smoke has a strong, distinctive smell, one that evokes powerful memories of home, especially for those who have moved away from peat-burning districts. Peat smoke translates into flavour wherever it comes into contact with food, particularly dairy produce or other animal fats (and whisky, of course). The smell is a product of chemicals from the peat's original plant materials, but its prevalence is mostly a function of the slow, cool-burning nature of a peat fire. Whatever calorific value is locked up within the material is released only slowly and at a considerably lower temperature than that of wood, straw or coal. The low temperature of combustion creates a great deal of partly burnt particles that we experience as smoke. In fact, the sheer abundance of fine particulates released by peat makes it one of the most damaging of all fuels for the lungs.

Staying power, unsurprisingly, is also a result of the cool-burning nature of peat. A single turf can burn for over an hour, which means a peat fire requires very little attention, not a small consideration for anyone running a busy household.

The loss of wetlands

Generally, the presence of peat in an area indicated a shortage of wood. Wet, boggy areas are not ideal for most tree growth. It works the other way round too. Where the land is very wet, felling trees that once sucked up excess water can make an area even more boggy, creating an accumulation of peat where once a straggly wood grew.

Before coal there were very many more peaty areas than there are today. Once useable coal supplies became widely available, fewer people were reliant upon peat. The ability and demand to put more land into agricultural production meant many wet areas were rapidly drained. The largest area that is still called 'the fens' – nearly 2.485 sq. miles (4,000 sq. km) in Lincolnshire, Cambridgeshire and Norfolk – is today prime cropland with only tattered fragments of wetland and peat formation surviving. But while this area is well known, there were once many small pockets of lowland fen scattered about in shallow valleys where drainage was poor and seasonal waterlogging was common. For example, Wallingfen, where the people of North Cave were cutting their turves in the sixteenth and seventeenth centuries, is now an area of flat agricultural development dotted with farmsteads as well as a completely new post-fen settlement called Newport. This township was built at the very end of the eighteenth century when, to provide transport and to drain the area, a canal was driven through the local wetlands. Natural England estimates that around three quarters of England's former fenland is now farmland.

Peat was also once widely available upon the high moors. Acidic soils and high rainfall make upland plateaus and shallow valleys into the perfect habitat for sphagnum, the moss that is the primary vector of upland peat formation in areas where harsh climate and thin soils combine to make tree growth slow and unproductive. Many of the communities farming in the fertile valleys surrounding the moors utilized these reserves of peat for fuel. Eskdale in the Lake District, for example, boasts as testimony to this past a scattering of small, stone-built huts, known as 'peat scales', high on the valley slopes. Still discernible alongside the peat scales are carefully graded sledge tracks leading up to the peat-cutting zone. Pockets of peat-burning also occurred in parts of Devon (near Dartmoor and Exmoor), in the Yorkshire Moors, high up in the valleys of Cumbria and across large swathes of Scotland, Ireland and Wales.

But for all this, peat burners did not constitute the majority of the population, probably no more than 10 per cent of those who lived within the boundaries of what is now the UK. Everywhere else, they used wood.

The reasons for this were obvious to John Norden. In 1607 he worried about the use of 'peats, turffe, heath, furze, broome and such like fuel for firing ... yea and neats dung' in those parts of Wiltshire where more conventional fuel was then in short supply. The dependence on such fuels spoke to him of severe poverty and, perhaps more crucially, of poor husbandry and inefficient land use. People who were using dung for fuel were clearly not using it to fertilize the fields, sacrificing future food crops for present warmth. Likewise the use of moors and heaths as sources of fuel discouraged people from ploughing up such areas and pressing them into food production. For Norden, wood represented the ideal of fuel efficacy and efficiency; nothing could be more perfect in terms of use or production cycle.

OUT OF THE WOODS

Wherever there was an unlimited choice of fuels, the people of the British Isles traditionally chose wood. They had lots of very good reasons for doing so. Wood is a renewable source of energy, fairly concentrated and easy to handle, and it burns in a clean, controllable and predictable fashion. The technologies required to harvest and prepare wood are simple and reliable. It stores well and compactly. It is extremely versatile as a fuel, suitable for a wide range of activities and provides a large range of temperatures, and quick, accurate changes within that range. Expanding and contracting the size of a wood fire is again both a simple and a rapid procedure; it's quick to light and easy to extinguish. There was also a long-standing skill base surrounding its production, preparation and use.

A thicket of decisions

Sophisticated managed production, rather than casual gathering or felling, was in evidence in Britain as far back as 4000 BC. It can be seen in the structure of the Sweet Track, a prehistoric wooden walkway discovered in 1970 by Ray Sweet while digging a ditch, which was preserved in the peat of the Somerset Levels. Along with some timber planks, the track utilizes two distinct groups of relatively uniform poles. Later tracks, dating back to around 3000 BC, employed woven hurdles instead of timber planks as the walking surface. These reveal even more carefully controlled wood management, as the walkways are made from very uniform hazel rods. Such uniformity could only be the result of regular, organized cropping and grazing regimes.

With the exception of pine, most trees native to Britain are not generally killed when the trunk is harvested. Many species send up new shoots from the stump, and many others produce them from the underground rootball. Only when the root system is severely damaged, diseased or removed during felling is a tree's life ended. In many cases regular harvesting, known as coppicing, lengthens a tree's lifespan. Left uncut, the natural lifespan of an ash tree, for example, is about two hundred years, but there are numerous ash coppice stools (comprising the base of the trunk and the root systems) which are a thousand years old and still living. So long as you leave the stumps and root systems alone, there is no need to replant felled deciduous woodland.

Ash, oak, hazel, hornbeam, lime, elder and wych elm are among the species that regrow from the stump after a felling. Sweet chestnut is another excellent coppicing wood, but was a later introduction to Britain and not much used in this way until the eighteenth century (when it became popular as a source of hop-growing poles). Different species respond to coppicing in different ways. Lime, for instance, is very easy to bring into a coppicing cycle at any stage in its life. Oak, in contrast, works well only if the first felling takes place within the first thirty years of growth. After the age of thirty, the bark of oak changes, becoming craggier and splitting around the trunk. It can no longer harbour the dormant buds that send forth new shoots if the main stem is cut down. Ash is generally easy to coppice, but if the felling takes place late in the spring, the stump will not bud until the next year, appearing dead until then. The shoots of all coppicing species grow out from the bark of the surviving stump, forming a loose ring of new growth. Successive fellings, after each new crop of shoots has had a few years to grow into usefully sized poles, tend to spread gradually outwards as the shoots seek light and space. Ancient rings can grow to about 16 feet (5 m) across.

How coppicing works: after the tree is cut close to the ground, leaving a stool; buds emerge from the stool and grow into a stand of shoots, which are harvested when they reach the desired length and diameter for use.

The species that sprout from an underground root system, such as cherry, aspen and most of the elms, form much less regular shapes. Elm in particular appears to become almost immortal through coppicing, forming huge, genetically identical patches known as 'clones'. All of these rootballs establish long-standing symbiotic relationships with the microorganisms and fungi in the surrounding soil, which helps to give coppicing a distinct edge in efficiency over replanting. New seedlings, whether naturally grown from seed in their eventual spot, or nurtured elsewhere and planted out as young saplings, take some time to find their feet. Much of their first few years' growth must necessarily be directed into extending and strengthening their hold underground. Coppice shoots, however, take advantage of the ready-grown water- and nutrient-collecting network of roots and rootlets spread over a considerable distance.

Regular grazing, or browsing, of new shoots can slow and even stop the regeneration of felled trees, so good management of a 'copse', or coppiced woodland, required good fencing. The instructions given in the 1598 edition of Fitzherbert's *This Ryghte Profytable Boke of Husbandry* are pertinent:

> before you fell your wood ... you must make a good sure hedge that no manner of cattell may get in, and soone as it is felde, let it be carried away before the spring come up, or else the cattell that doth carry the wood will eat the spring and the top is eaten or broken, it is a great hurt and hinderance with the goodness of the spring ...

Fitzherbert used the word 'cattell' to mean all browsing animals, from sheep to wild deer, and including the oxen or horses employed to transport the felled and trimmed products out of the copse. This was a quandary for woodland management. Carrying the wood by hand was not feasible. With no other option for removing harvested wood from the copse, he advised finishing up your work before any new shoots appeared, and keeping all browsers out of the copse for a year or two after the felling.

With protection in place, a felled area grows quickly and produces a rather straight and uniform crop. The shoots race for the light beginning in the same spring as those around them, so they grow in tandem, encouraged to stretch straight up to the open sunlight and discouraged from branching out sideways into the shade of their competitors. Woodland management for several thousand years, and in some areas continuing to this day, therefore consisted of dividing the woodlands into separate workable areas – known as 'fells', 'cants', 'coupes', 'haggs' or 'compartments' – that could be protected from overgrazing and felled in rotation. Oliver Rackham, the acclaimed botanist and historian of the British countryside, quoted a particularly explicit record of this practice from Cambridgeshire, where in 1356 an 80-acre patch of woodland was being managed on a seven-year rotation as a commercial proposition: 'a certain wood called Heylewode. Which contains eighty acres by estimate. Of the underwood of which there can be sold every year without causing waste or destruction. Eleven acres of underwood which are worth 55s at 5s an acre.'

Coppicing begins in late autumn once all the leaves have dropped. The poles are cut a few inches above the ground, traditionally at a slight angle so that the remaining stump will shed the rain, which helps to discourage rotting. How often you cut depends not only upon the sizes of pole that you want but also upon the mix of species present. Willow and hazel can have very short cycles, as they produce large numbers of shoots that grow very fast in the first year or two. The small, whippy stems of these two species were much in demand for basket- and fence-making, which encourages early harvesting. A single acre of purely hazel copse can – if it is healthy, in a suitable location and well managed – be cropped every three to four years to produce around 10,000 rods. This is enough to provide around 300 good-quality 6 feet (2 m) wattle 'hurdles', or panels of fencing, plus a large stack of slim rods for thatching spars, the short lengths which are pointed, split and twisted into staples to hold reeds or straw in place on the roof. Given a slightly longer cycle of five to seven years, the same hazel woodland would be used for firewood. Ash and oak are often worth leaving much longer before harvesting poles. This is because the number of shoots that appear around these felled stumps is fewer than those with hazel or willow, so they are less likely to crowd each other out as they grow bigger. If you are looking purely for volume rather than a specific size of pole, then hazel maximizes your yield at about ten years; ash and oak at thirty. Modern forestry commission guides suggest that thirty-year rotations with a mix of different tree species typically produce around a hundred tonnes of wood per hectare when felled.

Many expanses of woodland historically contained a wide variety of species and a mixture of cropping regimes. Timber for building houses, ships, mills, churches and furniture required trees with fifty to several hundred years' of growth. These older, larger trees, called 'standards', were often growing alongside smaller crops of 'underwood', used for fuel and fencing, that were turned over on a shorter cycle. The combination of a few well-spaced large trees growing among the denser, shorter and thinner stems of the main crop provided most of the materials that local communities needed. Oliver Rackham noted that the biological and the written records demonstrate a mix of standards and underwood was typical in coppicing before 1600.

In this boar hunt scene from Simon Bening's *Book of Hours* (c. 1540) an area of coppice has been felled, leaving the tall 'standards ' to grow on for timber. Beyond, another area of short, uniformly growing coppice awaits felling in another year.

The governing powers of the Tudor era worried about possible shortages of suitable timber 'for building, making, repayringe and mayntenyninge of Houses and Shippes, as also fewell and firewood'. From 1543 onwards a series of statutes were enacted to ensure the supply of woodland products on both the national and local levels, placing heavy emphasis upon the inclusion of standards. One act demanded that at least twelve timber trees be left upon every acre of felled coppice, and that the felled area be enclosed to protect the 'spring' from deer. Restrictions were put upon the admission of livestock into woodland enclosures during the critical period for new growth. Damage to fences was a particular sin.

Oak was commonly chosen as the standard tree for timber, but not exclusively. In areas where oak did not grow well, other species were allowed to develop into standards; hornbeam was favoured in some areas, elm in others. There was far more variety in the species cut on a quicker cycle. Underwood coppices often were not the result of ordered plantations but rather a happy combination taking root on a particular patch of land: of naturally seeded trees that thrived in the local soils and climate, together with the local grazing practices. People sometimes removed less useful species as they sprouted, but the remaining woodland was largely a product of happenstance.

The length of hiatus between fellings might suit some species more than others. When making the decision of when to fell a coppiced area, people had to weigh up the value of the standing wood in light of the current market price for particular shapes, sizes and species; the availability of labour for felling; and their own financial position (the ability to pay the upfront costs of felling before receiving the proceeds from its sale). In areas where certain industries or the domestic market created an especially strong demand, specializing in one species and felling in rotation, maximized profits.

In an ideal coppicing regime, the number of fells would equal the number of years' growth required to produce poles of a useful size, with each fell being of a size that the local workforce could manage in a single season. If seven years' growth produced the right size of pole for customers, the woodland's owner set up seven distinct, fenced areas of roughly equal size to be felled on a seven-year cycle. This sort of intensively managed coppice springs to prominence at the end of the sixteenth century in the Weald of southern England, where a newly invigorated iron industry was seeking a reliable supply of suitable fuel.

While ancient coppice stools can live for centuries, the productivity of such huge old stools falls after a time. When these less productive stools failed, they were often replaced with species then desirable to local industries. In some places, iron masters purchased existing copses themselves, replacing unwanted species with oak, which best suited their requirements. Elsewhere, they planted new woodlands entirely of oak. Pure oak coppice on a seven- to twelve-year cycle produced the perfect material to fuel their forges: charcoal. A consistent size – the most preferred poles were about 2 inches (5 cm) in diameter – permitted the wood to burn uniformly, so that all the wood was converted to charcoal. And oak converts into a particularly good charcoal, giving a hot, clean burn.

The variety of shapes, sizes and species of wood that suited the needs of a rural village were not the same as those of burgeoning towns and cities. Hazel rods for making hurdles and fences, for example, were of much more use in the countryside, while elm floorboards and oak boards for wainscoting were in much greater demand in urban centres. Firewood was wanted everywhere, but the appetite for fuel for city fires was enormous. Supplies had to be drawn from considerable distances, wherever roads and water transport allowed.

Fit for the fire

Firewood is a bulky commodity whose transportation is much eased if it is first trimmed and shaped into something that will stack easily and tightly. A load of wood that is bent, branched or composed of varying sizes is much harder to handle than a load of straight pieces of regular size. It's one thing to supply irregular loads to a cottage at the edge of the wood, another to fuel a city several or many miles away. Trimming off branches and twigs and cutting the wood into uniform lengths was essential if you wanted to load firewood onto carts or ships for urban markets. Commercially produced firewood also needed to fit the size and shape of the fireplaces it was to be used in, and be of a shape, size and species that combusted easily. Large oak logs of more than 10 inches (25 cm) in diameter are, for example, almost impossible to set light to.

A demonstration of large oak logs' non-flammability can be observed in Haddon Hall in Derbyshire. The partition wall between the hall's kitchen and pastry room is made of timber with wattle-and-daub infill. In the days before electric light, work at dingy times of day and night was carried out here by candle or rush light, the marks of which remain. In the wooden beam of the wall you can make out where very simple spiked iron candleholders were once placed. Higher up on the beam, and lining up with the holes left by the spikes, are the scorch marks of candle flame. There are several hundred scorch marks – some of them quite deep – not just in these two spaces but all over the building. Yet Haddon Hall did not burn down. Each mark represents the presence of candles in the same position, their flames repeatedly playing upon the wood beams, without ever managing to do more than gently char the surface of the oak.

Smaller diameter logs of oak burn more easily, although oak is never the easiest species to get started. Once alight, however, it is an excellent firewood, burning long, hot and steady. If you were intending to roast a large joint for dinner, you might well select oak as your fuel. There was a strong market for oak firewood so long as it was of a suitable size.

In 1601 an 'Acte concerning the Assize of Fewell' was passed specifying the sizes of firewood that could be offered for sale in any city, borough or incorporated town. Based upon an act of 1544 that had only applied to wood sold in London and Westminster, it was a codification of practices which were already largely in place throughout Britain. The usual term for a prepared piece of ready-made firewood was a 'billet'. The act required all billets be sawn to a uniform length of 3 feet 4 inches (102 cm). There were three acceptable circumferences, described as the 'greatness' of the billet: a 'single' billet with a circumference of 7½ inches (19 cm); a 'caste' billet of 10 inches (25 cm); and, less typical, a 'two caste' billet of 14 inches (35.5 cm). These measurements seem a little odd until you realize they roughly match diameters of 2, 3 and 4 inches respectively. Of course, trees are never perfectly round; further, billets could be made from a whole stem or a stem that had been split in two or four. A string passed around a log, split or whole, gave a very simple and accurate measure of the volume of combustible fuel contained in the billet. Clarifications of the act sought to make the measures even more accurate, demanding that single billets be formed only of whole, not cleft, wood, and that one-caste billets should be 11 inches (28 cm) around if they were composed of uncleft wood; 12 inches (30.5 cm) if there were quarter-cleft lengths included; and 13 inches (33 cm) if they were a mix of whole and half-cleft pieces. Similar variations were also given for two-caste billets.

These standard billets provided most of the needs of a person tending an open fire (with the exception of kindling). The two smaller sizes were general-use logs that provided a degree of flexibility in shaping a fire. The largest size, the two-caste, would only be used to maintain a large fire once it was burning well. It could also act as a brake upon a smaller conflagration, smothering it.

Billets could be made from a single stem or a stem cut in half or in quarters.

Still larger pieces of wood, which were not generally intended for firewood, were called 'tallwood'. These had to be 4 feet (1.2 m) in length, so that they were immediately discernible from ordinary billets. Tallwood was sometimes also known as 'cord wood', as it could be sold 'by the cord', the amount of prepared wood in a stack around which a 24-foot (7.3 m) cord can pass. It is rare in Britain for wood to be sold by the cord these days, but in the US, Canada and New Zealand the measure is still very much in use. This is because, particularly in the US and Canada, the firewood on sale is mostly pine of one species or another. Pine catches fire more easily than the usual firewood species of England and Wales. It also burns away more quickly, so pieces of tallwood with a diameter of 5, 6 or 7 inches (12.5 cm, 15 cm or 18 cm) are much more suitable.

When it comes to firewood, not all trees are equal. Hazel, for example, catches light very easily and burns brightly and quickly, sometimes a little too quickly. Willow burns quite well in terms of heat release but produces acrid smoke that, in even small amounts, makes eyes sting and water alarmingly. This makes it very difficult to live with willow as the fuel for your fireplace, and it should be avoided. Alder is also best avoided on the fire if you have any choice, being very sluggish to burn and very smoky. You spend ages coaxing it into life and then, when it does get going, it drives you away in search of a few lungfuls of clean air. By the time you have got your breath back, the fire has wound down to a recalcitrant smoulder.

There are those who will try and tell you that it is simply a matter of permitting such species sufficient time to dry out before setting light to them. Purely in terms of energy release, there is something in that. If you are intending to burn these species inside a well-designed modern wood burner, all will be fine. In the hearths and fireplaces of sixteenth- and seventeenth-century Britain, however, smoke was a serious problem. There were also the factors of time and space. Cutting wood at the end of one winter for use in the next was already a challenge in the growing confines of London and other urban environments. Doing so two years in advance was extremely awkward. The woodmonger who sold the billets might claim that his willow or alder had been seasoned for two years, but there was no easy way of checking if he was telling the truth. (Even today, you need a special wood moisture-measuring gadget to do this.) And he too needed a reasonably quick turnaround if he wanted to make a living.

There is a superstar of firewood – ash, which burns beautifully and fairly cleanly even when quite green. It burns almost as hotly and steadily as oak but is much easier to get going. It also requires very little in the way of fire management, just getting on with the job with scant need for human interference (with small chance of anything going drastically wrong). The small 2-inch (5 cm) diameter single billets will take straight from your kindling, especially if you have scraped a few bits of charcoal and charred ends together from a previous fire. The fire will move quickly from one single billet to another, giving you a good blaze within five minutes. The next size up, the one-caste billets, maintain a good, sustainable fire, giving you about twenty minutes of useful action before needing to be stoked. Enlarging or reducing the size of an ash-wood fire is a relatively speedy affair, as you simply adjust the size and number of billets you're adding.

In his influential work on forestry and the trees of Britain, *Sylva: or A Discourse of Forest-Trees and the Propagation of Timber*, published in book form in 1664, John Evelyn called ash 'the sweetest of our forest fuelling, and the fittest for ladies chambers'. A few years later, Moses Cook wrote: 'Of all the wood that I know, there is none burns so well green, as the Ash.'

The best-managed households kept stocks of ash, oak and hazel on hand in all three billet sizes, with probably more ash than oak or hazel. The ash would be the main firewood, with a few oak billets placed at the heart of any fire for long-term staying power. The hazel would help to get the fire going quickly in the morning and be good for raising a bit of extra heat when frying or grilling. When roasting, the hazel would be held back and more oak would be put on. This is all very simple in principle and endlessly subtle in practice. Much of this wood-fire management I have learnt through long experience, much as I suppose our forebears did (although they surely had more access to good advice from their elders). But, as a result, it came as absolutely no surprise to me that the most common coppice woods in Britain turned out to be the very species that I would turn to when making a fire.

Oak, ash and hazel dominated the underwood produced in coppices across the length and breadth of Britain, particularly those areas that were serving the needs of larger urban populations. There were of course coppice woods that contained not a stick of oak, ash or hazel, and small pockets grew prolific amounts of willow, hornbeam, elm, birch or beech. But overall, oak, ash and hazel were the top species. The British treescape did not merely supply the population with firewood; it was itself shaped by this function. Anyone looking at the landscape before coal would have seen prospects dominated by these species of trees growing in woodlands actively managed, fenced and felled on a regular schedule to produce a huge supply of small, straight, evenly grown trunks and branches.

I mentioned in the foreword my work on the reconstructed cooking galleys for Henry VIII's flagship *Mary Rose*. In the underwater wreckage, six hundred pieces of firewood survived from 1545. Most of it was found in the area next to the ruined galleys. Now this was not firewood intended for an open hearth in somebody's home; the crew cooked on two large brick fireboxes, or 'furnaces', identical in size and set side-by-side near the bottom of the ship. Each square structure supported a large jam pan-shaped pot with a gently rounded, flattish base. Below the pot the firebox was fully enclosed, apart from an opening at the front akin to an oven door. Wood was burnt within the enclosed space, heating the pots and their contents. It was, as I said, very similar to Edwardian laundry coppers, except that the door on the *Mary Rose*'s fireboxes was a little larger in proportion to the overall structure than its more modern siblings. The ship's pots and furnaces are large, much larger than you would likely find in any household. One of the pots has a capacity of 360 gallons (1636 litres) – and that's the small pot. The other could hold around 600 gallons (2727 litres).

Most of the written accounts of using firewood in big furnaces like the ship's come from industrial contexts. For example, Peder Månsson's guide to glassmaking from 1530 dictated building a furnace to a particular size – with a firebox of 20 inches (50 cm) across – and instructed that 'you should stoke it with dry wood, the length of which corresponds to the inner breadth of the furnace'. This is rather interesting, because this length was exactly half the length of the standard billet prescribed by law. It seems that this very precise stipulation about the size of the furnace was only partly due to technical requirements. Something this size would do the job, but it was the readily available fuel that got the final say: just buy standard billets and chop them in half.

The *Mary Rose*'s furnaces had to fit the ship, of course. But I think they were also designed to fit the available firewood. This wasn't a case of a perfect fit, as recommended in Månsson's guide, but a deliberate degree of mismatch that would help in the management of a fire at sea. This is a conclusion I reached by trying it out.

The *Mary Rose*'s replica furnace is regularly furnished with a stack of firewood that matches the wood found in the wreck (birch predominated). Here, there is no need to cut the regular billets in half; they fit in quite nicely at full length – well, not quite all the way in. In fact, they stick out through the furnace's opening by about 4 inches (10 cm) even when they are pushed right up against the back. But this traps the logs in place, so that they are unable to roll either backwards or forwards. On land this would be a wasteful arrangement – or, at least, a mildly inconvenient one – as you would need to knock the protruding ends of the logs into the fire as each billet burnt through. But on board a ship, I can see it would be extremely sensible: it renders fire management almost idiot-proof (for anyone raised around fires).

With your kindling placed at the front of the firebox, where you can reach it easily, the fire, once started, will build up quickly to a cheerily burning pile of about 12 inches (30 cm) in diameter. This fire can be pushed backwards into the centre of the firebox and the first of the billets – three or four of them only, so that you don't smother your little fire – can be slipped in on top. They will only fit into the opening one way round, and therefore have to lie parallel to each other, front to back, and have no room to roll or, worse, spill out. In addition to preventing the billets from rolling around, this also concentrates the combustion immediately underneath the centre of the gently rounded base of the pot. The firebox was impeccably designed to match the burn characteristics of its fuel.

Wood fires like to blend their flames together into a pyramid or spire shape, producing a single, concentrated hot spot. If you interrupt this formation with the base of a pot somewhere between one half and one third of the height of the spire of flame, the flame will fan outwards in all directions and hug the surface of the obstruction. And if you keep the fire in the spot right beneath your pot, you can achieve an extremely efficient transfer of heat. A rounded bottom to your pot adds quite noticeably to the effectiveness, leading the flames out to hug a much greater surface area than you would get with a flat-bottomed vessel. Pots with a round, or sometimes even a globular, bottom were intended to be used over a wood fire. On the *Mary Rose*, there was, however, the extra consideration of safety at sea. You really didn't want hot liquid to slop around too easily. The firebox design, combined with flattish, only gently rounded bases to the pots and firewood slighter longer than the furnace, maximized fuel efficiency while also providing a degree of fire safety.

Once the fire is going well, you can maintain it with remarkable ease and consistency. Every twenty minutes or so, just knock in the loose, unburnt ends and add two more billets. That is it. You do not need to stoke the fire, or fiddle about with the placement of logs; nor do you need to rake or operate bellows. Light it and use the standard fuel of the day and the *Mary Rose*'s galley is almost as reliable and undemanding as a modern gas or electric cooker.

Of faggots and furze

Billets were merely one portion of commercial wood fuel provision. The other major woodland fuel products were 'faggots' – tied bundles of small sticks, twigs and brushwood. From the sixteenth century onwards, faggots were, like billets, subject to legal restrictions on their dimensions when they were put up for sale. Commercial faggots had to be 36 inches (91.5 cm) in length and 26 inches (66 cm) in circumference.

Faggots could be made of any species. They were generally a secondary, or by-product, of something else. When people cut coppice wood for billets, tallwood or fencing poles, all of the trimmings were put to one side for faggot-making. Likewise, trees that were felled for timber were cut into useful pieces and the small wood went into faggot-making too. Hedge trimmings and orchard prunings were also utilized in this way. The estate and household accounts of Sir Thomas Puckering, a landed gentleman, Member of Parliament and son of one of Queen Elizabeth's Privy Councillors, were particularly clear upon this point. On 4 May 1620, he paid a man called Mellowes 'for cutting down the sallowes growing in my great reedy poole, and for making them into faggots, and fire wood'. Ten and a half loads of faggots were produced 'in my wood at Weston' in November, and after felling '2 okes' for timber, there was a payment two weeks later for 'faggotting the loppe therof'. In the following February, he enlisted labour 'for making into fagots the prunings of the trees in my orchard'.

The first step in making faggots is selecting two widely forked poles. These are cut about 18 inches (45 cm) from the fork, both on the main stem and the two diverging branches. When the stems are pushed into the ground about 24 inches (60 cm) apart, a crude cradle is formed. In this you lay your sticks and twiggy bits. When the cradle is full, you bind the contents at each end, just inside each forked stick cradling it, with two thin whippy split rods. Hazel, birch and willow are best for binding, but the stems of clematis, known as 'old man's beard', are also good for this job, as is honeysuckle, if there is any about. It is much easier to tie the binding if you first use a length of thin rope to compress the bundle and hold it in place. I have had most success using a 6-foot (1.8 m) length of cord, at one end of which I have tied a 3-inch-long

(7.5 cm) loop. I pass the looped end around the bundle, slip the free end of cord through the loop and then pull tight, compressing the brushwood as much as I can. Next I pull the loose end back towards me and trap it under my foot. The thin length of rod can then be pushed through the bundle, whipped around several times and pushed back through the bundle to secure the binding before the cord is released. Once securely tied, the bundle can be trimmed at each end, creating a tidy, easy-to-transport product.

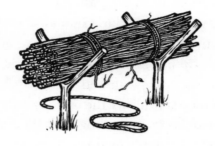

How to make a faggot: sticks and twigs are laid into a cradle formed from two forked branches, then bound with whippy rods.

Faggots were much in demand for lighting fires and stoking a wide range of ovens, furnaces and kilns. Small sticks and twigs burn hot and fast with plenty of flame – just what is needed to get a fire going, to spread it from that first single fragile flame into a blaze that will set light to a block of peat or a billet of firewood. But they also burn away very rapidly. Upon an open fire, faggots are very wasteful things. When the fire is trapped within an enclosed space, they are highly efficient.

Ovens and faggots had been perfect partners for centuries. Indeed, the only real difficulty in managing a faggot fire within an oven was maintaining the flow of oxygen to the centre of the oven.

If, for example, you permit the fire to burn up across the entrance of the oven, all of the oxygen is consumed there, and fuel is left behind, unburnt, within the body of the oven.

Introducing a new faggot can also block the flow of air if you are not careful. As the faggots catch, they burn fiercely, quickly and at a high temperature. A good firing produces a mushroom cloud of flame, rising in a central column and then fanning out around the dome of the oven's roof, licking against the walls. The more sophisticated brick and stone ovens that have survived down the centuries are frequently not perfect hemispheres but rather flattened domes. In these structures, the mushroom of flame can be made to reach right back down to the floor of the oven, curling under and delivering the waste gases and unburnt particles into the centre of the conflagration, to yield up all of their energy. The smoke escaping the oven is minimal, and the heat of combustion is delivered directly to the cooking surfaces. Once the oven surfaces are hot enough, the fire is allowed to die away. The ashes are swept out, a wet mop is run over the oven floor, the food is popped inside and the door is closed, sealing in the radiant heat.

I have had the privilege to fire several original ovens from the late medieval through to the Victorian period, as well as to work on a range of modern replicas. I have used billets, faggots and other traditional and modern shapes and sizes of woodland and heathland fuel. One of my most immediate observations is that, right up until the end of the eighteenth century when commercial faggot production began to peter out, there is a very strong tendency for the dimensions of ovens to match the legal specifications for faggots. The openings just barely permit a 26-inch (66 cm) circumference faggot to pass through. The internal dimensions of the ovens vary, but two of the most common are 30 inches (76 cm) and 36 inches (91 cm) in diameter. The smaller of the two is particularly good for burning a single faggot at a time, while the larger one allows you to tuck the faggots in at an angle, with three or four faggots in a pile. The smaller, one-at-a-time method works particularly well alongside a second fire. You pick up a faggot and hold one end in the fire until it is burning brightly, then carry it over to your oven and pop in the burning end, angling it upwards and a little to one side. The end you are holding can then be pushed in to the bottom of the oven. This removes the need to mess about trying to light a fire within the oven, and the angle ensures excellent oxygen flow. As one faggot burns away you replace it with another until you have reached the temperature you want. An oven with a diameter of 30 inches usually needs three faggots to reach bread-baking heat.

Equally common are ovens with a 36-inch diameter. These work best with a stacking method. Your first faggot, being just the same length as the oven is wide, easily sits flat upon the oven floor. I like to pop it in and then rotate it so that it runs diagonal to the door. The next faggot can be laid on top at ninety degrees and then a third goes straight in, propped up in the middle by the two previous bundles. This configuration allows hot embers to be introduced at the oven's front. The orientation of the twigs within the faggot also helps to move the fire towards the centre of the oven.

In great aristocratic households, bread ovens can be very much bigger than that. (Presumably this was also true of the ovens in commercial bakeries, but no such ovens survive from earlier than the nineteenth century.) Even for these larger ovens, the dimensions match multiples of standard-sized faggots rather well. Ovens markedly smaller than a standard faggot were more likely to be found in small rural cottages, and generally were later in date. Their owners were probably gathering their own twigs rather than buying a commercial product.

We can catch a glimpse of the scale of the commercial faggot market by looking at the probate inventory of a single baker in the town of Banbury. Robert Symons died in March 1586/7. In addition to having both a large stock of 'fyerwood' and '5 quarters of Coles', he had two hovels full of faggots and an entire rick of 'furs'. The faggots, lumped in with a couple of pig sties, are valued at £9; the rick of 'furs', or furze, was worth £10 – each the equivalent of a year's earnings for a skilled worker. In Symons' case, the furze had not yet been processed into faggots, but Sir Thomas Puckering's accounts show us the labour costs involved. In July 1620, he began making payments for 'furse kids at the Aspes'. By the end of the summer, well over 3,000 faggots have been produced from the furze that was grown 'at the Aspes', an area of 'common waste' within the parish of Bishop's Tachbrook, three miles south of Warwick. The man doing the work received something in the region of a shilling for every hundred that he bound. Sir Thomas's portion of land in the Aspes must have included heathland, and it looks rather like he was deliberately managing it for furze production.

Furze is another name for gorse, or *Ulex europaeus*. The scrub-like vegetation of a heath – particularly furze, broom and heather (often known as ling) – can be coppiced in a manner similar to trees in woodland. These shrubs normally live about twenty to thirty years, but if they are regularly cut or burnt down (grazing is generally not severe enough), they will continue to put forward new growth. Each cut effectively resets the ageing clock, just as it does for many tree species. There are references to formal furze coppicing in the medieval period. In the thirteenth century, the manor of Elmswell in Suffolk, for example, operated a seven-year cycle of furze coppicing over a 7-acre area, from which a profit of 18d per year was expected. Two centuries later, 'a certain piece of heath which every seventh year is worth 5s – that is 8½d per annum' was coppiced in Norfolk.

Heathland is not a naturally occurring habitat. It is a landscape produced by human activity upon poor, thin soils that suppresses tree growth and encourages furze, broom, ling and bracken to flourish. Pollen analysis indicates that 6,000 years ago Britain was without any discernible heathland at all. The plant species were present but in tiny volumes, scattered about rather than occurring in large, consistent plant communities. By the end of the Bronze Age, however, evidence of heathland becomes more common. As a landscape it offers people a range of very useful resources, including considerably more grazing than woodland, the provision of coarse thatching material and animal bedding and, of course, a ready source of quick, hot-burning fuel. Many people seem to have supplemented and mitigated the disadvantages of slow, cool peat-burning with an admixture of furze.

The pre-coal landscape was dotted with patches of useful heathland, both large and small. Local communities jealously guarded their right to cut particular areas according to complex rules governing who could cut, when it could be cut, how much could be taken and how often each area was to be cropped, much as we saw with the harvesting of peat as fuel. Then along came coal, and people no longer needed furze and its kindred for fuel, and the cuttings became less regular, in some places ending altogether. With fewer cuttings, the heathlands changed.

It is generally estimated that since 1800, nearly 80 per cent of Britain's lowland heaths have been lost. Sir Thomas Puckering's share of heathland at the Aspes, for instance, is now a rather unremarkable area of ordinary rough pasture and arable fields. There is not so much as a sprig of heather to be seen, and just a few isolated gorse bushes sit by the roadside.

The trade in charcoal

Commercial charcoal-burning was a significant part of woodland management schemes in areas where there was a good market for this premium fuel. Charcoal is a very steady and predictable burner, as well as being rather hotter than raw wood. Better yet, it produces almost no smoke. The heavier industries tended to favour charcoal for its high temperature profile when seeking to smelt, work and forge metal or glass. But there was also a domestic market for this wood product.

Home users were drawn to charcoal for the cleanliness of its burn and its steady heat. It was widely employed in households that made their own malt and brewed their own ale. Until the sixteenth century, brewing was primarily a domestic job. Small, regular batches of ale were made mostly by women at home. It was only during the 1500s that a more urban, industrial model, run by men making large batches of hop-flavoured beer, became routine.

Once barley has been watered and allowed to sprout, converting all of the starches within the grain into sugars (the process known as malting), it must be dried out quickly over a low heat to prevent further growth. Malted grain is particularly prone to holding on to smoke flavours, which taint the finished tipple. Killing the sprout and drying out the malt therefore had to be done with minimal smoke. In poorer households, this was done by using straw for fuel. But if a household could afford it, charcoal was far more reliable. Wealthy households were also likely to employ charcoal for a portion of their heating and cooking requirements.

As anyone who has used a charcoal-fired barbeque knows, a charcoal-fire can be both small and portable. It is easily contained within a bowl or tray of almost any non-combustible material. It can even, with care, be moved around while alight. You do not need a chimney or a dedicated fireplace, although both are handy if they are available. However, burning charcoal does give off carbon monoxide, so ventilation of some sort is essential. That was not much of a problem in the porous homes of the sixteenth and seventeenth centuries.

Earthenware 'chafing' dishes were particularly popular in the home. They allowed portable charcoal fires to be carried into any unheated room. The pottery was light to carry, and the earthenware handles remained cool enough to hold safely if a fire was lit in the dish. These small fires were an obvious improvement in conditions for the small, chimney-free rooms, chambers and closets that proliferated in the homes of the wealthy. They were also used for transitional or 'spot' heat in spaces with hearths or chimneys. If a room was only to be used for a brief segment of the day, perhaps while dressing, a charcoal-fired chafing dish could take the chill off for half an hour much more economically than lighting the main fire. Or perhaps the gentleman of the house would be better served by having a chafing dish at his feet under the desk as he looked over the latest correspondence from his country estate rather than wait for the fire on the other side of the room to get going.

In the kitchens charcoal stoves offered both cleanliness and predictable, steady heat for cooking. Cooking upon such stoves was very easy. Elite cooks preparing elaborate dishes were especially reliant upon them. There are many examples of brick-built charcoal fired stoves surviving in grand country houses up and down the length of the country. Many were in use for centuries, even during the first decades of coal-burning, often alongside and complementary to the main fireplace, and were only fully superseded when coal-fired cast-iron ranges reached their apogee of sophistication and practicality in the early twentieth century. There is, for example, a good one at Cowdray Park in Midhurst, West Sussex, which is open to the public. Inserted into this wood-burning medieval kitchen

A series of iron baskets for burning charcoal set in a brick structure provided the perfect stove for more elaborate cookery, as shown in this detail from a 1757 etching.

probably near the end of the seventeenth century, it may well have replaced an earlier incarnation. Hardwick Hall in Derbyshire also has an extensive survival in very good condition.

The charcoal stove at Kew Palace – which was constructed after London had been a coal-burning city for over 150 years – is today regularly used during demonstrations of historical cookery. I have made a few dishes on it, and in my experience the only difficulty is in timing the addition of fresh fuel to the fire. Anyone who has cooked upon a barbeque will have some sense of the challenges. Modern barbeque advice generally consists of lighting the fire well in advance and then waiting for a white ash to form across the upper surface of your pile of charcoal before commencing with your cooking. The heat at this stage will be high, evenly distributed and steady. You will be able to cook uninterrupted for around half an hour, almost as if you were using a gas-flame grill, before the heat begins to die away. For most home barbecues, this single burn is quite sufficient. A sustained campaign such as that required by the cooks of the grand kitchens of the past meant regular additions of fuel to the fire. If you wait until the fire grows short of fuel and then replenish with enough charcoal to cover the burning surface, you will experience a sudden and large drop in heat output. A single layer of fresh charcoal can almost instantly drop the temperature low enough that you might lay your bare hand upon it (but do be careful if you try to do so). It then takes ten to fifteen minutes for the charcoal to burn through, at which point you're back at a decent cooking temperature. Alternatively, you can engage in a programme of almost continuous feeding, one lump of charcoal at a time. This will successfully keep a fire burning evenly, but it also involves constant lifting and replacing of cooking pans.

Surviving brick-built charcoal stoves invariably have multiple charcoal-burning baskets spaced along the working surface. This permitted the cook to operate a simple regime with multiple charcoal fires at staggered stages of fuel combustion. When one batch of charcoal began to burn down, the pan or pot was moved across to another so that the nearly exhausted fire could be replenished with fuel. In this way, precise, technically challenging and fiddly cookery could be carried out seamlessly. And since such stoves did not require a chimney, they could be sited well away from the smoke and heat of the kitchen's main fires, aiding the creation of the most delicate recipes. Professional chefs working in the biggest and most fashionable establishments worked extensively with charcoal from the medieval period right up to the end of the nineteenth century.

Yet, for all its benefits, charcoal was a relatively expensive fuel. Its production begins with the selection of high-quality firewood, which must be dry, uniform in size and shape and, for the best results, all of the same species in each distinct burn. You clear an area of ground and set up a large post in the centre; alternatively, you can form a central flue by stacking wood horizontally in a triangular format. You then stack firewood around the post or triangular flue, paying very careful attention to the direction in which each piece lie in order to channel air and waste gases throughout the entire mass, and eventually lead it up and away. (In Romania and other places where this tradition is still widely practised, the exact method of stacking differs from region to region, but every version delivers an even movement of air and gases around the wood.) You then cover the constructed wood pile with turf or thatch it with foliage before sealing it up with sand, clay or earth that is packed down to form an almost airtight crust. Now, you can remove the central post, if there is one, leaving a hole. You open a couple of small vents at strategic points in the crust, then introduce kindling and a few burning embers into the central hole or flue, encouraging a good airflow until the stack is well alight. When your fire is established, you block up the central flue with earth, clay or turf and reduce the size of the vents in the crust, which allows the 'cooking' process to begin. If the airflow is successfully managed over the next few days and nights, all of the

Vannoccio Biringuccio's *De la pirotechnia* (1540) demonstrated a superior method for producing charcoal, by building a pyramid of wood covered with sand, earth or clay.

wood within the pile – also known as the 'clamp' or 'kiln' – will burn in such a way that it is converted to charcoal. Too much air and the wood will simply burn away to ash; too little and the fire will go out.

Over the years I have been involved in around a dozen charcoal burns, all of which produced at least some charcoal. Initially, the smoke from the clamp appears white, as the water vapour within the wood is burnt off. Over time, it turns yellow, as the tar is burnt. Finally, a thin blue smoke appears, as the wood starts to convert to charcoal. You can't leave the clamp untended for a moment, as there is a danger that the layers will slip or settle and the clamp will burst into flame. After it appears that the wood has been converted, the fire must be put out, either by comprehensively smothering the clamp with more sand, clay or earth, or by pouring water on it. Sometimes both methods are used in combination. It is amazing how quickly you learn to interpret the smoke signals rising from the clamp.

Skilled charcoal burners can generally convert around 80 to 90 per cent of the wood within a clamp into charcoal. A little more is lost in the cleaning and sorting process, as some of the charcoal falls away to powder when being handled. Only two of my burns have approached anything like this level of efficiency, but I don't have the breadth of experience of past generations.

Beyond the woods

Much of our discussion so far has centred upon the commercial fuel markets. This is in part because they are much better documented than more casual provision, but it is also in part because they form the supply of cities and towns, and the story of coal is very much bound up with the urban experience. However, most – about 95 per cent – of the British population did not live in an urban environment. They got the wood for their fires from other, less commercial sources.

Most people outside of towns and cities had some access to land and the resources that grew upon it. Yet, as we saw with the Wallingfen of North Cave, the countryside was not an open larder for all to plunder. Every scrap of earth, every twig and leaf growing upon it, was subject to ownership and carefully guarded rights of exploitation. Landlords, for instance, generally had the right to all of the timber growing upon their land, but their tenants had the right to all of the underwood. Most farmers were tenants of one sort or another, so the majority of the cultivated land had a minimum of two competing agendas. In addition, common land rights could be very complicated. Different groups of people had the right to different resources, which could only be accessed at particular times or in particular ways. Many commons, for example, permitted the taking of dead wood – but only if it could be extracted without recourse to a blade of any sort. It was allowed if the wood was extracted 'by hook or by crook', which is the origin of the saying.

Beyond the woods, there were a great many other trees available to the country dweller looking to fuel the domestic fires. Trees lined the roads and lanes, the rivers and streams. They graced the edges of greens and ponds and dotted the hedgerows. All were potential sources of fuel. There were also the hedgerows themselves, which needed an annual trim that yielded more combustible material. And then there were the pollards.

Pollards are trees that are periodically cut like coppice stools, but the cut is made not at ground level but further up the main trunk. This produces a very distinctive shape of tree, one that nowadays is seen infrequently. Most of the extant examples are quite old, even ancient, the most visible of which are willows lining riverbanks. They have a troll-like quality, with thick, gnarly trunks that often lean at a drunken angle, abruptly morphing about 6 feet (2 m) up, where the main stem is replaced with a mass of young rods and poles sprouting like wild, woody hair from between the healed scars of previous cuttings. Many people think them ugly, even 'maimed'. But like coppice stools, pollards can have a much longer life than an uncut tree because each cut resets the tree's natural lifespan. Pollards can be four or five times older than uncut specimens. They were once very common because

Like coppicing, pollarding extends the lifespan of a tree and provides a useful crop of small branches.

they satisfied the needs of both landlords and tenants, as well as livestock keepers and fuel users.

Since landlords retained the right to any timber on their land, regardless of any rental agreements, they understandably wanted as many trees as possible to grow to full size. Felling and selling timber could supply a great cash boost for an estate. (Profligate heirs, grand building projects and backing the wrong side on the political stage tended to result in major felling programmes.) In good times, a prudent landowner encouraged tree growth as a form of dynastic insurance. Consider that the late seventeenth-century writer Joseph Blagrave advised his gentleman-farmer readers to plant 'Fuell and Firewood sufficient to maintain many families, besides the Timber which may be raised in the Hedge-rows, if here and there in every Pearch be but planted an Ash, Oak, Elm'. Since a perch is a length of 16½ feet (5 m), fitting a full-sized timber tree into every perch of hedgerow was pretty dense planting.

Tenants saw it rather differently. Full-sized trees inhibited the growth of arable crops and offered them no compensatory benefits. Tenants were, however, permitted to cut and use the small growth of pollards, hedges and coppice on the land they rented (the trunk remained the property of the landlord). A pollarded tree produced good, usable poles and rods, perhaps not with quite the same efficiency as a coppice stool but still with a reasonable yield. Pollards also cast less shade over a planted field and drew less water from the ground. A sort of low-grade battle ensued wherein rental agreements contained clauses requiring tenants to plant, or at least permit, saplings to grow up into timber trees, while tenants quietly and surreptitiously converted them into pollards by cutting off the tops when the trees reached about fifteen or twenty years of age.

Records brought together by Tom Williamson, Gerry Barnes and Toby Pillatt in their study of *Trees in England* reveal this conflict in action. One lease, for a farm in Barnet in Hertfordshire dating to the early eighteenth century, required the tenant to 'do every Thing in his Power for the Encouragement, and growth of the young Timber Shoots, under the Penalty of Twenty Shillings for every Shoot of Sapling which shall be wilfully hinder'd from growing'. There were further financial penalties if the tenant were to 'stub up, prune, or injure any Sapling'. Five pounds was the punishment for outright destruction of a timber tree.

The second trade-off was between grazing and fuel production. As we have seen, a well-managed copse required secure fencing to prevent animals from eating the young shoots after a felling. But what if fencing an area off was not an option, as was often the case upon common land? Pollarding placed new shoot growth several feet off the ground, out of the reach of browsers. This type of commons was known as wood pasture. The more densely packed were the pollards, the more fuel could be produced, and the more widely spaced the managed trees, the better quality the grazing. Such wood pasture was a good compromise where competing common rights were shared between members of the community.

Wood pasture was once very common among the landscapes of Britain. In his *History of the Countryside*, Oliver Rackham pointed out that the Domesday Book of 1086 listed wood pasture separately from other types of woodland in some counties. In Lincolnshire coppiced wood and wood pasture occupied similar acreages – around 2 per cent of the land area. In Nottinghamshire there was five times more wood pasture than coppiced woodland, while in Derbyshire there was twelve times more, with 24 per cent of the total land area given over to wood pasture versus 2 per cent for coppicing.

From the late sixteenth century onwards, many landowners commissioned detailed surveys of their holdings, and these frequently included both written and pictorial representations of their timber trees, with the age and species noted. Some of these surveys, particularly those from the eighteenth century, can be utilized to locate and enumerate hedgerow trees. *Trees in England*

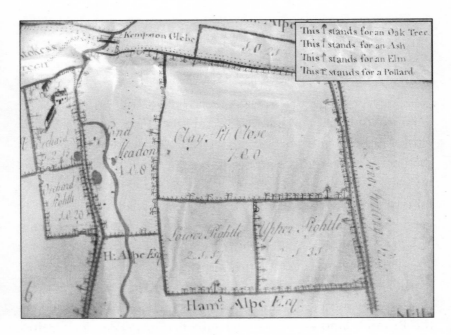

This † stands for an Oak Tree
This † stands for an Ash
This † stands for an Elm
This † stands for a Pollard

A 1764 map of Beeston-next-Mileham, in Norfolk, surveyed to show the species of hedge trees: oak, ash, elm or pollard.

gave the example of Henry Keymer, a surveyor working in Norfolk who prepared maps for several estates. Each hedge upon his maps was carefully marked with the location of standing trees that he divided into four types, allocating a different symbol to each. Oak, ash and elm were given a unique stylized tree icon, while the fourth symbol was 'for a pollard' of any species. The hedgerows on Keymer's maps bristled with these drawings. A 2½-acre square field on a farm in Beeston-next-Mileham had forty-seven tree symbols drawn within its hedge lines, all but eleven of which were pollards.

Some areas of the country boasted more hedges than others, with open, strip-farming areas having far fewer hedges than areas of small enclosed fields. Still, there were plenty of hedges around the farmyards, villages and roads of sixteenth-century Britain.

Once upon a land of trees

The provision of firewood entailed regular work for agricultural workers who might otherwise have been idle and unpaid through the depths of winter. The dependable financial return that could be gained from a scrap of woodland within reach of a ready market encouraged people to manage coppices and leave them to grow on a set schedule rather than grub them up in the hungriest of times. Townspeople too saw the benefit of preserving a little woodland close to home. Many a town council argued loudly and long in defence of these resources. And London, unsurprisingly, exerted the most extensive pressure upon the management of the Britain's landscape. It drew supplies from as far as 50 miles (80 km) away and rewarded landlords who, year in and year out, produced the sizes and species of firewood that were most convenient to transport and burn.

While wood remained the primary fuel of Britain, trees, woodlands and hedges were jealously guarded and carefully tended. Whenever and wherever demand for fuel was modest, care was looser, and arrangements were a little less formal. A wilder mix of species and growth was permitted. Closer to towns and cities, woods were more intensively and intently managed.

The switch to coal had a huge impact upon the natural world and the management of it. Coal replaced coppice wood, faggots, furze, peat, ling, pollards and all other organic fuels. As these resources were no longer needed, the landscapes that produced them were transformed.

Managed woodland suffered the least. There were many uses for good quality, straight-grained wood. If the economy had remained static when the switch to coal took place, there probably would have been a major change in these woodlands, as firewood was no longer wanted in such quantities. But that is not what happened. The population was on the rise, quite dramatically so, and the economy was growing. More people wanted more things, and more were in a position to have at least some of them. London's switch to coal came just as surges of activity happened in some older industries that used wood or charcoal in their kilns, forges and furnaces, such as glassblowing and iron casting. So as the capital's demand for commercial firewood plateaued, charcoal-burning actually increased.

The building industry was also benefiting from the expanding urban population. The growth of London called for more timber for house building, more planks for flooring, more poles for scaffolding and, later, more wood for crafting doors and window frames and furniture. The managed woodlands of Kent, Buckinghamshire and Hertfordshire were able to adapt to meet these new demands with ease. If anything, the management of woodland in these areas intensified in the ensuing centuries. As coal took over, woodlands were planted to produce materials suitable for building rather than fuel. The Chiltern Hills, once a major supplier of London's firewood, gained a new reputation as a centre of furniture-making.

Other landscapes fared less well. Heathland and moors were particularly vulnerable to the march of coal. When locals stopped cutting the furze, broom and heather, heathland was viewed differently. The supply of grazing and craft materials was not enough to justify maintaining its plants. Farmers stopped thinking of such land as useful, and the word 'waste' creeps into treatises upon agriculture. Moreover, the heathland becomes waste that can be 'improved'. From the middle of the seventeenth century, the draining and ploughing up of 'waste' becomes the goal. Landowners and tenants invested money and labour in converting heathland into cropland to meet urban demand for food.

The hedgerow and field trees fared no better. Wood pasture had been disappearing for centuries as population pressures encouraged more intensive agriculture. When pollards were no longer desperately needed for firewood, many of the surviving stands were furtively removed by farmers looking to improve the grazing on commons or newly enclosed pastureland. Though hedges and trees continued to serve a range of other functions – such as providing boundaries and barriers between areas of land, giving shade and shelter to livestock and binding the soil along river and stream edges – these did not require quite so many pollards or such wide, thick shaggy hedgerows. Farmers were keen to cut back hedges and cut down pollards, allowing more light into their fields and reducing the drain on water and nutrients. The landscape was quietly, but successively, thinned.

What emerged was a countryside focused upon food production – a little bit tidier, a little bit more uniform. Not a landscape stripped of trees, or totally devoid of moor and heath, but definitely a land of more universal agriculture dependent on fossil fuels. Coal tipped the age-old balance away from short-term energy. And over the past two centuries, oil, gas and electricity have done nothing to upset this new status quo.

Fuel for thought

Fossil fuels in all their forms may now have passed their zenith. The threat of climate change, concerns about national fuel security, environmental degradation and dwindling reserves have inspired a hunt for renewable energy sources for the future. Yet, for a variety of reasons, we are unlikely to revert to a complete reliance upon wood, peat and dung or, to give them their more modern name, 'biomass energy'.

Researchers have made great strides in recent years in improving processes and technologies in order to maximize efficiency in the use of plant- and animal-based energy sources. Anaerobic digesters are busily turning food waste, garden waste, cattle farming slurry and dung from poultry farms into biogas and fertilizer. Dry biomass materials – such as straw, wood from tree surgeons and household recycling centres, and willow grown upon a short coppice cycle – are burnt in highly efficient ovens and furnaces. Waste vegetable oils and animal fats are converted into biodiesel. Wood pellets fire power stations that once ran on coal. In 2019, Britain's Renewable Energy Association announced that 11 per cent of the country's energy was supplied by biomass sources, and there is considerable political pressure for that figure to rise. Meanwhile, the last two decades have seen a return of the domestic wood-fired stove, with about 1.5 million homes, or about 10 per cent, in Britain owning one in 2018. Sales stand at around 200,000 stoves annually.

Setting aside the issues of carbon sequestration and fine-particulate air pollution, there remain a bevy of questions about how a return to wood-burning would affect the planet and the lives of the people upon it. The ancient tension between using land for food production versus using land for fuel production has not gone away. The British landscape as yet shows little sign of the renewed competition for space and sunlight, with just a handful of willow and poplar coppices being planted and harvested for fuel. Instead, most of the competition between food and fuel is happening on the world stage, with many of the UK's needs outsourced to other nations. The majority of the wood being burnt in Britain's converted power stations, for example, is imported from the US. Crops deliberately grown for biofuels are speeding deforestation on a massive scale and threatening food security on several continents far from Britain's shores. The best way forward is by no means clear. Fuel, food, landscape and environment are intricately linked, as they always have been.

There are many historical narratives about the development of the British countryside, each playing their part in defining the present. Much has been written about the enclosure of open medieval fields, which were worked in strips side-by-side with neighbours, into separate and hedged, fenced or walled ones, worked by individual independent farmers, or about the large-scale deforestation that allegedly ensued in order to feed the ship-building of the Royal Navy – a history that today is juxtaposed with analyses of surviving ancient woodlands and the changing fashions of planting various species for building and furniture-making. Wide-reaching drainage schemes that 'reclaimed' land from the fens and marshes are discussed as part of a tale of increasing agricultural productivity. In each of these stories, domestic coal is an unwritten character.

Coal did not just change the landscape, climate and environment with its slag heaps, smoke and industrial expansion. It also changed the hedgerows and woods, fields and farming, the species mixes and plant communities, that make up the green and pleasant land of the UK.

THE DRAW OF COAL

For centuries coal was rarely Britain's fuel of choice.

There were some places where people chose to burn coal from early on. In Pembrokeshire and Carmarthenshire, where the highest-quality 'stone coal', or anthracite, is found, it was in regular use when the traveller and chronicler John Leland visited in the 1540s. To his surprise, people were burning coal 'though there be plenty wood'. Sixty years later, the Welsh lawyer and antiquarian George Owen, in his *Description of Penbrokeshire*, described the local coal as 'very good'. Unlike other types of coal, he claimed, it 'made a ready fire' that was 'voyde of smoake' and produced 'greater heate than light'. He also noted how it 'burneth apart and clyngeth not together' rather than smothering the fire in ash as some coals did.

In addition to its ease in burning, the coal in this corner of Wales was incredibly convenient to source. Sometimes also known as 'peacock coal', it had an almost oily, darkly iridescent surface and was often found in easy-to-access surface outcroppings. Gathering it was less onerous than chopping down trees for firewood. It 'doth not require man's labour to cleve wood and feede the fiere continually', wrote Owen. Better yet, it was sufficiently clean-burning that 'fyne camericke or lawne' cloth could be dried in front of it 'without any staine or blemish'. It was even considered as suitable 'to rost and boyle meate'. Here – and for centuries, here alone – coal was considered to be the superior fuel, with few of the drawbacks people everywhere else associated with it.

Leland's bewilderment was more typical of the experience most people across Britain had with coal than was Owen's gushing endorsement. From Northumberland to Kent, most English coal did not make 'a ready fire' that was 'voyde of smoake'. Quite the opposite. The coal in the rest of Wales was equally poor. Owen himself wrote that other Welsh coal was 'noysome for smoake and loathsome for the smell'. He moaned how 'ring coal' from the more easterly areas of Wales 'melteth and runneth as waxe and growth into one clodde'. The same was said of the coal then being used in Scotland.

Three hundred years of experimentation and technical development would turn domestic coal-burning into a homely art that is looked back upon with a degree of nostalgia. But it did not start out that way. Coal was not an easy fuel to use without the tools, techniques and appliances that were to come later.

Stoking the coal fire

The first problem was getting coal to burn at all. Tip out a pile of the stuff onto the ground and attempt to set fire to it without an accelerant and you will begin to see the problem. Now have a go at lighting a small wood fire directly on the same ground – a much easier proposition – and then add the coal on top; there's a strong possibility the coal will still fail to take. It requires a fairly substantial and long-lasting wood blaze to get coal started. And once it has caught, your problems are not necessarily over.

A coal fire flat on the ground can be a sluggish thing whose vigour is sapped by the build-up of its ash and clinker. Oxygen is the key factor here. Modern coal fires are burnt in a grate that exposes coal surfaces to the air by lifting the pile of fuel up off the ground and letting the ash and clinker fall away. Cold air is actively drawn up through the grate by the very act of combustion, with the rising heat creating a vacuum, or 'draw'. This draught is transformative. Coal with and without the use of a grate is almost unrecognizable as the same fuel.

A simple basket grate is essential for coal-fire management. The grate lifts the coals off the ground, ensuring good airflow to the fire.

The people of Pembrokeshire and Carmarthenshire, provided as they were with high-quality, hard anthracite, probably managed to burn coal without a grate, but it was still hard work. It would have required a combination of adjusting the size and shape of the coal lumps and forming the wood of the initial fire into an open and supportive framework – akin to building a grate out of firewood. As the wood burnt away, discrete lumps of smouldering anthracite would maintain their shape, including the integrity of the air gaps between the lumps, allowing oxygen in to feed the fire. Most other coal would smother itself. George Owen sang his praise for the coal of west Wales, saying it 'clyngeth not together'. For everyone else, dependent on the many varying grades and types of coal in the rest of the British Isles, burning coal without a grate was a frustrating business.

Now, people had long been aware that wood burnt better when lifted off the ground to encourage this draw. The simplest method was to use two 'sacrificial' logs set flat upon the hearth across which you balanced other firewood. As the fire burnt, the upper logs combusted merrily away, while the two base logs slowly smouldered or charred. New fuel was dropped regularly on top to sustain the blaze, while the base logs needed only infrequent replacement. Fire management involved keeping an eye on the overall shape of the fire and being ready to slot in a new base log when required.

One of the great innovations and status symbols of the Iron Age was to replace these two base logs with an iron fire support, or a pair of them. Archaeologists believe the earliest surviving examples of such iron supports were typically placed in the centre of a roughly circular open fire. These early irons were shaped something like a capital H. A cross bar was supported about 4 inches (10 cm) off the ground, with the firewood propped up and held at an angle in the middle of the fire circle. With pieces of wood propped up on both sides, a sort of tunnel was formed beneath the bar that encouraged cold air to be drawn in from both ends; the upright bars at the sides prevented the wood from rolling off.

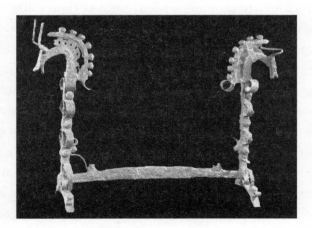

This Iron Age firedog, discovered on a farm near Capel Garmon, in Conwy, Wales, must have been the property of a powerful chieftain; archaeologists estimate that it may have taken the smith about three years to construct it.

Thus the idea that raising a fire off the ground improves the rate of combustion was neither strange nor new. It may well have seemed an obvious thing to try. But it's much harder to raise up burning coal than it is to raise up flaming logs. You need an extensive structure, one that is more complicated to manufacture, and which utilizes a lot more metal. For a long time it was probably not worth the effort or the expense to burn coal.

The problem with smoke

Once you got your coal burning, the next great technical problem to overcome was the smoke. Recall George Owen's frustration with how 'noysome for smoake' most coal was. He was not alone in his ill opinion; coal smoke was universally detested. In the 1660s, John Evelyn called it a 'feluginous and filthy vapour'. Other commentators said it was 'noxious', 'unwholesome', 'unsavoury', 'offensive' and 'sulphurous', an 'arsenical vehicle' with 'corrosive particles' that 'annoyed' and 'corrupted'.

Peat smoke, wood smoke and coal smoke can all be difficult to live with and all are harmful to your health. But experience tells me that wood smoke is the least unpleasant and difficult to live with, while coal smoke is the most problematic. Peat, as mentioned earlier, produces large volumes of smoke that are particularly high in harmful fine particulates because it burns at lower temperatures. Peat smoke tends to create a much bigger if more diffuse cloud than does wood. The smoke is less visible and less distinct. One lives in a fine haze. Wood is more likely to burn with a hotter, clean flame producing fewer emissions, although this is partly dependent on how well the fire is managed. When the air is still, wood smoke rises with ease, leaving clean air at head height. Coal, in contrast, burns hot but produces a collection of chemicals that are particularly liable to hang low, gathering in places where people need to breathe. The high sulphur content of coal smoke affects the eyes as well as the lungs. When it mixes with water, a mild sulphuric acid is formed – what, on an atmospheric level, we call 'acid rain'. The more immediate human experience is stinging eyes as the smoke makes contact with the wetness of the eyeball. When your eyes try to flush out the irritant by producing tears, the stinging gets worse.

The solution to the problem of smoke is the chimney, but most homes prior to about 1550 rarely had one. Domestic fires typically sat upon an open hearth in the middle of the room. All the heat generated by such a blaze was trapped within the living space while the smoke rose, cooled and slowly drifted up and out through any gap it could. Since windows were largely unglazed and roofs were generally thatched, a special opening in the roof was not always necessary. Smoke simply hung in the roof space until it could gently percolate out of the structure.

The quality and behaviour of smoke within domestic environments was no small matter. In the relatively still milieu of an interior space, wood smoke creates a distinct and visible horizon, below which the air is fairly clear and above which asphyxiation is a real possibility. The height of this horizon line is critical to living without a chimney. The exact dynamics vary from building to building and from hour to hour as the weather outside changes. Winds can cause cross-draughts that stir things up; doors and shutters opening and closing can buffet smoke in various directions.

Coal smoke is more like peat smoke in some respects and like wood smoke in others. Initially, when the exhaust from a coal fire is hot, the smoke is dark and distinct, rising and roiling like wood smoke but far more visible. Then as it begins to cool, it spreads out and drops somewhat, creating a more diffused atmosphere, present at all levels but becoming denser further up, like the smoke from a peat fire. Smoke management is one of those unspoken daily realities that we have next to no written record of, and yet it must have been a very pressing issue and life skill. From my experiences managing fires in a multitude of buildings in many different weather conditions, I can attest to the annoyance of a small change in the angle of a propped-open door, the opening of a shutter or the shifting of a piece of furniture that you had placed just so to quiet the air. And as for people standing in doorways, don't get me started.

Over time households would have developed strategies for dealing with the prevailing winds, planting or removing trees around the house, blocking up old doors and windows and opening new ones in more suitable spots. They might even, where possible, adjust the angle and position of new buildings to take into account the local wind patterns.

But it's not just about the wind. Temperature, air pressure and humidity levels have an impact as well. On cold, damp mornings, smoke hangs low to the ground, quickly losing the heat that helps it rise. Hot sunny afternoons, in contrast, help speed smoke up and away. Damp air acts like a lid, holding the smoke down. A rainy day means the smoke horizon drops; a clear frosty morning means it lifts. A well-managed wood fire in a well-managed home can produce a virtually smoke-free living experience so long as you are burning well-seasoned wood and are content to live life at ground level. No rooms above the ground floor was the norm during the era of open hearths. Naturally, there were moments when it didn't go as planned, when gusts of wind blew the smoke into every corner of the room, or a bad batch of wood and a change in the weather pulled the smoke horizon uncomfortably – and dangerously – low. But in general, the situation was tolerable. People lived like this for millennia.

Replacing wood with coal, with no other adaptations to the home, made life a lot harder. Coal meant more smoke within the living area, and it meant smoke that stung the eyes and affected breathing. People burning coal upon open hearths probably coughed a great deal more and had to deal with running noses too. In short, until they came up with a new way of organizing their living structures, their lives became quite a bit more miserable.

The cost of wood

For reasons that historians cannot quite put a finger on, population growth in the sixteenth century was increasingly concentrated in just one place – London. Other towns and cities were growing, but at very modest rates. The imbalance became more and more marked, and the ancient city of London became both larger and more densely populated. The Domesday Book, completed in 1086 by command of William the Conqueror, reported London's population as roughly 15,000 people. That figure rose to 80,000 before the plague struck in the mid-1300s and halved the number of Londoners. Gradually, through the first half of the sixteenth century, the city recovered, to about 50,000 residents. By the end of Elizabeth I's reign in 1603, the population had quadrupled to 200,000. This urban population boom created unprecedented demand for fuel supplies with hardly any time for adjustments in the chains of supply. It was a crisis in the making.

Looking back at the dawn of the fourteenth century, when London's medieval population was at its peak, we can see that problems with the fuel supply were already developing. In the decade between 1270 and 1280, for example, the price of faggots produced in the demesne of Hampstead, just five miles from London and listed among the accounts of Westminster Abbey, was 20*d* per hundred. Only a decade later, the same demesne was valuing them at 38*d* per hundred. Three manors in Surrey, all within 20 miles (32 km) of London, saw a 50 per cent rise in fuel prices between the 1280s and 1330s. The rising price of fuel is especially noticeable compared to the almost entirely stable price of wheat. Food supplies for the capital were keeping pace with demand, but fuel supplies were under pressure.

Nor was this simply a problem of haphazard and inefficient provision. A well-established and organized trade was in place, centred upstream from London Bridge around Wood Wharf, in the parish of St Peter the Less, and dominated by a group of men known as *buscarii* in the Latin texts – the woodmongers. These merchants had links with the owners of woodland and estates stretching far along the Thames and into surrounding counties. The closer these woods were to London, the more likely they were to specialize in short-cycle cropping.

Transport costs played a huge role in determining wood production in these areas. The bulkiest forms of firewood were bavins and faggots, both of which required a great deal of cart or barge space. Bavins, an especially small form of faggot used almost exclusively for lighting fires and composed of the smallest of twigs, could be produced in a single year; for the London market, they were produced primarily in Middlesex. Faggots arrived in the capital mostly from Middlesex, Surrey and Essex, as well as some of the more accessible parts of Buckinghamshire, Hertfordshire and Kent, not more than about 12 miles (19 km) away. There was little profit in carrying such bulky fuels any great distance but their relatively quick production cycle made them an appealing prospect to those with woodlands close to the city. Billets and tallwood held more value per load, so were worth the higher transport costs entailed in hauling them from more distant woods to market. Charcoal, being lighter and easier to transport, might come from as much as 26 miles (41 km) away. It was light enough to permit the use of a packhorse to carry the burden. To some degree, rising prices encouraged people from outside the capital's usual wood-supplying districts to expand or redirect their business. But venture far beyond the reaches of the Thames and transport became much more difficult and costly.

By the mid-sixteenth century, when London's population was once again nearing 80,000, problems in the supply of wood were reasserting themselves. Firewood prices were ticking up rapidly, outstripping price rises for pretty much every other commodity, and concerns were being voiced from many quarters. According to the *Chronicle of the Grey Friars* of 1542/3, the Lord Mayor of London was reported to have been visiting the wood wharves daily, putting pressure upon the merchants to supply wood to the poor at reasonable rates. A number of local government officials were trying to cut out the middlemen in an effort to hold down prices. Statutes were passed to address the cost and availability of both fuel and timber.

William Harrison, writing his *Description of the Island of Britain* in 1576, worried that firewood was running out, and that before long 'broom, turf, gale, heath, furze, brakes, whins, ling, dies, hassocks, flags, straw, sedge, reed, rush, and also sea coal will be good merchandise even in the city of London, whereunto some of them even now have gotten ready passage and taken up their inns in the greatest merchants' parlours'. These less desirable fuels had all been used at various times and in various places across the country. But London had grown accustomed to receiving regular commercial wood supplies via a sophisticated supply chain. The idea that Londoners might have to resort to the fuels of the rural poor was unsettling.

At this difficult and pivotal moment we get a snapshot of the capital's fuel market from the probate inventory of Thomas West, a merchant, based in Wallingford, roughly 50 miles (80 km) from London (then in Berkshire, now in Oxfordshire), who died in 1573. The inventory includes a long list of his debts and business dealings over the last eight years of his life. West seems to have had depots upstream on the River Thames at Burcot, where he had an agent working on his behalf, and at Culham, just south of Abingdon, in Oxfordshire. Downstream, he maintained a presence at Pangbourne, in Berkshire. He moved a reasonable volume of agricultural produce (around 20 per cent of the entries that specify any particular good), a small but noticeable amount of fish (6 per cent) and a fairly sizeable volume of coal (20 per cent). But the main bulk of his business, representing 40 per cent of the entries that specify any particular good, was in transporting wood down the Thames towards London. In fact, West's wood, and most of his agricultural produce, was sent downstream, while the fish and coal, along with a myriad of tiny quantities of various other goods, came upstream, out of London, before being distributed to settlements across the surrounding countryside.

Fifty miles – the actual journey following the course of the river is actually considerably longer – is an awfully long way to be shipping firewood, yet that was what the majority of West's wood cargoes seem to have consisted of. Reference was made in some cases to 'timber', meaning the much higher value, large straight pieces of wood used by the construction industry, but much of the wood was described as billet or tallwood. An important part of his trade involved supplying the royal court in London with firewood. While this may well have involved some gratifyingly large orders, it did come with its own difficulties. A significant number of the debts listed in his probate inventory were from the Board of Green Cloth and its assignees. One of these debts, incurred by John Manwood on behalf of the royal household, had been outstanding for two years and was recorded as having been partly paid off in cheese!

The vigour and extent of Thomas West's trade in firewood in a region so far from the city centre mirrored contemporary records of rising prices and elite concerns. London was looking to augment its fuel supplies by reaching further out, and as a result, was forced to pay the higher transport costs involved. But what of the coal that West was also shipping? This coal was travelling out of London and being delivered to a variety of landings and stagings along the river's banks. Most of the coal debts in West's inventory were from blacksmiths. It was the smithies' trade that he was supplying, and he was doing so with coal purchased in London.

Coal had certainly arrived in London by the turn of the thirteenth century. Several records mentioned it being used by lime burners in 1180. Within fifty to seventy-five years, London smiths were using coal sufficiently regularly for it to become the specialist cargo of a few wharves downstream of London Bridge – and for it to attract the attention of the tax collectors. It came in the main from the outcroppings of surface coal in and around the Tyne and Wear estuaries.

By sea or by land

Britain is very well endowed with coal deposits. There are the easily accessible anthracites of south-west Wales; large deposits of differing types of coal running in broad bands across much of south Wales; and another, smaller deposit in the north, on the coast in Flintshire. Scotland has coalfields that stretch in a belt from Ayr to Glasgow, Stirling, Kirkcaldy and Edinburgh. Nottinghamshire and Derbyshire are blessed with their own swathe of accessible coal, while smaller coalfields are scattered throughout the Midlands at Wolverhampton and Stoke-on-Trent and to the north of Manchester. On the north-west coast of England lies the small coalfield around Whitehaven, while the area around Bath and Frome and that around Coventry are the two sources of coal that are geographically closest to the capital.

But in the early days of the trade, London drew its coal almost exclusively from Newcastle. For all that Newcastle seems remote from London, it had the closest of the outcroppings by the sea route to London. In some places near Newcastle, the coal was right on the water's edge, eroding out of the cliffs and riverbanks to be gathered on the beaches. Simple and cheap to extract, sea coal was also simple and cheap to load onto boats and carry to other ports.

Scotland was three days' sail further north and, as a separate country then under its own king, it was often politically at odds with England and Wales. So, very little Scottish coal made its way to London in these early years. The Welsh coalfields, despite fewer political and trading difficulties, were nearly twice as far from London by sea than Newcastle, and the voyage involved piloting the dangerous seas around Land's End. Overland transport meanwhile was extortionately expensive in comparison to transport over water. If you spent £1 on coal at the Newcastle pithead, it would cost you a further £3 to ship it to London, 250 miles (402 km) away. If you asked a carter to transport your £1's worth of coal overland, £3 would get it less than 10 miles (16 km) from your starting point. In other words, London was lucky. Coal could be had in the heart of the city at the same sort of cost that would have prevailed if a great surface outcropping

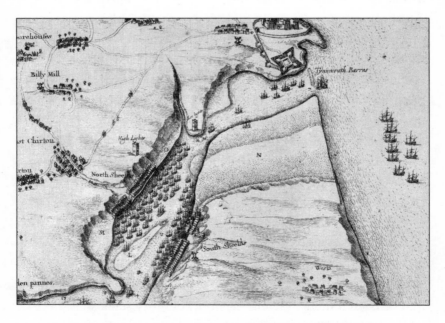

The River of Tyne Leading from the Sea (c. 1651) by Wenceslaus Hollar, showing ships waiting to be loaded with 'sea coal' for the journey to London.

had naturally occurred within a 10-mile radius. To all intents and purposes, there was an untapped fuel resource sitting on the capital's doorstep.

This was not the high-quality anthracite of Pembrokeshire, but a softer, more sulphurous version that caked when burnt and gave off a plentiful supply of stinging black smoke. Still, it suited the needs of the lime burners and the blacksmiths very well, despite the plentiful complaints about the smoke from their neighbours in local records.

London's lime burners, who supplied lime mortar for the building trade and limewash for paint, liked the sea coal from Newcastle because it was a more concentrated form of fuel than wood and was cheaper than charcoal. Limekilns work best with large batches of fuel. The fuel is stuffed into the bottom of the kiln with limestone packed on top, followed by more fuel and limestone, in alternating layers. Once the kiln has been filled, the fire is lit. The heat initiates a reaction with the limestone (calcium carbonate), producing both carbon dioxide and lumps of calcium oxide. After the fuel has burnt away and the carbon dioxide has wafted into the atmosphere, the limestone has, hopefully, been converted into pure quicklime (calcium oxide). Coal neatly packed into a kiln takes up far less space than does wood, and it burns long and steady, releasing more heat and thus ensuring more limestone is converted to quicklime in each campaign of burning. It also allows for near continuous production, since more layers can be added to the top of a burn as the finished material is removed from the bottom.

As far as the early lime burners were concerned, the ideal coal was a so-called 'nutty slack' – some of the cheaper, more broken-up loads of coal from Newcastle. The 'slack' was essentially coal dust, while the 'nutty' elements were small lumps of coal mixed in. For each 5 inches (12 cm) of depth of nutty slack shovelled into a kiln, around 10 inches (25 cm) of limestone was loaded on top of it. Many builders considered the quicklime produced with nutty slack to be a superior product to that produced with wood.

For blacksmiths, the caking qualities of Newcastle sea coal were invaluable. Recall how smiths can create different shapes of fire, including a sort of cavern or oven shape. Watered and tamped down, fires of sea coal could be shaped very accurately to provide particular areas with precise temperatures. The ash and clinker could also be manipulated within the forge to a smith's advantage, creating cooler areas to rest the work, or acting as insulators around hot spots. And most importantly, coal didn't burn away as rapidly as its main historical rival, charcoal.

By the time of Elizabeth's reign, word had spread across the country of the technical advantages of burning coal in these two industries. As a result, wherever a supply could be had at not too great a cost, coal was finding a market. Thomas West's customers in Berkshire and Oxfordshire were among the lime burners and blacksmiths who had heard about the wonders of coal. His coal was certainly well-travelled, having been gathered near Newcastle, loaded onto a barge and carried down the Tyne, reloaded onto coastal vessels for the journey down to London, then transferred back onto a barge and sailed up the Thames.

Chimneys and their cousins

Two key technological developments were needed to transform domestic coal-burning from a difficult, horribly smoky experience into a daily ritual that could be not only tolerated but adopted across the city: the iron grate and the chimney. Of these, it was the chimney that involved the biggest and most immediate investment and upheaval in living arrangements. And again, a certain serendipity came into play.

Castles, monasteries and other great houses began to have chimneys not long after the Norman Conquest. But building in stone, even just the stone for a chimney stack, was supremely expensive, and for centuries, chimneys were restricted to the super elite. There were very few people living in stone dwellings, with the majority of even the aristocracy living in more traditionally British wooden abodes.

These earliest chimneys were perhaps viewed more as status symbols, following imported patterns rather than developing organically to solve a domestic problem. A fire on the floor in the centre of the room is very heat efficient. All of the energy released by the fire radiates out evenly into the living space. Chimneys, on the other hand, channel around 70 per cent of the heat of a fire straight up and out of the building. Moreover, these structures are typically located at the edge of the room, creating an unevenly heated space. They also produce a draw, which sucks cold air in at the base, creating a cold draught at floor level. With so much inefficiency built into the design, those who built chimneys needed considerable means to contend with the original capital investment of building and the significantly higher ongoing fuel costs. It came down to a choice of burning considerably more fuel or accepting a much colder home.

London may well have been at the very forefront of the development of the chimney in more modest homes. Chimneys began to be mentioned in London with some frequency in documentary evidence from the fifteenth century. Regulations gathered together and copied out in the *Liber Albus* of 1419 by John Carpenter, the town clerk of London, insisted that chimneys should no longer be made of wood. Instead they were to be constructed of stone, tiles or plaster. It's not clear if these were chimneys in the modern sense, or one of a myriad of 'interim' chimney forms being experimented with. There is less ambiguity in the will left in 1488 by a London mason called Stephen Burton. It included a stock of pre-made stone fire surrounds, known as 'parells', that were meant to be inserted into the chimneys of his wealthy customers. Images from the mid-sixteenth century – including the famous

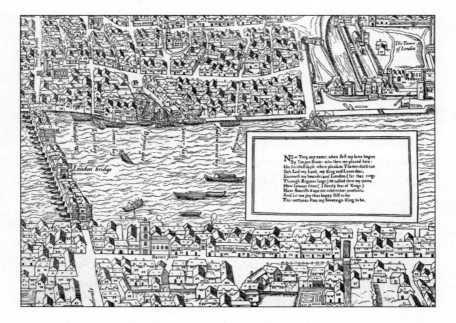

Detail from the map of London, drawn by surveyor Ralph Agas in 1561, showing the area around Southwark, London Bridge and the Tower of London. Already, a number of buildings had chimneys.

Wyngaerde Panorama of 1543/4, another panorama of London by an unknown artist made *c.* 1550 and held by the Ashmolean Museum in Oxford and the Agas map of 1561 – clearly depict a considerable number of chimneys on the city's skyline. However, a certain, very inconvenient fire in 1666 destroyed the vast majority of the physical evidence of them.

Domestic chimneys did not sprout up all at once, although it may have sometimes seemed that way to contemporaries. For instance, in 1577 William Harrison of Essex reported fussily on the 'multitude of chimneys lately erected'. The old men in his village remembered 'in their young days there were not above two or three, if so many, in most uplands towns of the realm (the religious houses and manor places of their lords always excepted, and peradventure some great personages)'. Instead, Harrison wrote, 'each one made his fire against a reredos in the hall, where he dined and dressed his meat'.

Not everyone made the switch from open hearth in the middle of the room to a chimney set against a wall in one fell swoop. There were a range of considerably cheaper 'transitional' forms that were much less disruptive to instal. Harrison's reredos were a sort of fireback, generally chest high and 4–6 feet (1.2–1.8 m) long. In some places it was a large flat upright stone, but it could also be a short section of fire-resistant wall, even one of wattle and thick daub, against which the fire was built. The short wall helped channel air around the fire and was particularly useful in counteracting the sudden changes in draught caused by opening and closing a door.

Another option was the smoke bay, which the people of Kent seem to have found particularly congenial based on the number of homes sporting them between the end of the fifteenth century (when wood was still king) and the mid-seventeenth century (when

Central hearth with reredos in a croft on Birsay, Orkney
(photograph c. 1900).

coal began to arrive). A smoke bay was created by the addition
of rooms within part of the roof space, leaving a smaller, more
constricted but still open passage for smoke to rise up from the
fire to the rafters.

An especially good survivor of this sort of domestic arrangement,
in an unusually ordinary and modest home at that, can be found
in the Weaver's House in Spon End, near Coventry. The house
was built in 1455 by Coventry Priory as a speculative investment,
one of six in a continuous row, or terrace, intended to be rented
out to local craftspeople. On the ground floor at the front there
is a reasonably sized room that would have been the hall or
'houseplace'. This room would have contained the home's hearth,
either located in the middle of the room or, given the modest
space, pushed to the room's side with a reredos behind. The other
ground-floor room is the size of a small bedroom. It is presented
today with a small bed in situ, but it may have been used as a

Sketch of the layout of the interior of the Weaver's House at Spon End,
near Coventry, with the smoke bay above the main hearth and a first-floor
room to the side, providing a smoke-free living space that also helps to
channel smoke up into the rafters.

buttery, a storage area for foodstuffs and household equipment like tubs and churns. From this room a steep staircase – more a ladder, really – ascends to the only room on the first 'floor'. This room is a little larger than the room below it and overhangs part of the hall. It currently houses a loom and may well have been a dedicated working area. The timber frame indicates this was the building's original configuration, with one upstairs room perched in the traditional smoke space, usable because the walls seal it off from the area over the fire. The smoke from the hearth was left free to waft about and percolate its way out through the roof, untrammelled by any sort of chimney.

Another urban model can be found in Tewkesbury among the Abbey Lawn Cottages. Managed by the John Moore Museum, the Merchant's House is one of a row of late-fifteenth-century buildings. Open to the public, it is presented with its original room layout, including a large hall open to the roof but partially subdivided by an upstairs room.

I have been lucky enough to spend time in buildings with a smoke bay, cooking, brewing, baking and generally hanging out doing historic stuff. The effects of these structures for managing smoke are intriguing. The areas beneath the jettied-out upstairs rooms were considerably less smoky than those areas open to the rafters. The smoke bay changed the normal flow of air within the space. The upstairs room acted as a lid, preventing the air beneath the jetty from rising, and causing it to become really still, so that very little smoke gathered there. The air in the open area could rise freely and move out through the roof, which ensured the smoke-laden air was usually drawn up and away from the fire. Despite there being no physical barrier between the two areas up to first-floor level, the two bodies of air barely commingled. One created a gentle, upwards-moving, smoke-laden current, the other a static, smoke-free volume.

Differing more in degree than in fundamentals was the smoke hood, another halfway-house smoke management system. A fine one can be found in the Avoncroft Museum of Historic Buildings in Bromsgrove. The fifteenth-century town house has a hall with a hearth located in one corner. Over it sits a large wattle-and-daub hood, roughly 6 sq. feet (2 sq. m), which ushers smoke up and away. Though the hall remained open to the rafters, the hood reduced the amount of smoke that gathered in the room, and because there was no constriction around the fire itself, no great draw was created. Like the smoke bay, the smoke hood was more of a smoke collection and channelling apparatus.

Those smoke hoods which have survived are generally constructed of wattle and daub, lath and plaster or wood – the sort of chimneys described in the *Liber Albus* regulations. They were typically sited about 6 feet (2 m) above the fire, or at ceiling height, and continued up through the building to an opening in the roof, much like a primitive chimney. The fairly wide funnel they create –

Constructed of wattle and daub, lath and plaster or wood, a smoke hood could be easily inserted into the home, at much less cost than a true chimney.

usually between 4–6 sq. feet (1.2–2 sq. m) – allowed the smoke to cool as it ascended, meaning that the smoke hood was much less likely to catch fire than people today often expect.

If you are burning wood, a hood offers distinct smoke management advantages over an open fire, without costing too much in terms of construction or ongoing fuel costs. It is also relatively easy to insert one into an existing building. Without a draw, the majority of your fire's heat remains within the room, and with no ground-level side walls, your access to the fire for cooking is fairly free. A hood is less of a help in controlling coal smoke, which is much less eager to rise once cool, nonetheless there is something to be gained from one.

That simple smoke hoods were often called 'chimneys' in period sources is made clear by the accounts for the construction of a 'chimney in widdowe Cox her house in Saltisford' to provide separate accommodation for 'Widdoe Whood' in the same building. A carpenter was employed for four days, along with two sawyers for one day, and a load of rods and laths was bought in order to insert this new 'chimney'. Once the chimney had been built, a tiler by the name of Barnes was paid to 'tear' the chimney and make the hearth. Constructed of a combination of sawn wooden planks as well as the rods and laths, and then plastered, with a hearth that was probably lined with tiles, the whole accommodation could be inserted into an existing building quite quickly.

When I think about these changes in the home, and the uneven and ad hoc nature of the solutions people were devising to address common domestic problems, I am reminded of the great double glazing and central heating installation frenzy of my own youth. Central heating systems had been in use in churches and grand houses in Britain for nearly a century, but in the 1960s, most people's homes still relied on coal, gas or electric fires that essentially heated only one room. Then, suddenly, things began to change. By 1970, 30 per cent of homes in Britain had some form of central heating. Double glazing, originally a Scottish idea, became quite popular in the 1970s and really took off with the introduction of a uPVC version in the 1980s. Within a couple of decades both had become widespread. Central heating take-up was particularly quick: by 1990 around 95 per cent of homes had a system, a proportion that has remained pretty stable to the present day.

Many families went through a stage of having partial central heating systems, which didn't reach all areas of the home, or of having 'secondary' double glazing, which involved fitting a relatively cheap extra layer of window over the top of your existing panes. It didn't look as neat, or have quite the thermal efficiency of true double glazing, but it involved much less expense and disruption to instal. New builds, however, soon came to include both central heating and double glazing – initially as much vaunted and advertised selling points, and later as standard features.

These changes had a profound impact upon the way homes are utilized. When heat was available in just one room, there was a distinct pressure on families to spend time together communally in this single space. As the heat spread out, so did the inhabitants. The rise of games consoles and on-demand entertainment systems, for example, probably owes as much to the rise of central heating as it does to any other technology. There have been a whole host of other indirect responses. Larger houses with more bedrooms and other separate spaces became more attractive propositions when all of those spaces could be heated, fuelling a boom in construction. Meanwhile, bathrooms have become much more desirable places, ones in which people are willing to spend more time, helping to stimulate the personal care industry.

With the benefit of hindsight, these overhauls of living spaces and lifestyles appear to be obvious, perhaps inevitable improvements, part of the great forward march of technology. Living through such a transformation, however, feels much less obvious, inevitable or even all that beneficial. The changes were costly; people vacillated over whether or not to make the improvements, unconvinced that they would see any long-term pay-off. Early adopters struggled to learn how to use the new systems. Others held on to the traditional ways out of emotional attachment. But once the ball started rolling, neighbour followed example of neighbour, and homes and home life were reconfigured.

Back in the fifteenth and sixteenth centuries, a similar pattern held. Architectural surveys of the old housing stock of the British Isles show an enormous volume of adaptation and remodelling of homes in order to include chimneys where once there had been none, particularly between 1550 and 1650. In the more prosperous south-east of England, including William Harrison's village in Essex, where reredos were being lamented, such changes came early. In remoter and poorer districts further from London, the changes came a little later.

People adapted their homes in fits and starts, as they could afford, especially within the urban environment. Reredos were cheap and easy to instal. Smoke bays required much more investment and greater upheaval but were undoubtedly more desirable, since they increased the amount of living space with the insertion of the upstairs room. Both the Weaver's House at Spon End and the Merchant's House in Tewkesbury were built as speculative ventures. They were designed to attract rent-paying tenants and offered with the 'new' smoke bay layout as standard – much as builders of the early 1980s included central heating and double glazing in their developments. The speculators knew that more and more people would want these features in their home.

First movers (and furnishers)

Already the most densely populated city in Britain, the pressure to maximize living space was always strongest in London. Smoke bays and smoke hoods, including those 'wooden chimneys' banned in the *Liber Albus*, were steadily being replaced by substantial true chimneys built of stone or brick. As early as 1370, a row of eighteen shops built by the Dean and Chapter of St Paul's next to their brewery boasted a chimney on each unit. The contract for the mason specified ten chimney stacks, eight of which were attached to doubled, back-to-back fireplaces facing into two separate retail units, thus serving all of the properties. The fireplace surrounds were to be lined with Flemish tiles and the hearths were to be of stone and tile shards.

In homes where chimneys had been installed during the wood-burning era, the desire for more heating may have been a spur to switch to coal. A fireplace was fixed in size by the brick- or stonework and its chimney. A roaring blaze could be expanded only up to a point. There was a very real limit to the amount of fuel you could add to your fire. If you wanted more heat to compensate for the 70 per cent that was escaping straight up the chimney, you needed to burn something that produced a hotter flame. Coal delivered more heat.

Another complementary response to the heating problem was to subdivide your space. If you could no longer afford to heat the whole of your living accommodations with a single central hearth in an open hall, you could at least heat one portion of it around a fireplace, walling the immediate area in to trap the heat. The rest of the house might well be freezing, but you had somewhere to thaw out at the end of a hard day.

There was also the issue of furniture to consider. With an open central hearth the most comfortable area within the home is close to the floor. Sitting in a tall chair on a rainy day, when the cooler, damp air pulled the smoke horizon down low in the hall to below your chin, ensured bouts of coughing and spluttering and general discomfort. It was much better to furnish your home with low stools, or better yet, to cover the floor with a warm, insulating layer of soft rushes and sit directly upon them. The same approach was taken to sleeping arrangements, with your 'bed' (what we would call a mattress or pallet) placed directly on the floor.

Surviving probate inventories hint (but no more than hint) at these practical realities. It is extremely hard to tell from a list of someone's possessions at the time of their death whether they were living in a house with or without a chimney. The buildings were rarely described in detail. That was not, after all, the purpose of the document; it was not a bill of sale. You can make a reasonable guess about how many separate rooms there were by the way items were grouped together and many, but not all, inventories did name some of the separate spaces. References to 'upper chambers' are particularly suggestive. In a few, very rare cases, it's possible to link an inventory with a surviving building. There does, however, seem to be a loose relationship between central hearths and small, low furniture in regions where the surviving houses show that chimneys were only adopted late in history. Similarly, there seems to be a relationship between chimneys and rather more substantial volumes and styles of furniture in regions where the still extant buildings show earlier chimney adoption.

It wasn't just that central hearths discouraged tall, substantial furniture; chimneys actively called for it. The floor-level draught that a chimney produced was no pleasant thing if you had to sit and sleep on the floor. Once you had installed a chimney, you were subject to a cold insinuating incentive to visit the carpenter and invest in some furniture that could raise you up a few inches. Bedsteads that lifted your mattress or pallet up off the newly draughty floor significantly improved your comfort.

These everyday practicalities actively slowed the adoption of chimneys when wood and peat remained the dominant domestic fuels. Building a chimney alone entailed a large initial outlay in building works. With new furniture added to the costs, a chimney more than doubled people's bills. Chimneys were worth this financial burden for the Norman monarchy, upper aristocracy and religious houses, all of which sought to make a statement about their superior cultural heritage through the sophistication of their buildings. These elite were naturally more likely to invest their wealth in large 'statement' pieces of furniture such as thrones and banqueting tables. They used their rooms for ceremonies and other large gatherings of people. A chimney, housing the fire at the side of a room rather than in the centre, was an asset in such spaces if only for snob value. The reduced heat could be easily mitigated by burning enormous quantities of wood and, later, coal.

But if these were the practical issues surrounding chimney installation there were also more nebulous cultural questions. Take, for example, Penshurst Place, the home of Sir John de Pulteney, a very wealthy Londoner who was elected mayor of the city on four separate occasions. Built in 1341 on a grand scale with no expense spared, it is a stone-walled building whose great hall measures 60 x 40 feet (18 x 12 m). The hall is capped by a magnificent 60-foot-high chestnut beamed roof. High tracery windows provide a lovely light. At one end of the hall lies the 'solar', or private family wing. Here Sir John and his family could retire from the public congregating in the hall itself. At the other end of the hall are the remains of a service wing, now comprised of a buttery and pantry along with a passage that once led to the kitchens (sadly demolished). Despite very ample financial resources, and the example of a couple of centuries of chimney experimentation around Britain in buildings of a similar status, the Pulteney family chose to erect a central hearth in their brand-new, statement-piece hall. Hearths were ancient symbols of home and hospitality, stability and tradition. They harked back to the days of chieftains and feasting. Good fellowship, open and honest dealing and strong community values were all embodied by gathering around an open central hearth. There may even have been a feeling that a fire in a chimney was an indication of a withdrawal from the common good, a selfish layout that restricted warmth – literal and proverbial – to a small group clustered in front of it, leaving everyone else out in the cold.

The Pulteneys were an exception among the elite, but their choice reflected the status quo. For most people across wood-burning Britain, warmth produced cheaply was much more valuable than stone cold status. Affordable heating throughout the living quarters of a home was worth the unpleasantness of the handful of smoky days to be expected from a central hearth.

There were, however, several rather powerful and practical points in favour of chimney technology. A chimney reduced the amount of smoke at ground level, where people were used to living, but even more radically, it did so higher up in the room, lifting the smoke horizon. With a chimney it was possible to make use of the space above head height. A full upstairs area could be employed in the home, doubling or trebling the size of your living space within the same four walls. This was a very attractive prospect for families packed cheek by jowl in tight, often awkward urban plots. Chimneys also offered improved fire safety – a boon after the Great Fire.

So, near the end of the sixteenth century, the pace of chimney building began to accelerate. It began, as we have seen, in the prosperous south-east, where more people could afford to invest in a status symbol, and in London, where population pressures were changing the economics of housing. With more and more people living in the capital, rents were rising and more people were squeezing onto each and every piece of land. The only option left was to build upwards. A three- or four-storey building was increasingly the norm in London. With rooms stacked upon rooms, smoke control became essential.

Perhaps these two factors – a mixture of social aspiration and fashion in the countryside with the population pressure upon urban living spaces – would have been enough to usher in chimneys right across the country. But there was a third driver:

coal. While coal cannot be blamed or lauded as the originator of the move over to chimneys, it was central to the spread of this new approach to inhabiting the indoor realm. If you wanted to burn coal in your home, you were going to have to find a way of dealing with the sulphurous and particularly low-hanging smoke. Chimneys were the answer.

Once a household made the switch to coal, they quickly found many good reasons to build, maintain and upgrade chimneys. Because coal burns hotter than wood, the resultant smoke is hotter too. The smuts get sticky in a way that wood smuts and ash do not. Coal smoke also lays down a thick black coating upon the surfaces of any flue that it passes through. Hot and clogged with combustible soot and coal tar, the chimneys used while burning coal are therefore at higher risk of catching fire than those used while burning wood. The makeshift wood-and-plaster smoke bays and smoke hoods were much more vulnerable to catching ablaze once people adopted coal in the home. Experiments in smoke management like the smoke bay and smoke hood facilitated the uptake of coal-burning in more homes, since they made it marginally safer to use this fuel. But these interim systems were soon shown to be insufficient, resulting in the adoption of substantial, sealed brick- and stonework chimneys in even modest abodes. These true chimneys created more of a draw, keeping the air clearer of smoke but pulling in cold air at ground level. This in turn encouraged people to invest in more furnishings and subdivide their spaces. By this point, they were committed to this new fuel and its accompanying lifestyle.

The shift from wood to coal thus transformed homes from bigger open spaces where a wide range of activities took place into collections of several smaller, furniture-filled rooms. It is only now in the late twentieth and early twenty-first centuries, with central heating, that the spaces in which we live are once again widening and broadening.

As London's population surge took off in earnest, we see a city where the lack of space was already encouraging a patchwork of developments in fire and smoke management. More than anywhere else, the capital's residents had a good number of homes that could cope with coal reasonably well. Others, if not exactly perfect, were better equipped than most of their rural brethren to deal with the foul, acrid smoke of their new fuel of choice. But once Londoners made the switch, the rest of the country followed.

LONDON,
TRANSFORMED

It is the gathering of taxes upon the imports of Newcastle coal which gives us our clearest picture of the big switch that was happening in the great capital. Until the mid-sixteenth century, somewhere between 10,000 and 15,000 tonnes of coal was arriving at the city wharves annually. This then is our baseline: the amount of coal sufficient to fuel a couple of specialist industries within the city and supply some forward-looking (and relatively prosperous) blacksmiths along the upper reaches of the Thames.

By 1581/2, however, a dramatic rise was under way. That year, 27,000 tonnes of coal arrived. By the end of the decade, the haul was close to 50,000 tonnes annually. After that, the trade increased by leaps and bounds: 68,000 tonnes in 1591/2, 144,000 tonnes in 1605/6, 288,000 tonnes in 1637/8. By the late 1680s, more than 500,000 tonnes of coal was landing upon the city shores – and being taxed.

When you plot the rise in coal imports alongside the rise in London's population, the picture becomes even more dramatic. As early as 1577, William Harrison, in *An Historical Description of the*

Island of Britain, noted that coal use 'beginneth now to grow from the forge into the kitchen and hall'. In the mid-sixteenth century, when the population hovered somewhere between 80,000 and 100,000 people, less than 20,000 tonnes of coal were brought into the capital, enough for approximately one quarter of a tonne per capita. By the 1610s, when the population stood at a little over 200,000, there was three quarters of a tonne of coal available per person. It was as if each individual Londoner was consuming three times as much coal as had their parents, and now there were twice as many Londoners as there had been then.

But was this increase in coal consumption really down to individual Londoners? Historians who study the development of the nascent coal industry are convinced that, in the main, it was – or, at least, it was down to individual households. John Hatcher, for example, concluded that 'the most important transition of all was the progressive adoption of coal for domestic heating'. Similarly, William M. Cavert argued that 'the early modern world's leading coal market was driven primarily by domestic rather than industrial consumption'.

Coal on the horizon

Another way of looking at the question is to take a close look at London itself during this transitory period. As a first stop, consider the view of London taken from the property surveys drawn up by Ralph Treswell around 1610. Treswell, a member of the Worshipful Company of Painter-Strainers, had managed to pick up the skills of a surveyor and cartographer and gained employment drawing up plans of land holdings and buildings. In central London his two main clients were Christ's Hospital and the clothworkers' guild, storied institutions that owned large and varied portfolios of sites within the city that they rented out to a long and equally varied list of tenants. Treswell's surveys give us a detailed portrait of London's housing stock before the Great Fire swept almost all of it away in 1666.

All of his surviving plans depicted the ground floor of the building, although many contained notes about the number and name of the rooms above. He differentiated between stone walls, brick walls and 'standard' walls (presumably, timber-framed walls with wattle-and-daub or lath-and-plaster infill). Wooden fences were also represented. Every well was marked, and so too

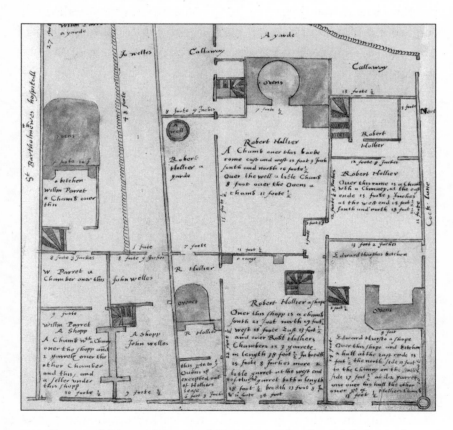

Survey of Giltspur Street and Cock Lane taken by Ralph Treswell for Christ's Hospital *Evidence Book* (1611). We can see ovens, fireplaces, and 'a range' in the centre.

were ground-floor privies and staircases. Most excitingly for our purposes, he also marked the fireplaces.

These were not generic symbols. Each fireplace was shown with its position within the room. The illustrations varied in size according to the size of the fireplace, and differing thicknesses of brickwork were carefully drawn, with a number of unusual shapes, alterations and adaptations discernible. While some included ovens, many did not. For those with ovens, the oven doors were depicted, some facing in to the fireplace and others facing out to the room. There were no central hearths marked for any of the properties, nor was this simply an oversight, as almost half of all the ground-floor rooms in the surveys had a fireplace instead. In fact, I have yet to find a room described as a 'kitchen' that did not have a fireplace.

There were brick fireplaces in rooms named as chambers, halls and parlours; in wash houses and a few shops, which were perhaps catering establishments; and in drinking rooms in taverns and alehouses. They also appeared in many rooms labelled only with the name of the tenant.

Thirty years later, London, as drawn by Wenceslaus Hollar, bristled with brick chimneys, very much in line with Treswell's interior surveys. Between the mid-sixteenth century and the mid-seventeenth, a generous scattering of chimneys had grown into a positive forest of them. Did a city that was already practised in building brick chimneys experience a chimney-building spree as more and more people made the switch to coal starting around the 1570s? Or did the existing chimneys encourage households to start using coal? Or could it have been a bit of both? Either way, by 1610 London was a city superbly, and perhaps uniquely, equipped for domestic coal-burning.

As London switched to coal, worries about the supply of wood faded somewhat. Wood was increasingly expensive, but so many were using coal, particularly in poorer households, that it was changes in the price of coal that now needed to be watched

Detail from *A Long View of London from Bankside* by Wenceslaus Hollar, showing the proliferation of chimneys across the city's skyline by 1647.

carefully. In 1601 the Privy Council tried to reassure the Lord Mayor of London that Her Majesty took concerns about coal supply very seriously and was well aware that high prices could have serious consequences for the capital. By 1610, Parliament described coal as the 'ordinary and necessary' fuel of the city, 'spent almost everywhere in every man's house'.

Throughout the city, households had made the switch from being wood-burners to being coal-burners, and there were more

Londoners than ever before. The change proved to be both swift and for the long haul.

For every man, woman and child?

By 1600, London was a coal city and would remain so well into the twentieth century. And as the city grew, its appetite for coal grew with it. It would be illuminating to be able to see how exactly the big switch occurred for this generation of Londoners and how it remodelled city life. But beyond the bare totals, we know very little about the dynamics of how each household made the decision.

We do not know for certain which sectors of the population were quickest to change. Was it the poor, the middling or the wealthy who first decided to use coal instead of wood? Did dockworkers, blacksmiths and lime burners, who had greater access to coal, carry a bit of this fuel to their homes, and its use spread from there? Was there perhaps a small community from a traditional coal-burning area – like Pembrokeshire – who introduced it to their neighbours? We have nothing to tell us whether people made the move incrementally or wholesale, if some swapped completely or if most mixed their fuel consumption, at least for a time.

Nor do we know who within the household was responsible for making the purchase. When it came to spending money, men were typically in charge of all large capital expenditures, such as the purchase of land and livestock, while women took responsibility for day-to-day expenses of items like bread and candles. Fuel supplies sit right on the gender divide. A large stock of fuel to last the year might be a capital outlay; smaller, weekly deliveries more like the purchase of cheese and butter. Was the switch to coal led by men or women? It is an intriguing question – and unanswerable at present.

In his influential volume *The Industrious Revolution*, the historian Jan de Vries looked at consumer behaviour and household economy since 1650. Although he did not cover fuel use, he highlighted the importance of considering 'the behaviour of ordinary working people in the context of their aspirations and of their choices. This is not to deny that these choices are often highly constrained, but it does reject the view that they do not exist.' Such a way of thinking reminds us that simply because coal was much cheaper than wood, this does not necessarily mean poorer members of society switched to it. Choices were available to them: they could use coal exclusively, prioritize certain wood-burning occasions, skimp heavily on some other expense to fund a wood habit, use a mixture of fuels or manage without any fire at all. I would argue that the figures themselves hint at a complex collection of choices.

An average consumption per head that rises from one quarter to three quarters of a tonne of coal annually within thirty years speaks of a significant aggregate shift, but three quarters of a tonne per person leaves quite some room for individual decision-making. I asked two solid fuel suppliers about average orders today, and modern demand suggests that a single fire used only during the winter months in an efficiently designed grate and chimney consumes about 2 tonnes of coal. People who try to heat both their home and their water entirely by coal generally use more than double that amount. Those who use a coal-fired AGA or Rayburn range as their main cooker tend to go through between 3½ and 4½ tonnes annually.

Of course, in the past people typically lived in households rather than separately, so if we want a more realistic picture to measure against the modern experience we must lump together individual shares of average coal usage. According to the Cambridge Group for the History of Population and Social Structure, the average household size in the late sixteenth century was around 4.75 persons, although the figure may have been more or less in urban contexts. There was also a small amount of coal use in brewing and other industries, which historian William Cavert has estimated at just under one quarter of London's total coal supply. So, the average household would therefore have consumed around 2½ to 3 tonnes of coal per year. Based on modern experience using coal, this level of provision would have allowed each household, with careful management, to maintain one coal fire sufficient to cook upon throughout the year.

Slightly more rooted in reality are the rations of contemporaries. In 1620, the bakers' guild described the typical member's household as including a master, mistress, children, servants and apprentices, and declared that for a year they needed four 'chaldrons' (or 'chalders') – a measure specific to coal that is just under 6½ tonnes. This household would have been larger and more prosperous than the average in London, keeping a warmer home and doing a great deal more cooking. Compare it to the almshouses maintained by the merchant tailors' company, who gave one chaldron (just over 1½ tonnes) to their resident almswomen, or those kept by their less generous compatriots, the brewers' company, who doled out half a chaldron.

One indication of people making choices about where and how they spent their money can be seen in the plethora of commercial catering establishments, from pie shops to taverns, dotting London. Sixteenth- and seventeenth-century Londoners who required no fire at home, whether on a particular day or as a regular habit, could bring home a takeaway or eat out. It might seem odd that a poorer person would choose to eat out rather than cook at home, but after factoring in fuel costs, the time spent cooking (rather than being engaged in money-earning work) and the likelihood of living in crowded accommodation without basic facilities (such as a chimney), then daily bread from the baker and the occasional hot pie from the shop on the corner, washed down with a jug of ale, was a sensible option. If they did not need to depend on a fire to feed themselves, there may well have been a large number of poorer people who 'chose' not to burn very much of anything at all.

Will ye buy my sack o' small Coals, or will ye buy a - ny great Coals?

A seventeenth-century coal seller, captured by Marcellus Laroon
for *The Cryes of the City of London, Drawne after the Life* (c. 1688).
The cry 'Small coals!' appeared in the very first broadside versions of
Cryes of London, dating to the 1620s, suggesting a street trade was
well-established by then.

Looking 'inside' individual homes is difficult due to the legacy
of the Great Fire, which erased a large body of evidence about
the lives of ordinary folk. Just as the housing stock went up in
smoke, so too did the vast majority of local records. Many other
areas of the country boast large collections of wills and inventories
describing the possessions and household interiors of the middling
and better-off members of sixteenth-century society, but such
surviving records are much rarer from within the city. The very
wealthy are more likely to have left a trace, probably because
their records were considerably more copious in the first place,
and because they were often deposited in a variety of locations,
sometimes far from the capital.

An interesting slice of life in London in 1620 comes from the
household account books of Sir Thomas Puckering, the Member

of Parliament whose use of faggots and furze helped us to understand woodland management. Sir Thomas lived in rented accommodation in London for part of the year, spending the rest of his time at his main home in Warwick. Fortuitously, his accounts thus probably rested in Warwick when the fire broke out in Pudding Lane.

On 11 January 1620, Sir Thomas was preparing to move up to his lodgings in London where he was 'going thither to Parliament'. In anticipation his servants laid in a stock of fuel, purchasing one chaldron of sea coal for 18s and a thousand oak billets for 20s. The following week, after he'd arrived, saw purchases of a handsaw 'to saw our billets with' and a sawhorse 'to saw them on'. There was also a payment of 1s 6d to his bailiff 'for dressing the wood in my woodyard and carrying it into my woodhouse'. Most of the family and servants had stayed behind in Warwick on this occasion, so the fuel was intended for use by a fairly small group. Yet, both types of fuel were essential to maintaining a gentleman's London home, and they were both bought in bulk.

One of the earliest London inventories taken by the Court of Orphans (who looked after the inheritances of the underage orphans of freemen of the city and whose records do survive), that of Robert Manne from 1623, did not list the fuel in the house. However, it did allude to fuel choices through the inventory of household equipment, including 'an Iron for seacoles' in the kitchen and 'an iron grate' in the 'long garret'. The other fire furniture within the house – and it was a big and richly equipped home – were more suitable for wood-burning. This provides a clue to interpreting the inventory of Gregory Isham's estate in 1558. Like Manne, Isham was a wealthy London mercer with a large and well-furnished home in the city. (In this case, the family also had a house in the country, where copies of the inventory were preserved.) Here there was a particularly early reference to possible coal-burning consisting of an 'Irene harthe' in 'the garrettes'. The

Earl of Rutland's London pad was much grander than either of these men's homes. In 1630 alone, the household consumed a colossal volume of fuel: 30 chaldrons of sea coal (equivalent to 42 tonnes), 6 tonnes of a cleaner variety called 'scotch coal' (from Scotland), 26 loads of faggots and 12,000 billets.

That the wealthy felt the need to continue the practice of wood-burning is no great surprise. Sea coal was smelly and dirty, a fact of life about which people moaned repeatedly. High-quality firewood and charcoal remained readily available in London, if you could afford it. The rising price, I imagine, might have lent wood fires a sheen of status and exclusivity. But why were they also burning coal? Both mercers appear to have used coal in the lower-status areas of their homes: the kitchen and the garret. Parlours, halls and chambers, which were more likely to be occupied by the master and mistress, were furnished with andirons to support wood within a fireplace. This pattern continued for decades: coal for the kitchen and servants' areas, wood for the spaces occupied by more 'important' household members and their guests.

Each according to degree

That the wealthy aspired to manage households noted for both fine hospitality and frugal housekeeping might seem contradictory. But these aspirations were tightly bound up with the belief in socially appropriate provision, the idea that what was suitable, and indeed necessary, for a lord was not the same as for a labourer. Differentiated provision was a moral good in Britain (and wider Europe), allowing lavish spending on entertainment and economizing in housekeeping to sit comfortably, side-by-side. Indeed, we see this worldview holding in many aspects of British life through to the nineteenth century.

Sixteenth-century British society still followed a legal code for appropriate dress, called the sumptuary laws, which stipulated cloth types, colours and even cuts of clothing according to a person's social status. The restrictions were laid out most precisely at the upper reaches of society, where the clothes of a duke were distinguished from the clothes of an earl and so on, but even commoners' dress was prescribed. Apprentices were required to stick to a more restricted range of styles and cloths than those allowed for their masters, in whose homes they lived. This public, visual stratification was seen as a virtue; it helped to produce a 'well-ordered society'.

Food preparation fulfilled a similar philosophical function and was backed up by contemporary medical understandings. Food suitable for your station in life was considered to be healthy, while food for a different walk of life was wasted on you. Medical men even argued that the digestive processes of labourers and lords worked differently. Labourers were said to have 'hotter' stomachs that cooked and broke down coarse fare, turning it into good, digestible 'chile'. If they ate more dainty meats, it was believed their stomachs would scorch and ruin the food, providing no nutritive value.

Within the wealthier households of the day different dishes were served to people based on their social status. The lord and his fellow diners at the top table enjoyed a large, varied array of dishes, many of which employed great labour on the part of the cooks. Plain, cheap, hearty food was offered to the 'lower' servants, while a larger, more mixed menu was laid out for higher-ranking ones. The very top echelons of domestic staff were favoured with a few additional dishes from the lord's table itself. Since most members of the household, regardless of their status, ate together in the main hall, the different provisions of food were very obvious. They were supposed to be. Social cohesion and hierarchy were understood to be strengthened by the daily ritual of eating together, 'each according to one's degree'.

Over time these two aspects of living life 'according to degree' fell out of use. Sumptuary laws were no longer enforced, and communal but stratified dining lingered only in university colleges and similar hierarchical institutions. But the general feeling that there was an appropriate level of provision for differing social levels continued into the early twentieth century, particularly in households where servants were clothed in graded uniforms and fed plainer, cheaper food.

The arrival of coal into domestic spaces may well have offered a new arena for performance of the powerful old notion of 'each according to degree'. William Harrison, in the 1587 edition of his *Description of England*, wrote with concern about wood shortages and the possibility that people might be forced to burn inferior fuels such as dung, reeds, straw and coal – even in the city of London. Coal was already associated with the poor; the shock to Harrison and his ilk was that this 'poverty fuel' was being adopted by other social classes. Yet, at the same time, the initial upsurge in coal supplies may have given wealthier households a new means for upholding the social order. Now that there was a luxury fuel and a lesser, common fuel, it may have seemed morally right to incorporate the difference into the management of their homes.

Returning to Sir Thomas Puckering's accounts, we find patterns of fuel provisioning that fit with the concept of one fuel for the masters and another for the servants. Among the estate documents that have survived is the inventory of his possessions at his death in 1637, which can be used to paint a picture of his Warwick home and its heating.

Sir Thomas should not have had any trouble fuelling this home entirely with wood if he had chosen to do so. He owned a wood at Weston from which he sold large quantities of faggots, and another area that yielded large quantities of furze. The accounts for building works on his properties suggest he was also able to draw a significant volume of timber from his own land. When summing up his household expenses, he indicated the regular use of fuel grown on his estate with the phrase: 'Besides all maner of wood, and furzes burnt in my house at Warwick, being of my own growth and not rated.'

Yet wood was not the only fuel in use. From the beginning of May until mid-August, every entry in the section of accounts entitled 'Weekly expenses in the charge of my house viz in diet, fewell, candles, washing etc' included 'pitt-coles'. Not 'sea coal', like that which arrived in London from Newcastle via the sea route, but coal from a pit in the Coventry coalfield a few miles distant. Unfortunately, we don't know which pit the coal came from, so we don't know exactly how far it had to travel. The amounts varied from half a load up to six 'lodes', week to week, for a total of twenty-nine loads over sixteen weeks. Since all but one of the entries included a fraction of a load – measured in halves or quarters – it seems that a load was a recognized unit of sale. From May until August most farmers needed their horses on the land far less than during the rest of the year. So, rather than being a weekly supply of coal, the loads, which were probably conveyed by cart, may represent delivery of the coming year's stock of coal supplies.

Then, from the end of August through to the beginning of November, Sir Thomas's estate paid for five substantial deliveries of charcoal. The pit coal cost him around 13½*s* a load, while bags of charcoal (again, we don't know how big a bag was) cost him 11*d* each.

The home where all this fuel was burnt was called 'The Priory' and, after the Castle, it was the largest residence in Warwick, with over fifty rooms plus a host of outbuildings. Outside there was ample provision for many different types of fuel. A 'Coalehouse' was home to both 'Seacoales and charcoales' and featured a weighing beam. More charcoal was housed in the brewhouse; the 'Woodyard' contained eight loads of firewood and another weighing beam. Timber was housed in two separate buildings, with another load of wood up at the mill.

Sir Thomas Puckering's Priory, in Warwick, as it appeared about 1656. Sir Thomas's household accounts showed wood, charcoal and 'pit coal' from a colliery in Coventry, each fuel being used in different areas of the Priory.

The charcoal appears to have been primarily associated with brewing beer, since one entry specifically gave the purpose 'to drie my hoppes with'. It may have also been used within the house in chambers without chimneys, because it gave off little smoke. But apart from two chafing dishes in the kitchen and the possibility that 'twoe Iron fire panns' in the wardrobe were for charcoal, there were no other suitable containers listed.

There may have been charcoal stoves built into the kitchen, and these would not have appeared in an inventory of movable goods. Large-scale boiling and roasting – as would be customary in such an extensive household – would have required large fires, with unimpeded access for turning, stirring, basting and regulating temperature. Having an array of small pots full of sauces and dainty dishes – destined for Sir Thomas's table – sitting around the edge of these main fires would have been a nuisance and, in my experience, resulted in lots of spills. Many of the surviving kitchens of the era show evidence of having had charcoal-fired built-in stoves. In the brewhouse, using charcoal would of course have ensured the flavour of the brew was not tainted with smoke.

The wardrobe, meanwhile, would have been jam-packed with textiles: bed hangings, coverlets, turkey carpets, tapestries, quilts and curtains. It needed to be kept free of damp and cloth moths. The contents would have been regularly aired and brushed in front of a non-smoky fire, with perhaps a handful of herbs tossed on now and again to fumigate the room. Charcoal was a specialist fuel, worth its expense to the wealthy because of its technical properties. Most of the rooms were equipped with andirons, sometimes termed 'cobirons', and one entry in the inventory, for a small room adjoining the nursery, suggests that these were indeed for burning wood, since the space was described as 'where wood was usually layd for the use of the said chamber'. Fire furniture appropriate for wood-burning was present in sixteen parlours and chambers, while a similar number of rooms appear to have been unheated. Those with wood fires were especially well furnished, with a number of textiles and upholstered chairs – the very latest thing in 1637. These were high-status spaces where Sir Thomas entertained his best guests.

However, two chambers, one occupied by 'Tobias' and the other by 'Mr Brotherton', as well as a closet used by Sir Thomas himself, had iron grates. So too did the rather empty-sounding 'Hall', which had nothing but some tables and benches, a bit of armour on the walls and a grate. The pantry also contained an 'old' iron grate, and there was another in the 'wool house'. The fire furniture within the kitchen would seem inconclusive, comprising of no more than 'twoe Iron barrs', if it were not for the presence of a 'coal hammer', an instrument used to break up large lumps of coal into more manageable sizes. Why was Sir Thomas willing to spend good money bringing coal into his house when he had such ample wood supplies? Why was coal being used in particular spaces within his home while wood was used in others? Coal was being used at The Priory in seven separate spaces, three of them in service areas – the kitchen, pantry and wool house. It was also used in the hall, a sort of crossover space. Traditionally, the hall would have been the main receiving space for guests, but by 1637 this function had largely faded away. Sir Thomas's hall, like many halls in wealthy homes, had devolved into little more than an anteroom. It was still somewhere his tenants might come if they had important issues to discuss with their lord, and all guests would enter the house through it. But the best guests would be invited through into one of the more private (wood-burning) parlours, leaving their own servants to wait in the hall (with its iron grate for coal). On a practical note, a coal-burning fire in this largely uninhabited space required very little tending. Indeed, the coal grate in Sir Thomas's closet may have been set up with this in mind. A closet was a private space, visited by neither guests nor servants. Think of it perhaps as the lord's version of a 'man cave'. Sir Thomas kept his books in his, along with three little cabinets, a small table, a stool and 'an old Cloth Chaire'. A fire that necessitated little attention may well have afforded the seclusion he sought in this space.

Among the elite he was not alone in his fuel choices. The surviving household accounts of the Earl and Countess of Bath cover both their rented London town house and their main country residence, down in Devon. For their Lincoln's Inn Fields town house, they purchased sea coal, scotch coal, billets and faggots. Payments to the woodmonger featured about four times as often as those for coal, but the quantity of sea coal was still substantial, with a few smaller purchases of scotch coal. Like The Priory, the house in Devon of the Earl and Countess of Bath was very well provided with a variety of wood. Sales of surplus faggots, timber and billets brought in a substantial revenue. Yet almost as soon as the accounts began, in 1637, they were also buying coal. Its usage within the house can be deduced from not one but three inventories taken: one in January 1638, when the old countess, Lady Anne, died; a second in March of the following year, a little before the new countess, Lady Rachel, first visited the house; and a third in 1655, when Henry, the fifth earl, died. In all three, coal appears to have been confined to the service areas of the house.

In Hertfordshire yet another wealthy household was firing its service areas with coal. The House at Gorhambury, near St Albans, rented at that time by Sir Edward Radcliffe, heir to the Earl of Sussex, had twelve chaldrons of sea coal in stock on 1 October 1637. There was an iron grate in the scullery and another in the kitchen, which may or may not have been the same set-up as the 'kitchen range' with an iron back that had to be mended twice within the next two years. Much larger stocks of wood of six different types strongly suggest the rest of the house was fuelled by wood.

All three of these households were led by people who spent part of their time in London and part of it upon their country estates. Was it their life as Londoners that got them to seek coal for use out in the country?

Coal copycats

Coal had come to be seen by the wealthy as perfectly appropriate for kitchens and servants. Perhaps some had even begun to think of coal as 'better' suited for cooking, particularly in a few important contexts.

For many years, historians have pointed to the uptake of coal by the poor to show that this change came from the bottom up rather than the top down. Indeed, I made this argument myself. One of the most persuasive sources of evidence for this view were

A coal merchant's trade card, showing heavers unloading coal from a barge on the River Thames (*c.* 1720–1760). Was the big switch to coal made first by wealthy or poorer households?

the records of how various public and charitable bodies provided coal as a free or cheap fuel to alleviate the hardships of the poor. These of course tell us that some of those living in poverty were being provided with coal – and presumably, using it – but it also tells us that this is what their wealthier neighbours thought was suitable for someone in their predicament. Widespread endorsement by the great and the good of coal as fuel for the poor can only have eased the passage of more coal into the city. It is easy to imagine the odd case where coal was urged upon a resistant and conservative householder in financial difficulties by those who professed to know what was best for them. Certainly those who accepted a position within an almshouse were left with no choice but to take whatever fuel was offered, or enjoy a very cold and bitter winter.

But as London's wealthy families took to using coal in the service areas of their homes, they inadvertently raised the social status of this fuel and provided an arena for the young women (and a few young men) working for them to gain a good deal of experience in the new art of coaxing coal fires into life. Service was not seen in quite such an unremittingly derogatory light as we in the twenty-first century might imagine. Much depended on where you worked and who was your master. The life of a servant in a great house was wholly different to that of one in an inn or tavern, and equally different from that of a lone servant in a craftsman's home. In the late sixteenth and early seventeenth centuries, many young people spent a number of years working in someone else's house before marrying and setting up on their own. Out in the countryside, where much of the work was agricultural rather than purely domestic, as many as 70 per cent of young people did so.

These young servants came from a variety of backgrounds. Those in London were often from outside the city, having grown up as the daughters (or sons) of middling and small-scale country farmers. Others were the children of craftsmen or labourers. Most hoped one day to be mistresses (or masters) themselves, and a minor but significant proportion succeeded. Service was not considered to be for 'the lowest of the low'; it was an occupation for young people who thought of themselves as of the middling sort. Naturally, youngsters with connections were able to gain the most sought-after positions, generally within the wealthiest households. These young people were most decidedly not 'poor'. They came from comfortable homes and were paid good wages, clothed well and fed well. Thus, it was a servant elite who were working within the coal-burning service areas in the homes of men like Sir Thomas Puckering. Coal may have begun its rise by being associated with poverty, but by the 1600s it was becoming linked with wealthy kitchens, brewhouses, sculleries, garrets – the world of the elite domestic servant.

These former servants would have been in a good position to bring coal to the wider population. Trained in its use, and perhaps seeing their skill as emblematic of a higher-status profession and class, they were likely advocates for the adoption of coal within their own, more modest homes. A new generation was eager to make the switch to coal. The question now was how to satisfy their demand for it.

THE SPREADING BLAZE

Supplying the country's growing demand for coal necessitated expansion upon an unprecedented scale. More than that, it required the importation and development of new technologies, the building of transportation infrastructure and the recruitment of workers, both in the mines and on the sea and waterways.

'There are scant signs of rapid growth in the north-east coalfield before 1570,' said the industrial historian John Hatcher. The same could be said of other coalfields as well. Small-scale workings supplying largely local needs were the order of the day until the big switch at the end of the sixteenth century. Several local workings were the subject of antiquarian and historian John Leland's *Itinerary* in the 1530s and 1540s. A typical entry read: 'From Redden burn along the Tweed to Berwick there is virtually no woodland, but coal is dug for fuel at Murton, a small village in Glendale, two miles from Berwick.' The Tyne and Wear estuaries had coalfields supplying London by the medieval period, which made this area stand out. Indeed, it is estimated that half of all coal dug in Britain prior to 1570 came from this field alone.

The Newcastle experience was extraordinary. In Pembrokeshire, which boasted the best coal in Wales and outcrops that were perhaps even easier to extract than those of Newcastle, very little was exported by sea. Customs records along the coast noted only very small amounts with the exception of the port of Swansea, which exported more than a thousand tonnes per year before 1600. Newcastle, however, was dispatching more than twenty times that amount. The journey around Land's End was just too long and too much of a risk to make Welsh coal viable in London at this date. One contemporary commentator, quoted in Ronald Rees's *The Black Mystery*, related:

> This cole, for the rare properties thereof, was carried out of this country, to the citie of London, to the Lord treasurer Burley, by a gentleman of experience, to showe how farre the same excelled that of Newcastel, wherewith the citie of London is served; and I thinke, if the passage were not soe tedious, there would be greate use made of it.

The workings

In the heartlands of England, far from the sea, the coalfield around Leicestershire was also constrained in finding markets for its product. We know a good deal about operations in this area from an exciting discovery made at the 'Lounge' coal mine in the parish of Coleorton. In 1985, the site was being worked by British Coal Opencast when excavators uncovered a continuous series of old workings covering an area of around half a square kilometre. The access shafts were lined with timber. Using dendrochronology, it was possible to ascertain that they had been sunk at different times between 1450 and 1600.

Fragments of the pit props, tools, equipment and clothing excavated at Coleorton give us a picture of a Tudor coal mine in action. There were two important treatises upon mining written in the period: *De la pirotechnia* by Vannoccio Biringuccio, published in Venice in 1540, and *De re metallica* by Georgius Agricola, first published in Latin in Basel in 1556. The archaeological remains at Coleorton accord well with the simpler techniques outlined in both of these works. The authors had evidently seen many mining operations in practice. Agricola, in particular, spent considerable time in the Erzgebirge (or 'ore bearing') mountains of Saxony, Bohemia and Hungary, an area renowned for developing cutting-edge mining and metallurgy technologies.

Instructional diagram for digging a mine shaft, from
De re metallica by Georgius Agricola (1556).

Underground at Coleorton, the men worked in 'stalls' separated by 'pillars' of uncut coal. These pillars supported the roof of the mine. Such a form of working could leave as much coal underground as was extracted, but it also spared the expense of extensive pit props. A series of parallel stalls were burrowed into the coal seam, broken roughly every 100 feet (30 m), where a cross passage was knocked through a set of adjacent stalls to help maintain airflow through the mine.

Each 'hewer', or coal miner, worked in his own stall, chopping coal out of the face with a wooden-handled iron pick. He'd pass freed coal back to his companions, generally wives, daughters or sons or boys employed by him directly – who hauled it to the pithead. Shovels carved from a single piece of wood were used to move the loosened coal from place to place, and the site was lit with tallow (beef- and mutton-fat) candles. Among the remains at Coleorton, a couple of small stools were also discovered, one of which seemed to bear the remains of some sort of cushion or padding. The stools may not have been for sitting on but instead for supporting a collier's weight, or perhaps just a knee or shoulder, when he was chopping in an awkward position.

Loose coal was loaded into a container, or 'corf', for hauling the coal to the pithead. Several fragments of these survived within the workings at Coleorton. For the most part, it was the corf's sturdy wooden runners that stood the test of time. Some have a strip of iron attached for running the containers like sledges. These runners were attached to hard-wearing wooden bases, and there is some evidence to suggest that the sides of the corf were woven basketware, about 20 inches (50 cm) square and 12 inches (30.5 cm) deep. Tracks in the mine floor show where they were dragged.

In the most modern section of the Coleorton workings, at a slightly deeper level than the rest, a remnant of a timber-lined roadway for dragging corf containers has been dated to the 1620s. It is not a wooden railway as such, but it hints at future developments in the miners' art. Indeed, the workings here were not laid out in the stall-and-pillar arrangement found elsewhere in the mine, but in the more efficient 'longwall' formation, a technical development that was previously thought to have first appeared in Britain at the end of the seventeenth century. In a longwall working, instead of digging parallel holes into the coalface, the whole face was worked, leaving no uncut sections. A mixture of pit props and walls constructed of rubble and coal waste, known as 'gob' or 'goaf', were built behind the hewers to support the mine roof. This was much more labour-intensive, requiring another set of men to build the roof supports while the hewers extracted coal, but it ensured a much higher proportion of the coal was extracted from the mine.

The investment in these expensive methods hint at the growing market for – and profits in – coal. In the 1600 edition of *Britannia*, William Camden noted that the Coleorton mines 'yield much profit to the lords of the manor, and supply all the neighbourhood far and near with firing'. But the fate of Coleorton was bound up in the local economy. The mine, owned by the Beaumont family for much of the century, had been leased out to one John Wilkins, who had a substantial record in running some of the era's large-scale mines. Wilkins ramped up production at Coleorton to twenty-four loads a day before closing it entirely. It was alleged by the mine's aggrieved owners that he'd shut it down in order to focus on getting workings at two others, Silverhill and Swannington, up to full capacity. It seems it was easier here to produce coal than to get it to a market where it would sell at a profit. Demand rather than supply was the limiting factor.

The Newcastle coalfield was blessed in being able to supply both local and London demand. Already the most productive of Britain's fields, the volume of coal being exported began to rise rapidly, increasing fourfold between 1570 and 1600 to 200,000 tonnes annually. The next twenty-five years saw a further doubling of the trade, closely following the increase in imports to London.

The odd load arrived in the capital from elsewhere but these were exceptions, and very small exceptions at that. By the end of the 1620s, 400,000 tonnes of coal was leaving the area around Newcastle by sea, headed for London.

The collieries producing Newcastle's coal were clustered together, located predominantly on the south bank of the Tyne to the west of Gateshead. This area boasted, in the early stages of development, not only the cheapest transport but also the cheapest extraction. The River Tyne and its tributaries above Newcastle had carved steep valleys through layers of rock. This not only provided easy access to the coal, but also ensured good drainage. Flooding is one of the great hazards of mining. Water in a mine would quickly bring a halt to exploitation. Removing it from a mine could be done, but it cost time, labour and money.

Digging a drainage channel through solid rock was particularly difficult and expensive, but this removed more water and opened up new areas to mining than did hauling or winching water up to the surface. Known as 'adits' or 'soughs', these channels required some knowledge of surveying and engineering. A specialist team had to work out the mining position underground in relation to the planned aperture at the surface, which had to be below the starting point, sloping down and away from the lowest underground workings yet popping out above ground. Not every mine was suitably located for an adit. The mine had to be located upon higher ground, so that the channel would drain water out rather than letting water in. In 1603, George Owen described the draining of a mine with an adit in Pembrokeshire. The owners had instructed that 'a level, as they call it, which is by a way digged underground, somewhat lower than the work, to bring a passage for the water' be created. Owen was astounded by the cost, writing 'this is very chargeable and may cost sometimes £20 and oftentimes more'.

The Wollaton mines in Nottinghamshire appear to have embraced a range of emerging technologies. Adits were mentioned there as early as the late fifteenth century, with large ones under construction in 1509; in the 1550s, an adit running about a mile underground was built. The owners must have been particularly well capitalized. Accounts for 1553 also mentioned parts for an engine for 'pumping the water out of pits', while in 1573, two gangs of men were paid for operating a windlass in shifts, drawing water up out of the shafts. Not long afterwards, a more mechanical project was undertaken, requiring the enlistment of a 'pump maker' from Derbyshire, six specialists from Cornwall, seven stones of iron and a gang of labourers. Five years later, millwrights were working on a 'windmill' that powered a continuous chain studded with buckets which dipped down into the sump at the bottom of a shaft, hauling water up to the surface. The water was then emptied into a leat and thence a 'watermill', which was in fact a horse-powered 'rag-and-chain' pump. Hollowed-out logs provided the pipes through

A rag-and-chain pump for removing water was among the technological innovations suggested for mines by Georgius Agricola in *De re metallica* (1556).

which a chain, studded at intervals with a series of 'rags' (in this case, stiff leather discs, but sometimes a ball of tightly packed rag), was pulled. So long as the rags were tightly fitted within the pipe, water would be trapped and drawn up.

It is highly likely that the Derbyshire pump maker had experience in lead mines, and that the Cornishmen were veterans of tin mines, and they were importing this expertise into the coal industry. Wollaton was looking to horses and wind for power to raise water from its workings, but in many areas water itself offered a solution. The copious woodcuts found within the pages of *De re metallica* overflow with detailed examples of mining engines – usually water-powered, but adaptable to horse and wind power too. These could provide the muscle needed for everything from pumping water to bellowing or ore stamping. And there is evidence that at least one forward-thinking British mine owner, the Willoughbys of Wollaton, were studying the diagrams with great care.

At Keswick, in Cumberland, a group of highly skilled migrants, sponsored by Queen Elizabeth herself, had in the 1560s arrived from one of the most technologically advanced areas of Europe with the specific aim of improving British mining technology. The workers hailed from Schwaz in the Tyrol, where silver, copper and iron were mined and where a state-of-the-art rod engine had recently been introduced. With their guidance, deposits that had once been out of reach would soon come into view.

Such cutting-edge techniques often coexisted with the simplest of methods. As some mines were installing water-powered pumping engines, others were still being emptied by hand by the colliers' families and servants, who carried buckets of water up long ladders. Much depended upon the nature of a mine's layout and conditions, as well as the potential for profit. Many coal reserves were simply not viable, being too costly to drain, or located too far from water-based routes for transporting coal to London.

The Newcastle coalfield, despite its size and importance, was not at the forefront of new mining technologies. It did not need to be. It was close to the sea and, in most places, the seams drained naturally. Yet, even on the Tyne and Wear, new technologies started to take off in the 1570s, as London's domestic habits changed and the demand for coal increased. Enough Londoners were buying coal to encourage pit owners to invest in any contraption that would give them access to more coal within a short distance of the Newcastle ports.

One window into this investment spree comes from the rush to legal proceedings as pit- and landowners contested water rights. In his study of coalmills, Eric Clavering identified around twenty-five water-powered pumping mills serving Tyne and Wear coal mines in the first half of the seventeenth century. Finding sufficient streams to power so many machines stretched the resources in the area. The courts were confronted with a plethora of disputes about dammed and diverted watercourses. Channels were being cut across hillsides to gather run-off. Wells were running dry. Water mills were left idle, and some mines drowned.

The seventeenth century might be seen as a pump-priming exercise as far as coal was concerned. Historian John Hatcher has estimated that by the late seventeenth century, around 15,000 people were working as coal miners. At least as many more were employed transporting coal from pit to market. Domestic use prepared the way for coal's starring role in the industrial economy. What had once been a localized, rather backward industry, of less importance nationally than, say, candle-making, had emerged as a major employer, a crucial economic powerhouse, a new necessity.

In the national interest

Not all Newcastle coal went to London. In the mid-sixteenth century, when the overall volume of traffic was still small, only about 20 per cent of coal from fields along the Tyne and Wear estuaries ended up in the capital. A sizeable proportion was used locally, and the rest found a market in Europe. But as London's appetite for coal grew, demand in these local and foreign markets remained fairly static, so that by the mid-seventeenth century, London was consuming some 60 per cent of the coal leaving the north-east of England, even though the amount of coal being mined had increased hugely. This left some supply to be sold in other markets along the sea route.

The town of Ipswich lies on the east coast directly upon the Newcastle–London sea route, so it is little surprise that coal should turn up there. Moreover, while the port of Newcastle in 1612 was home to thirty ships capable of carrying coal up and down the coast, the port of Ipswich had over fifty ships – with capacity to haul over 230,000 tonnes of coal. Less than 2 per cent of the coal that left the region around Newcastle over the next thirty years was actually unloaded at Ipswich, but as a home port, many of the ships called in there, often waiting for London prices to rise before completing the final leg of the journey. By 1639, Ipswich was sufficiently important in the coal trade that unrest there was a cause for concern in Newcastle. That year, the mayor of Newcastle complained: 'the Ipswich Puritans have so wrought with the shipmen that for six weeks I did not load one chaldron of coals so that my staiths are so full that they are like to fire'.

For the most part, Ipswich had been fuelled by wood, as seen in the town's finances and the accounts of two local charitable institutions. The large feast provided by the town to honour the Master of the Rolls when he visited in 1568, for example, was cooked upon wood that cost the town more than seven shillings. Wood provided warmth for a number of smaller civic occasions too. Load after load was purchased by the Tooley Foundation and Christ's Hospital for their respective poor inmates. But then in the middle of 1586, Christ's Hospital switched over to coal, buying three chaldrons in June and another ten in July. Later accounts demonstrate that this was a long-term change. Small volumes of coal had been sailing past on the way to London for at least three centuries, and then, just as the London trade was growing rapidly, the people in charge of one of Ipswich's most important charities decided to switch their fuel supply.

All along the east coast, something similar was going on. The port of Yarmouth also furnished ships for the coastal coal trade, with around 7 per cent of the coal arriving at its docks being transferred onto smaller vessels for transport upriver towards what was then Britain's second largest city, Norwich. Port by port, the numbers added up. By 1650, 400,000 tonnes of coal were being delivered to London every year, but another 200,000 tonnes were being distributed at other stops up and down the coast. Coal was gaining a toehold beyond the capital.

In the opinion of the contemporary commentator Robert Kayll, there were many advantages to the expansion in commercial maritime activities to support the coal trade. 'The Newcastle voyage, if not the only, yet is the especial nursery and school of sea-men,' he wrote in *The Trades Increase*. 'For as it is the chiefest in employment of seamen, so it is the gentlest and most open to land men; they never grudging in their smallest vessels to entertain some two freshmen or learners.'

The government had long advocated support for the commercial fishing trade as a means of training sailors who could be pressed into naval service should the need arise. Previously, this policy had mostly taken the form of 'patriotic' fish-eating. Many puritanical elements in this Protestant nation had wanted to abandon the old Catholic practice of observing meat-free days. But Queen Elizabeth, near the start of her reign, had decreed that Wednesdays, Fridays and Saturdays were still to be 'fish days' – not for religious reasons, she proclaimed, but as a way of providing ample employ for her country's fishermen and thus training for young sailors. Now, the coal trade was showing that it too could help to fulfil this vital national security function.

A government survey of the country's merchant shipping in 1582 recorded 1,204 small ships with capacity to carry between 10 and 80 tonnes of coal cargo; 73 mid-sized ships with capacity of 80 and 100 tonnes; and 178 large ships with capacity over 100 tonnes. The government was most interested in supporting trade on the larger, 100-tonne ships, which might be particularly useful in wartime. In an attempt to defend themselves from pirates (and potentially engage in a bit of privateering on their own account), most of these seagoing ships, even the small ones, carried cannon of some sort. The sailors who manned these vessels therefore had experience not just in hauling on sails and loading cargoes, but in a wide range of the skills needed for a fight at sea. And as it happens, well over two thirds of the ships that saw off the Spanish Armada in 1588 were private merchant ships rather than government-owned naval vessels.

Regular trade on the Newcastle run sustained the market for new ships and new routes, as well as new sailors. Some ship owners confined their activities exclusively to the coal run, but a number used it as fill-in work between trips carrying other commodities. It gave them an opportunity to sign up more landsmen and train up crew members. The Newcastle run was a scruffy, dependable business, but it helped to broaden Britain's base as a shipping and trading power.

Meandering inland

Further inland, natural waterways were also providing routes for coal to slowly make its way into new markets. King's College Cambridge has a good set of records documenting fuel use in this period. Trinity College has another, rather more sporadic set. Both indicated the difficulties in sourcing fuel at reasonable prices.

By the early 1580s, King's was largely reliant upon a mixture of turf, sedge and charcoal rather than wood. In his *Description of England* published in 1587, William Harrison commented upon the college's problem and various solutions employed. 'Only wood is the chief want to such as study there, whereof this kind of provision is brought to them either from Essex and other places thereabouts …', he wrote, 'otherwise the necessity thereof is supplied with gale.' In contrast, the students had no want of 'seacoal, whereof they have great plenty'. From this, we know that peat and a variety of fenland vegetation – what he called 'gale' – were procured fairly locally, while wood came from further away, and sea coal arrived by boat, having made its way into the Wash, through King's Lynn and up the River Grant, otherwise known as the Cam. Over the next few decades the price of turf in Cambridge rose substantially as, like firewood before it, supplies came under pressure. Coal prices rose more slowly.

Up until 1653, when a sluice was erected at Denver, at the base of the New Bedford River, small sailing boats built and rigged for trading around the Wash could make their way up to Cambridge as far as the common hithe, on the bank opposite Magdalene College. The sluice, once operational, slowed down the journey and necessitated a change of vessel. The price of coal in Cambridge rose that year by 33*d* per chaldron – around 15 per cent. The following year, it settled back down to

Detail from David Loggan's engraving of Magdalene College Cambridge (*c.* 1690), with coal barges visible on the River Cam. William Harrison said the city's students were well supplied with this new fuel – 'whereof they have great plenty'.

previous levels, the flow of traffic having become regular enough to absorb the extra expense and difficulties. So, in the 1580s, when Harrison wrote his report, around one quarter of King's College fuel was sea coal, some 40 tonnes of it. Forty years later, around 200 tonnes per year were being used by the college, representing around three quarters of their total fuel consumption. The same sort of pattern can be seen in Trinity's accounts.

Coal also spread by routes over land to districts far from the reach of Newcastle. The town of Banbury, in Oxfordshire, is a good example. Lying some 28 miles (45 km) from the nearest coal pit, in Bedworth, Banbury had a long tradition of being a wood-burning settlement. But at the turn of the seventeenth century, just a couple of decades behind London, fuel use began to shift. It was not as sudden or complete a switch as instigated by Londoners, but because records survive, we can see who led the way. For example, accounts from 1602 summarized the charitable bequests and trusts for providing cheap coal for the poor. Coal was to be purchased by the town in the summer months, when prices were low, then sold on to the poor at cost price in the winter when other fuels were expensive. Coal, being easy to store unsheltered in quantity, was more practical than wood for such a system. Twenty-eight miles was a long way to haul such a heavy and bulky commodity overland, which gives a strong indication that other fuel sources around the town were getting tight.

The poor for whom the coal supplies were intended were the least likely group of residents to leave any record of their domestic situation, but one individual who died in 1645 spent the end of his life in relative poverty. In the inventories, George Hawtayne was described as an innholder, so he can't always have been poor. At his death, however, he was listed as possessing, besides his clothing, a very modest number of possessions: only one bed, with workaday textiles upon it, one stool, one old brass pot and a kettle, two platters and two candlesticks, a 'cowl' (or wooden tub), half a hogshead of beer and 'a small parcel of pitt coles'. No fire furniture of any sort was mentioned, and the whole value of his movables amounted to just over £5. It sounds rather like the retirement provision for an elderly person, no longer running a full household but instead living quite modestly in a single room. Without a will to accompany the inventory, or indeed any other information about the man, it is hard to know whether he had other assets, such as property or leases, that might have lifted him out of poverty. Regardless, towards the end of his life, it appears Hawtayne may have been one of the poor who burnt the town's coal provisions, and that he did so without the benefit of a grate.

If Hawtayne had not had a small stock of coal in hand when he died we would have been unable to ascertain what fuel he'd been using. This is one of the many problems in reconstructing the fuel habits of the poorest in society. Even where there was an inventory or other description of poorer people's homes and possessions, the lack of coal-burning fire furniture does not mean they were not burning coal. The poor would not have had the money to buy grates. They were more likely to have found a makeshift solution requiring minimal or no investment.

The inventory of another man, this one living in the parish of Westerleigh, in Gloucestershire, provides a particularly good example of this conundrum. John Robbins was described in the probate inventory of his worldly possessions in 1624 as a collier, and indeed his possessions bear strong testament to that fact. He owned a 'Colpitt bucket', a rope, a couple of sledgehammers, four wedges, seven 'Colepitt mattockes' and what was probably a 'Colpitt pick', although the last three letters at the edge of the manuscript have been eaten away. He was not a rich man. He appears to have lived in a one-room house furnished with a bed, two coffers, a trestle table and a basic set of cookware. His fire furniture was skimpy too, consisting only of a pothook, a fire shovel and pair of tongs. He had neither andirons (usually associated with wood) nor a grate (associated with coal). Yet surely a coal miner would have been burning coal at home?

Grates did cost money. They were not hugely expensive though, being cheaper usually than brass cooking pots and tables, and much cheaper than beds. Where both andirons and coal grates were valued in a single inventory, they seem to be given about the same value. But many households would have had andirons, since they had long been in use and were the sort of almost unbreakable item that got passed down generation to generation, whereas a household that had made the switch to coal would need to make an investment in a grate. If a family was switching to coal due to an urgent need to save money, it is unlikely they were in a

A brass from the parish church in Newland, Gloucestershire, commemorating a miner, complete with pick shovel.

position to buy new equipment to do so. The lack of a grate therefore cannot be taken as proof that people were not burning coal, and nor can the presence of a pair of andirons be taken as proof that they were burning wood.

Those with ample resources would have started to make more adjustments as coal became available at scale. Indeed, the very first recorded domestic coal user in the area of Banbury was one Thomas Homan, a fairly prosperous farmer in Wroxton. He had his own plough, harrow, 'longecart' and muck cart, which set him apart as master of one of the better equipped households by the standards of the day. The inventory of his property, taken in 1581, was at times frustratingly brief, with things lumped together, such as 'the bedding' and 'the brass and pewter', with no further detail given. Yet his fire irons were listed separately, perhaps because they were so unusual at this time in this locality. Homan had 'a grate of Iron' as well as andirons, pothooks and spits. He also had 'one loade of coles' in addition to timber and wood. And the use of the word 'loade' indicated that this was coal, not charcoal. Recall how Sir Thomas Puckering bought his pit coal in loads and his charcoal by the bag. The same split in terminology can be seen in other examples from the period as well.

Banbury boasted other early coal adopters, and all appear to have been quite prosperous. Robert Poope (died 1592), Thomas Harrys (died 1595) and George Richards (died 1598) headed up households with sufficient resources to cover the upfront costs of transporting coal over those 28 miles. They would have had to buy their coal in bulk too. The distribution system for coal did not yet allow bit-by-bit purchasing this far inland. Like the town corporation, well-off households would have sent a man and cart off to Bedworth, gradually establishing a route and local habit. Early inland adopters were people with the facilities and enterprise to fetch coal from the pits and landing stages themselves.

In this way a rather distinctive, mixed pattern of early coal use was established outside the capital. Some of the first people to burn coal at home were the very poorest members of society, recipients of charitable donations of fuel. But alongside them were a number of wealthier, well-informed and often fashion-driven people, possibly the very people who funded or administered the charitable institutions donating coal to the impoverished. With carts, horses and men at their disposal, the cost of transporting coal themselves could be absorbed into general household expenses, making a load of coal for the service areas of the home seem very cheap indeed.

People with an eye to business opportunities were not slow in noticing these developments. From 1612 onwards, all of the inventories that mentioned stocks of coal in Banbury (except poor George Hawtayne's) also mentioned grates to burn it in. Prosperous people were investing in equipment with the expectation of a continued, regular coal supply. With a dozen or so merchants, craftsmen and local landowners now frequently burning coal, and the local charitable foundations buying it for the poor, it was but a short, profit-seeking hop for someone to begin to fetch coal for his neighbours as well as himself. Before you knew it, coal was just another commodity for sale in town. Regular supply encouraged new customers, particularly the more numerous, slightly smaller households, to switch to coal too.

In his study of land travel in this period, Mark Brayshay highlights the steady rise of road maintenance, horse ownership and an increasingly comprehensive system of public carrier services. Carters and traders of many sorts were beginning to see a value in transporting and offering coal for sale. The heavy loads of coal being hauled from pits and landing stages naturally put pressure upon Britain's road network, but it also increased the volume of business and potential for profit. With more people involved in using the roads for bulk transport, there were more voices expressing concern about the state of the roads and agitating for local communities to do something about it. The coal trade spurred a strengthening in many transport links.

As coal-burning was adopted further away from London, it required vast improvements in Britain's roads to accommodate chaldron wagons, like these documented by the Swiss artist S. H. Grimm on a tour of Northumberland around 1778.

Between 1692 and 1703, the London apothecary John Houghton collected data about the price of coal in fifty-five places in the south of England for a weekly news-sheet. Prices varied widely. A mere 5*s* 8*d* bought a chaldron in Derby, at the heart of a productive coalfield, while the extortionate sum of 54*s* was the retail price in Hitchin, in Hertfordshire, situated far from the coalfields as well as the sea. Yet in Bedford, happily located on the Great Ouse, a chaldron could be had for just 22*s*. Houghton and his fellow Londoners, for their part, were forking out around 33*s* per chaldron.

The range of prices recorded by Houghton wonderfully illustrate the impact of transport costs upon the supply of such a heavy and bulky commodity, but it also indicates how much the use of coal had spread. The host of towns and cities for which he reported this retail data had had no tradition of coal-burning a few decades earlier. Coal might well be very expensive in Hitchin, but now it was available.

The opinion that coal was a suitable fuel for the home was new and circulating fast. Initially the spread of coal was concentrated along the east coast around sea ports and the most navigable rivers. A few inland coalfields also began to expand their output. This gave the idea of domestic coal space to take hold. Traditional forms of transport and traditional methods of doing business were then pressed into service, around the same time that other fuels were in shorter supply in many areas. The economies to be made by switching over to coal, particularly for those who could afford to buy in bulk, stimulated investments inside the home, in the form of fire furniture, and outside the home, in the form of improved roads. John Hatcher has estimated that by 1700, when industry rather abruptly became a major coal user, there were already more domestic households in England burning coal than were burning wood. The London habit had been taken up across the country.

The almost total domination of coal as a domestic fuel did not reach its height until around the 1850s, when railways finally made it possible to cheaply deliver coal to even the most landlocked pockets, where wood-burning had lingered out of financial necessity. In truth, the big switch was already history: by the mid-eighteenth century, Britain was essentially deemed to be a coal-burning nation.

The birth of cast-iron manufacturing

The growth in domestic demand for coal had also exerted its influence over several industries. Most notable of these was the iron industry. When Abraham Darby the Elder first started experimenting with cheaper and more efficient ways of producing iron at the end of the seventeenth century, he had been inspired to do so in order to make cooking pots suitable for coal fires.

People had moved over to metal pots, primarily made from brass, bronze and related alloys simply called 'pot metal', starting in the thirteenth century, leaving earthenware to be used upon the fire only for a small number of specialist functions. Surviving inventories suggest that when people moved over to metal cookware, they generally invested in two types: cast metal, which was poured as molten metal into a mould, or wrought ('worked') metal which was made into bars, then hammered and beaten out into sheets, before being shaped and riveted together. Cast pots required much more metal to produce, and were rather brittle and heavy, but they lasted well and the labour costs were lower. Wrought metal pots required much more labour to produce and wore out quite quickly, but they used far less expensive metal, and were lighter and much easier to mend if they got damaged.

Brass pots of either type were the most common. Cast-brass pots were particularly good for thicker mixtures and longer cooking

'Brass pot or iron pot to mend?' was among the common street-sellers' cries in *The Cryes of the City of London, Drawne after the Life* (*c.* 1688).

times, since their thick walls spread and held heat, providing a more even cooking temperature without hotspots. Beaten-brass kettles generally had much thinner walls, making it easier to heat their contents and making them ideal for bringing water up to the boil; they were, however, liable to 'catch' (start to stick) on the bottom when trying to make something like scrambled eggs or a thick, starchy mix. Most people had at least one brass pot of each type, giving them flexibility in their cooking. But as coal became more popular, people noticed that iron worked better than brass upon their fires.

Coal cookery involved much higher heat and rather more sulphurous fumes. Iron pots were slower to heat, being less thermally conductive, but they held the heat longer than a brass pan could. Most importantly, iron pots lasted much, much longer when employed over coal than brass ones did. When the switch began, there were very few iron pots in circulation, and almost all were made of wrought iron – light and thin-walled.

The higher heat and acidic chemicals generated by coal-burning compared to wood was taking a toll not just on pots but also the masonry of brick- and stonework chimneys. To protect against the damaging heat, more and more people were investing in a new piece of fire furniture, a separate cast-iron fireback. Cast iron stood up well to the abuse of coal-burning. It also lasted longer in coal fires than wrought iron as well as brass of either type. Manufacturing cast-iron pots might therefore seem like an obvious next step. But there were two major difficulties: getting enough cheap iron to cast pots, and gaining the know-how to do so. Abraham Darby would set out to tackle and successfully solve both problems, although not all at once, and not all by himself.

Abraham Darby (1678–1717) is often portrayed as a hero of the Industrial Revolution, and it's not hard to see why. He was an open-minded and energetic businessman willing to listen to and support others with knowledge, skill and ideas. As a lad he was apprenticed to a malt mill maker, a trade that was increasingly employing cast-iron rollers to crush malt rather than using millstones. Further, because of its close links with maltsters, people in the trade were familiar with using coke as a fuel.

Upon finishing his training, Darby married, moved to Bristol and set up business. Within a couple of years he decided to set up a brass works at Baptist Mills with the backing of some fellow Quaker businessmen. The vast majority of good brass, at that time, was imported from Europe. Although it was fairly well known in Britain that brass was an alloy of copper and zinc, most local manufacturers were working with impure ores and had difficulty in achieving consistent proportions of the two constituent metals to reliably produce the range of brass types that were wanted. In addition, European metalworkers were employing sophisticated casting techniques that involved pouring molten metal into hot moulds made from loam (a mixture of sand and clay), which allowed the metal to cool very slowly and produced a particular crystalline structure. This was a fairly expensive procedure, requiring fresh materials for each cast as the hot mould had to be smashed apart to get the metalwork out and could not be recycled. It also called for more fuel and labour. In comparison, British brass foundries were putting out much cruder, chunkier ware. Their pots relied on the methods used in bell founding, with pots cast in two halves and then welded together. A rough clay core formed the pot's internal void and a cold sand mould shaped the pot's wall. The pot walls had to be thick enough to retain their structural integrity through the production process. The approach worked well enough with brass and bronze, but it was not really feasible with iron. British cast brass fell by the wayside in competition with European techniques, and cast iron was used only with large slab or bar-like items like firebacks and simple grates.

Among Darby's partners in the mill were John and Thomas Coster, copper manufacturers. The Costers were familiar with the methods used in Dutch brass foundries, including the use of coal fires, and suggested they gather more information. Darby set off for the Netherlands where he combined a bit of what might be called industrial espionage with employee recruitment, persuading a number of skilled European foundry workers to up sticks and move to Bristol with their families. After much experimentation the Baptist Mills Brass Works began producing good-quality wrought brassware. The partners in the business were delighted, but Darby was also tinkering about with casting iron. Eventually, his investors got fed up with the amount of time and money he was spending on his efforts with iron, and Darby set up his own operation.

During his experiments, he had managed to secure the services of John Thomas, an apprentice with a particularly enquiring mind. Within another couple of years, they had come across a discovery important enough for them to 'stop the keyhole of the door' so that no one could overhear them, according to

John Thomas's daughter Hannah. Later that same year, 1707, Darby filed a patent (as an apprentice, all of Thomas's work and innovation belonged to his master):

> A new way of casting iron bellied potts, and other iron bellied ware in sand only, without loam or clay, by which iron pots, and other ware may be cast fine and with more ease and expedition, and may be afforded cheaper than they can be by the way commonly used, and in regard to their cheapnesse may be of great advantage to the poore of this our kingdome ...

The new method employed a fine, dry sand that was compressed into several sections of a mould box, which could be reused and relied upon a third less iron. This was a very valuable commercial breakthrough, and everyone knew it. John Thomas was offered double the wages if he would leave Darby's employ and bring his knowledge with him. He chose to stay. An 'Article of Agreement' was drawn up between the two men, increasing Thomas's wages, guaranteeing free board and lodgings and binding him for a period of three years not to divulge 'to any other person on or about casting Iron Potts nor will disclose the method to anyone'.

A simple cast-iron pot. Abraham Darby's breakthrough in casting iron opened the way to improved methods for cooking over coal – and a host of technologies associated with the Industrial Revolution.

Traditionally it has been thought that the next big innovation, producing pig iron, a cheap iron suitable for casting by smelting it with coke rather than charcoal, happened quite separately. However, it has recently been noticed by Dr Richard Williams that Darby's 1707 patent would not work if the liquid iron that was poured into his cold-sand moulds had been made with charcoal, as was the usual practice at the time. In order to successfully cast iron pots in his moulds, Darby needed iron made from coke.

When you smelt iron ready for casting, the iron and fuel are mixed and burnt together as one mass. Some elements within the fuel pass into the iron, changing its inherent properties. When the fuel used for this process is charcoal, a good deal of carbon binds with the metal, forming what is known as 'white cast iron'. It is extremely brittle, wholly unsuitable for rounded pot shapes. When coke is used as the fuel, a high proportion of silicon is present, and some of the carbon binds with it, forming graphite crystals within the molten iron. This 'grey cast iron' is much tougher and less brittle than its white counterpart. Grey cast iron could be made into pots and pans.

In 1709, Darby moved his operations to Coalbrookdale, in Shropshire, where he bought an unused iron furnace and forges. With two new partners who had experience in brass founding and a new financial backer, he and John Thomas set up a commercial operation to capitalize on their patent. The blast furnace at Coalbrookdale was run, from the first, upon coke. There is an account from someone who worked at the site which mentions charcoal being used to begin with, but the business accounts for the first two years survived intact. They show no sign of charcoal and fulsome mention of coke costs.

Abraham Darby had invented a viable production method and a suitable material to meet the demand of a ready, waiting market. It is this transition, from charcoal to coke, that gets industrial historians excited. This is one of the key innovations that sparked the Industrial Revolution, they say, although they don't generally have cooking pots in mind when they do. Casting intricate and strong shapes in coke-produced iron opened up a huge range of possibilities. By a stroke of pure luck, it turned out to be just what Thomas Newcomen needed for certain of his steam engine parts, what George Stephenson needed for his iron rails, what so many architects needed for their new ideas in construction. Cast-iron pots, kettles and grates provided the spur to further invention. And their sales provided the capital for further industrial experimentation and development.

As important as the technological leap was the economic one. Using coke rather than charcoal as a fuel removed the most significant brake upon iron production. Charcoal, being a wood product, was a renewable but limited resource; coke, being a coal product, was available in seemingly vast and largely untapped reserves. As mining technologies advanced and transportation infrastructure improved, switching to coke was a simple matter of money. Coke made cast iron not only a lot tougher but a lot cheaper. So, when, at the beginning of the 1750s, Darby's son, another Abraham, found a way of further improving the quality of iron, reducing its carbon content so that it could be wrought in the forges as well as moulded in castings, the brakes really came off. Iron was the base metal of the Industrial Revolution, thanks in large part to the domestic adoption of coal-burning and the need for iron pots.

Around 1700, the coal trade started to evolve once again. After a century fuelled by domestic consumption, with around three quarters of coal used in the home, the industrial demand for coal was finally catching up. By 1900, industrial consumption accounted for more than three quarters of coal use, while domestic consumption was just under one quarter, despite a greatly enlarged population.

Domestic demand for coal transformed the mining industry, the transportation industry and the retail fuel trade. A whole new supply chain developed, penetrating deep into the old wood-fired countryside and reconfiguring commerce. In addition to a surge in the numbers of people making a living from mining coal, carters, boatmen, dockers, traders and merchants found new business and forged new relationships. Out in open waters, there was increasing demand for ships and the men to sail them. Support and training was thrown towards development of maritime trade and technologies that permitted Britain to widen her horizons. Other industries benefited too as the profile and availability of coal rose on the back of domestic usage. Coal could be obtained in far more places and in far more convenient quantities. It became something that you hardly thought about.

Need more or cheaper fuel? Try coal.

6

COOKS' TOOLS

It is perfectly possible, with the requisite skill, ingenuity and equipment, to cook any foodstuff or recipe with any fuel. You can produce an edible oatcake in an electric oven, deep fat fry your chips over dung, or toast your bread on an induction hob. I have even successfully cooked salmon in a dishwasher and some potatoes and kippers on the engine of a Model T Ford. It would therefore be wrong to say that fuel completely dictates the food we cook and eat. But some things simply work better and taste nicer than do others.

Oatcakes are in fact not bad when popped in an electric oven, but they are not great either. They fall somewhere close to bland on the scale of tastiness. But bake them on a hot stone over a peat fire, and then dry them on a rack in front of that fire, and they absorb a little of the smoke's flavour and can be crisped to perfection. As for trying to deep fat fry chips over a dung fire, I don't recommend it. The only way to get the oil hot enough is to create a veritable wind tunnel, operating a bellows like crazy to get a sufficient blaze going. If you do ever give it a try, make sure you are outside and have very good fire-extinguishing equipment nearby, as sparks fly all round and the chances of igniting your oil are high. Petrol engines sadly taint the taste of everything, but dishwashers are great for large quantities of salmon – so long as you don't use any chemicals to clean your dishes for a cycle or two before cooking.

The food that is easiest and tastiest to cook upon your primary fuel source is naturally going to become considerably more popular. In the largest, best equipped and most comprehensively staffed kitchens, most technical difficulties can be overcome. In more modest homes – with less in the way of facilities, time and labour – small differences in convenience and practicality have a significant effect. Over time, people tend to find the range of recipes that suit not just their palates but their lifestyles. The shift from wood to coal would prove to be a major change in the kitchen, one that required considerable adjustment in technique and approach. Some traditional styles of cooking became much harder; others got easier. Kitchen skills changed, as much of the old fire management knowledge was lost and cooks instead learnt the careful choreography of juggling pans and pots.

Britain was the first Western country to comprehensively switch over to coal as a domestic fuel by a considerable margin. While London was domestically dependent upon coal by 1600, most US cities did not make the switch until around 1850, for example. Britain, partly because it is a fairly compact country, also became much more uniformly fired by coal, even in rural districts, than any other nation. By 1900, 95 per cent of all households were coal-burning, while elsewhere in the world, even in the most industrially developed cities of Northern Europe and North America, such a figure was rarely reached, and those cities stood like islands in a wood-burning mainstream. No other nation's cuisine developed quite along the same lines since no other nation was to have the same relationship with coal.

Coal cookery and British cookery are to some degree synonymous. It is not at the top of society that we encounter specific coal cookery, however, but rather in the everyday practice of poorer and middling families. As such, coal cookery is also the cookery of women. The male chefs employed in the great houses and grand hotels were able to maintain continental wood-burning traditions, utilizing expensive charcoal stoves and other state-of-the-art equipment. Coal cookery was developed and practised by the lone housewife, the general cook and the maid-of-all-work.

The all-essential grate

I have mentioned already the two technical aids to cooking on coal that made the big switch possible in the late sixteenth century: the chimney and the grate. But how did people come to the form of the grate? And how did they cook upon them?

When most of us think of cooking on coal, we imagine facing one of those big, black iron ranges beloved of historic houses and period dramas. But these built-in ranges were the result of centuries of experimentation and technical development. The first grates were very different and involved a lot less iron. Survivals of the first grates are very rare, and early descriptions were terse in the extreme. Prices for grates, however, suggest that most were rather small and made of low-quality metal.

It has been suggested by collectors of kitchen paraphernalia that the first fire grates were composed from a few loose iron bars laid in parallel between a pair of andirons. Such a set-up would indeed work in a makeshift way. There were countless probate inventories listing an iron bar or two along with andirons among the pots and pans, which at first glance seems to back up this idea. However, one or two bars would not have been much use in supporting a pile of coal up off the ground. Instead, they would have been extremely useful set into the brick- or stonework of a chimney, to hang pots from. More iron bars could have been used to make an ad hoc grate, but the number of early inventories with more than two iron bars was very small indeed. So we probably have to discount the 'andirons plus a number of bars' approach as a long-term or popular solution. The grate-less inventories that boasted an iron bar or two probably had those bars firmly fixed above the hearth, whether the household was burning coal or wood.

There were other types of grate in use that might have provided inspiration – or more prosaically, were pressed into service – for the grates that became common fire furniture in the early coal cookery era. So-called 'grates' made of iron were sometimes used to provide security on cellar windows or ventilation for warehouses. They were employed as covers over sinkholes and drain openings. A flat iron grate, liberated from its original use and either supported upon andirons or propped up on a couple of bricks or stones, may well have served as the 'proto' coal-fire grate.

A gridiron might have been the first step in devising fire equipment suitable for cooking on coal.

Households also might have experimented with a gridiron. This was a piece of cooking equipment used for grilling food, and fairly common in the wealthier households of the period. Think of it rather like a robust version of the wire insert that goes into a modern grill tray. A frame of parallel iron bars was seated upon four iron legs around 3 inches (7.5 cm) high. Typically, a handle was attached, so that the gridiron could be moved around with ease. The cook spread a few embers out to the side of the main fire and placed the gridiron over them, periodically raking a few fresh embers from the fire to position them under the frame, or introducing a handful of small twigs or some straw to create a 'flame-grilled' effect. Although a promising option, as a support for the weight of even a small coal fire, a gridiron would have been a bit flimsy.

The few surviving sixteenth- and early seventeenth-century fire grates are rather grand. In form they can be summed up as a square or rectangular high-sided iron basket supported about 3 inches off the ground. All hail from very wealthy houses and belonged more to the great hall rather than their service areas. A particularly fine example can be found in the fireplace in the hall at Charterhouse in London. It bears the coat of arms of Thomas Rutton, who founded Charterhouse and was the first holder of the 'Grand Lease' for the Whickham and Gateshead collieries.

I have tried to cook with simple basket grates of burning coal a number of times. They are not ideal. You can stand pots around them, but this results in painfully slow cooking, as in most cases the rounded sides of your pot, skillet or kettle present only a tiny surface area near the heat. You can try to nestle a pot directly in the burning coals much as you would with a wood fire, but this tends to cut down the oxygen flow around the coals, damping the fire down. The pot also takes up a lot of space within your grate.

In his satirical *Directions to Servants* (written in the 1730s and published posthumously), Jonathan Swift recommended all sorts of bad practice and misbehaviour that servants could possibly get up to. Among them he suggested that cooks should 'make room for the sauce-pan by wriggling it on the coals'. Plunging a pan into the coals and wriggling it about now and again will help to ensure it sinks down within the fire and any ash build-up is dispersed, and it does permit a rapid boil – but it does so at the expense of any other pots, pans and roasts. It frequently damages the pan

An early illustration of a simple basket grate, from *The History of Witches and Wizards*, published in London in 1720.

too. The sides of the grate also make it hard to get something with a large flat base and a long handle down in the basket.

What other options were left? Balancing a frying pan on the top bars of the basket is effective if the grate is almost full of burning coal, but it can be rather precarious. The simplest and most successful option is to suspend a pot over the top so that it hangs free with its bottom a few inches over the coals.

Stirring the pot

Recall how the flames from a wood fire tend to merge together in a single pyramid at the centre of the blaze, but the flames of coal rarely take this shape, instead forming a series of smaller, lower, hotter and bluer flames, spaced across the upper surface of the bed of embers. Pots need to be much closer to coal fuel if you want to maximize their take-up of this heat. This influenced the design of pots and pans.

Long legs upon a pot became something of a nuisance, as they lifted the pot away from the heat; since the pot cannot stand safely within the grate itself, these long legs no longer have a purpose. Long-legged pots, commonly used on wood fires, gradually disappeared as coal took over. In their place came pots with three short, stubby legs, just sufficient enough to stabilize them when placed upon the floor or another surface away from the fire. The shape of the base of pots and pans also changed in response to the burn characteristics of coal. Flames from a wood fire curl out and around a rounded vessel, heating its contents, but the many little points of flame produced by coal work most efficiently when presented with a broader, flatter profile. If you look at the cast-brass and cast-bronze pots of the fifteenth century held in the collection of the Dumfries Museum in Scotland, which were designed for use with wood or peat fires, you find 6-inch (15 cm) legs supporting a pot whose lower half is almost a perfect hemisphere. 'Sag bottom' cauldrons (they look rather like earlier globe pots that have sagged or slumped a little) were more common from the late sixteenth and early seventeenth centuries. As coal arrived, pots gradually became broader, flatter and shorter-legged.

Cooking within a broader-based pot, hung low over the fire, is fairly easy if you are boiling or simmering food. Stirring is not all that convenient, however. A pot standing within the hearth upon its own long legs stays still as you whizz the food around; a hanging pot swings about. This is more noticeable with thicker mixtures – often the very ones that need mixing the most. A successful stir requires that you hold on to the pot with your other hand, leaning over the fire. It is awkward. Easier by far is to add more liquid and leave the contents to simmer on their own, unstirred.

One advantage of this form of cooking is how well it complements the long burn time of coal. Coal fires require much less frequent attention than any of the wood-based fuels, but this is of little use to cooks if they have to remain at the hearth stirring or tending to the contents of the pot. A long simmer of a pot full of very liquid food allows the cook to turn her attention elsewhere. Naturally, there was less incentive to adopt this cooking method if she had to return frequently to the hearth to feed wood onto the fire and keep the simmer going. But with long-burning coal, boiling became king.

Suspending pots over a fire is generally more successful if in fact it is one pot, singular, being suspended. A row of pots spaced along a bar set in the chimney can be managed, but such a system creates a number of irritations. The first is the matter of access to the heat. Those pots at the ends of the row are likely to receive less energy from the fire than those in the middle. You can swap the pots around in order to regulate their temperatures, but

A basket grate – with a single pot hanging above it – was in use at Grieve's Farm when the Swiss artist S. H. Grimm visited there on his tour of Northumberland around 1778.

taking full hot pots on and off a fixed bar is a fraught business. It is all about your angle of attack. Almost everything that modern health and safety people tell you about safe lifting practice has to go out of the window. You cannot get your feet and legs too close to the fire, so you will be bent forward at either the hip or the waist. A pot full of hot liquid cannot be clutched close to the body during the manoeuvre but must instead be held some distance away and in front of you. Bracing your elbow against your body is a big help when making the lift, but this impedes your ability to move your lower body as every movement is transferred to the liquid in the pot by this rigid support. Then there is the problem of pots swinging and bumping. The iron chimney bar may well have been fixed, but pots were hung from it upon hooks or chains of one sort or another. Moving one pot risked knocking the others and setting everything sloshing about. Keeping a bit of distance between pots made this much less problematic. It also allowed the heat from the fire to move more freely around each pot, ensuring more even cooking. Too many pots in the kitchen created chaos.

One-pot cookery had a long tradition among poorer families, who relied on it out of necessity – either because they had only one pot or only enough food to fill a single cauldron. Now coal users in every wealth bracket were also seeing the value of this method.

Fixing the fire

When introduced into a kitchen, the simple basket grate was fixed in size and shape. People could of course ask the local blacksmith to make a grate of any size or shape, but once it was made, that was that. Today, with our modern appliances, we are perhaps accustomed to the idea of our heat source being a fixed size and shape, but I suspect this came as a bit of a shock to many a servant girl working with coal for the first time.

Wood and peat fires are entirely mutable. You can spread them out or concentrate them, funnel them into long thin trenches or rake them into wide circles. You can easily divide a big fire into several small separate fires or combine small fires into one. You can build a big ring of fire around a particularly large pot stood at one end of the hearth while a smaller, slower central fire is burning in the middle and a ring of little pots is simmering away at the far end. You can scrape out a pile of burning embers to pop beneath a gridiron when there is a bit of toasting to do, brushing the embers back into the main fire when the job is done.

The traditional open hearths, whether located in the centre of the room or at the side with a chimney, were large spaces that allowed such mobility. Moving the fire was very common, which is why fire shovels and tongs were very common too. Even when no other fire furniture was mentioned in an inventory – no grates or andirons, no cobirons or ranges, no iron bars – there will be shovels, rakes and tongs. Rather than moving heavy pots, people moved the fire.

Most cooking over wood and peat involved the use of a cast-brass pot upon three legs. Almost every household had one, and all but the poorest had several. These were virtually indestructible, and they were passed down from generation to generation. If they got too worn or damaged to be of use, they could be melted down and sold for scrap. Inventories frequently lump all pots together by weight, valuing the cookware purely by its scrap metal value: 'all the pot brass xxxli weight at iv*d* the lb'.

A cast-brass pot was heavy. The casting process required the metal to be of a certain thickness in order to maintain its integrity. Once full it was much heavier still. I currently own about a dozen replicas that I have been using for years, as well

146

as a couple of smaller originals, which I don't use to cook with but have lifted and shifted on many occasions. Each is outfitted with two lug handles, cast with the main body of the pot. These handles are small; they are decidedly not shaped for hands to hold. Rather, they were intended to serve as anchor points onto which removable handles could be hooked. It's a very practical arrangement. The handles, generally forged of iron, were formed of two curved bars linked together loosely at the top, with the two free ends bent over to form hooks. One handle would fit a large range of different-sized pots. When it comes time to move a pot, you grab a handle, hanging somewhere in your cooking space away from the fire, where it remains cool to the touch, and hook the ends onto the pot's hot lugs. When you're finished, you unhook the handle and hang it back up, out of the way. There is no chance of burning yourself upon a hot handle and you have less chance of spilling the contents of the pot. Whatever angle you lift the pot at, the pot swings level because the handle is not fixed.

How to move a fire: In the wood-burning era, people moved fires rather than pots. Embers were brushed to the side of the hearth for use with a gridiron; large pots were kept in place, with the fire built up and swept away as needed; and rakes and tongs were everyday necessities.

The largest of the replica pots I have dealt with on a regular basis has a cooking capacity of 4 gallons (18.2 litres). This one is cast. Even empty, the size and shape of the pot, which was by no means the largest size in use in the medieval and Tudor periods, means that I cannot lift it by myself. If necessary, I get someone to help me, and we stick a billet through the handle and use it as a carrying pole. Even when the pot is full of boiling broth, this works well, keeping us safely removed from both the scalding liquid and the fire. On my own, I can roll the pot about if I need to, but I rarely do. Instead, I roll the empty cool pot into place upon the hearth and leave it there. Liquids and foodstuffs are added in situ, and fished or ladled out when they are done cooking, without the pot moving an inch.

The fire is lit and managed around the pot too. Standing upon three legs, the body of the pot is suspended a few inches above the hearth, leaving room beneath it for a bed of hot embers. The active part of the fire is made up against the pot's side. If I need to bring a large volume of broth up to the boil, I add some wood around the pot to encourage the fire to form a ring. If I am in a real hurry, I periodically knock burning sections of wood beneath the pot. Achieving a 4–6-inch (12–15 cm) high fire all around the pot is much more effective for maintaining heat than a towering inferno to one side, but this requires considerably more skill and attention, and the towering inferno and a regular stir with a long-handled spoon or ladle will get the job done. And cooling the fire is easy: simply spread it out. With plenty of space around the hearth and some tongs and a rake, it's the work of a moment. It is not quite as instant as turning off the gas on a modern gas cooker, or switching off an induction hob, but it beats switching off a conventional electric hob every time.

The iron grate, with the coal fire fixed in size and shape, made these long-practised techniques of temperature control irrelevant. Moving the fire was simply impossible. You could not quickly reduce the temperature by spreading the fire out, nor could you quickly raise it by pulling together disparate elements. Creating different shapes of fire that could hug a pot or slide beneath it was no longer possible either. The method of keeping a semi-permanent pot upon the hearth, filling and emptying it in situ, was obsolete.

The simple basket grate and the coal-fired kitchen had a major impact upon cooking methods. The biggest pots disappear from the record. Instead, we see a steady rise in the use of the 'furnace', or built-in pot, such as the Victorian 'coppers'.

Furnaces had been around for centuries in the largest households and in industry. The galleys that provided the cooking facilities aboard the *Mary Rose*, Henry VIII's ill-fated flagship, were furnaces. Domestically, these fireboxes with built-in pots seem to have been rare outside the great country houses before the 1590s. Thereafter, more and more furnaces start to pop up in wealthier homes – exactly the sort of homes that show evidence of equipping their kitchens for use with a coal fire. The match is by no means perfect:

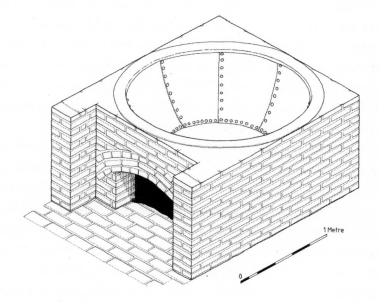

1 Metre

0

The fireboxes on the *Mary Rose*, with their built-in pots, were very similar in design to furnaces in use in the homes of the wealthy and prosperous in the early seventeenth century, when these households were mixing wood and coal fuel in the kitchen.

there were homes with furnaces that gave no indication of coal-burning, and coal-burning homes that lacked furnaces. However, the two technologies frequently appeared together. Sir Thomas Puckering, for example, had 'a copper boiler' and a 'great ladel' in his kitchen at The Priory in 1637, and the Earl and Countess of Bath had one 'copper' in their brewhouse at Tawstock in 1639. But it wasn't merely the great houses that were installing furnaces. Around the same time in Banbury, five of the six households with iron grates for burning coal also had built-in pots, two of which were described as made of lead and one of copper.

In this early period, furnaces were fuelled with wood, and particularly with faggots. Lead pots are very tricky to use with coal, due to the low melting point of the metal. You can use them if you are very careful to keep the water level high within the vessel, but if you let it boil mostly away, the pot will melt and dump the rest of its contents upon the fire. If you are lucky, you will be left with an extinguished fire and a ruined pot; if you are not so lucky, and the pot dumps its load in one go, the whole brick structure can explode. Thus, the Banbury furnaces almost certainly did not use coal as a fuel. This would only come later, when more pots were made of cast iron.

Furnaces were however often used in conjunction with coal grates, providing the sort of water-boiling facility that had previously been provided by a large pot on the main hearth. In very large households, it had long been sensible to free up cooking space upon the hearth by building a separate, dedicated hearth for boiling. A fixed brick support allowed for a much bigger pot than a free-standing, self-supporting cauldron. Such structures were not especially cheap to instal and they took up space, so while wood was still the king of the kitchen, there was little incentive for smaller homes, which typically didn't need the additional boiling capacity, to invest in them. Once coal became the principal cooking fuel, and the fire was contained within a relatively small fixed grate, it was much more attractive (or perhaps imperative) for medium-sized households to splash out on building a separate arrangement for boiling too. And once they'd invested in a purpose-built copper or lead furnace for boiling, it made sense to make full use of it.

When John Byng wrote from Kent in 1790 that 'A common cook here would not know how to manage a coal fire,' he was referring to just these sorts of challenges. Kent had remained a primarily wood-burning county long after much of the country had swapped over to coal. Traditional cooks confronted with a coal grate were flummoxed. How were they supposed to control the heat? How could they cook more than one thing at a time? How were they to prevent their recipes from catching on the bottom or side of their pans and pots?

Thick or thin?

As cooking methods changed in the years following the big switch, food changed as well. Surviving recipe books hint at a change in the texture of food with the rise in popularity of boiling. This was when ordinary British cookery (largely done by women), as opposed to elite fashionable cookery (frequently led by men), began to diverge from European tradition.

The pivot occurred first in London at the end of the sixteenth century. Printed recipe books of this time were written primarily by men based in the city for a city-based readership. They were printed and distributed initially within London before gradually being disseminated to other parts of the country. So it was unsurprising that it would be city tastes and city cooking (and the city sensibilities being catered for), which informed their advice. The recipe books captured the early struggles to adapt to coal in the kitchen and the consequent effects this would have upon British eating habits.

Boiling had naturally always been a popular method of cookery. Many of the recipes that appear in the earliest English cookery manuscripts, dating back to the 1390s, involved boiling meats and broth. Take, for example, the diced mushrooms mingled with finely chopped leeks and 'seethed' (simmered) in broth, then seasoned with a spice and given a dash of colour with saffron in a recipe simply called 'Funges'. Eggs were poached before being covered with a spiced egg custard under the name of 'Pochee' (we might see a certain similarity with the dish we know as eggs Benedict). Pigeons were stewed in a spiced broth sharpened with a dash of verjuice, which was ideally the juice of unripe grapes but in England was often crab-apple juice; the birds' bellies were then stuffed with herbs and whole peeled cloves of garlic. Every breed of meat and species of fish imaginable seems subject to being parboiled in broth or 'fair water' for at least one dish, and often several.

But alongside what might be called 'wet boil' cooking were a collection of thicker concoctions. Boasting names such as 'frumenty', 'purry' and 'mortrews', this family of recipes produced a range of textures that were moist but not liquid. Some were smooth and semi-solid like a modern mousse, others thicker like a pâté. Some had a grainy texture akin to a risotto or paella. The very first recipe given in *The Forme of Cury*, often identified as the cookbook of the court of King Richard II, is 'furmenty', wherein whole grains of wheat were dehusked, then seethed in water until the grains burst. The wheat was next strained and cooled. After that, it was returned to the pot and the fire, where broth and milk were added slowly, allowing the grain to absorb as much as possible. When the texture became soft and creamy, the pot was taken from the fire and egg yolks were stirred in with a pinch of salt. The text suggested serving the frumenty with venison or fresh fat mutton. A second version given later in the manuscript was said to be suitable for serving and eating upon fish days, when church law required that people eat neither meat nor eggs nor dairy products. Here the broth, milk and eggs were replaced with 'almond milk'. It is much like the 'farro risotto' and 'farro porridge' that foodies rave about today. Indeed, it may well be the same thing; the Italians are very good at hanging on to medieval recipes.

The Forme of Cury was clearly concerned with dishes suitable for the very grandest of tables. However, many food historians consider these two recipes to represent a posh version of what may have been the most widely eaten meal of medieval Europe. Whole, unmilled grains swelled and softened in whatever liquid was available, would have represented the least processing of food with the least equipment and the least fuel expenditure. For a grain-based economy, frumenty was the cheapest of foods.

And it needn't be dull or unappetizing. A pinch of salt and an ever seasonally changing variety of herbs and vegetables lifts it enormously. If you have a bit of meat or fish to add in, then so much the better. Dairy products are transformative. A big knob of butter is particularly good with chives, and lumps of partially melted cheese are one of my favourite things to stir in. Milk or cream invites a handful of fruit in season, or a drizzle of honey, if you are very lucky. How about shellfish? Cockles, mussels and shrimp, if you have them, can steam and cook as the grains absorb the cooking liquor. Frumenty in its almost endlessly different forms was England's paella, risotto and porridge.

The dish works particularly well with the rising and falling heat that is generally produced upon a wood fire. Add fresh fuel to the fire and the temperature quickly drops, only to build rapidly to a good high heat as the wood catches. The fire burns briskly for a while and then, as the fuel begins to be consumed, the heat starts gently to fall until you pop on some more wood. If you are quite attentive, you can minimize this cycle of rising and falling temperature by feeding the fire often, with small amounts. If you are busy then the cycle tends to be pronounced. Frumenty and other grain- and pulse-based thick dishes do very well with an initial period of high heat to get a boil going and then a 'resting' period of lower heat that allows them to absorb the liquid. In fact, this is exactly how good cooks approach making both risotto and paella. The realities of cooking like this, with a cycle of heat waxing first hot and then more gently, were alluded to in some sixteenth-century recipes, where cooks were instructed to give a dish 'a walm or two'.

Mimicking this heat regime upon a coal fire is possible – if you pay close attention. Bringing the pot up to an initial boil is fairly straightforward, but then you need to remove it from the fire and stand it to one side for a while before returning it to the fire for short blasts of heat from time to time. Using a flat-bottomed pan upon a great iron slab that crosses over a fire at one point but not at others – as you might find, for example, upon a modern AGA or Rayburn cooker, or upon the best of the early twentieth-century enclosed cast-iron ranges – this poses no great difficulty. But, as we discussed before, this is not what early coal adopters were faced with in the kitchen. Rather than sliding a pot on and off the heat, they had to manoeuvre it on and off a basket grate.

Around the time coal entered more domestic spaces, some areas of the country – for instance, Yorkshire – started to adopt a cooking aid known as a 'sway', or chimney crane. A sway helped a lot with the lifting and shifting of pots on and off a fire. Essentially it consisted of a couple of staples permanently fixed into the back of the chimney into which a cross-braced right angle of iron was slotted. This formed a hinged bracket that could both suspend a pot and be used to swing it in an arc above and way from the fire, and back again.

Cooking a frumenty over a basket grate of coal with the help of a sway is a reasonable proposition. You position the pot over the fire until the water boils, add your grain and swing the pot

In Thomas Rowlandson's engraving 'The Cook's Prayer!!' (1801), the long-time cook to 'Alderman Gobble' takes a break from her kitchen duties. Behind her, a pot hangs from a sway above an iron grate; in front of the grate, meat is roasting on a spit.

to the side, periodically nudging it nearer or further away from the grate as cooking proceeds. This still requires more labour – and more risk of spoiling your supper – than cooking a frumenty upon a wood fire. The bursts of heat from coal are fiercer and die away faster. Lose your focus for a moment or two – say, when a child cries or you have to shoo the chickens out of the house – and your mixture catches on the bottom.

Disasters can happen with any cooking operation, but the potential for problems cooking a thicker, starchy mix was considerably higher over a coal fire than over a wood one. The poorest could least afford such disasters. If you had nothing else, then a spoilt dish must be eaten or else you went hungry. The need for a safe, reliable cooking method was strongest among those who were under most pressure.

The accomplished cook

The thick and starchy style of recipe started to fade out of general use as coal took over. The last great blast of traditional frumenties and thick purees, at least as far as recipe books were concerned, came in Robert May's 1660 manual, *The Accomplisht Cooke*. 'Take wheat and wet it, then beat it in a sack with a wash beetle,' he advised his readers. The next step was to clean off the husks, then boil the grain on a 'soft' fire all night. The cooked grain was drained in the morning and then brought back to the boil with cream or milk and spices. Thickening it with egg yolk was optional; in May's view, it was best served with a scrape from the sugar cone. He recycled the recipe under a completely different name, 'French barley pottage', which used whole barley grains. He did it again, with oats, under the name 'gruel pottage'. Finally, he sketched out two more whole-oat versions: one made with raisins and rosewater and one with herbs and butter.

May was an interesting character, widely acknowledged to be the first professionally trained cook to write a printed cookery book in English. Earlier writers tended to be gentlemen with an interest in the subject, and many of them acknowledged quite openly in their text that they were heavily borrowing, or even just transcribing, the handwritten recipe collections of aristocratic and gentle-born women. May, however, had formal training in the households of the great. He'd spent five years in Paris in his late teens, followed by a spell in London and some time in the more rural context of Cowdray Park, near Midhurst, in West Sussex. His subsequent career oscillated between town and country. Service to the Countess of Kent, for example, led him to cook both at Wrest Park, in Bedfordshire, and in her

Portrait of Robert May, perhaps the first professionally trained cook to write a cookery book in English, from the frontispiece of the 1671 edition of his *Accomplisht Cooke*.

town house at Whitefriars, in London. (The kitchen at Cowdray still stands, and can be visited; the one at Wrest Park has sadly been completely rebuilt.)

Much is made of May's role in the rise of French cooking in England, but his experiences as a cook on the cusp of a major change in fuel use is much less discussed. Here was a cook who worked in London in the seventeenth century, when coal was newly on the rise, yet also worked in areas of the country, particularly at Cowdray, that continued to use wood. The households that he was employed in were not quite the biggest in the land, but they were not far off. He must have used both wood and coal, and upon a grand scale. While the installation of charcoal stoves in some of the more elite London kitchens may have softened the transition, he surely encountered some of the tensions between the old and the new ways of cooking.

Frumenty was by no means alone among the old thicker boiled offerings at table. A variety of pea and bean purees pepper the medieval recipe collections. 'Drawen benes' required parboiling, then grinding the beans to a puree with a pestle and mortar before cooking them in a little broth with very finely chopped onion and a stamen or two of saffron for colour. This produced a dish similar to that known in much of the Mediterranean as 'fava'. Another common dish, known as 'makke', consisted of boiling up ground beans to a thick, stiff paste, then stirring a little red wine into the cooked puree, which was served with a garnish of fried onions. A version made with peas, called 'perrey of pesoun', required a particularly fast boiling, so that the peas would burst and be soft enough to pass through a coarse straining cloth (no pestle and mortar needed). The resulting puree was again cooked through thoroughly, this time with a little oil, a pinch of salt and a pinch of sugar. The descendant of this dish is served to this day, with fish and chips, throughout the UK.

These were not the only thick and sticky styles of dish that held sway in England at the dawn of the sixteenth century. A significant proportion of the boiled meat and fish dishes were thickened either with breadcrumbs, rice flour or raw egg (the last stirred in as you would with a custard). Indeed, a lot of medieval food could be eaten heaped on a spoon. There were solid foods that could be sliced and picked up with the fingers, as well as a few wet dishes that had to be served upon 'sippets' (also known as 'sops', or in modern terms, toast), which sopped up the juice and made them easier to handle. However, the majority of cooked dishes were thick and moist. The most popular apple dish – it turns up, in one form or another, in pretty much every recipe collection through to the 1660s – was an apple moye, wherein apples were peeled, cored and stewed to a puree, then thickened with cream and eggs (or, for fasting days, rice flour) to make a sort of thick apple fool. Another standard, 'mortrews', a dish of diced meats in a thick sauce, could be made with chicken, rabbit or pork. One recipe reminded the cook to 'styre well for quelling'. Its semi-solid texture gloops and spits if it's not stirred while it cooks.

It is these thicker, stickier recipes that begin to disappear from the repertoire of cookery books at the same time as coal comes to the fore. Roughly 20 per cent of the medieval recipes fell into this category, but in *The Accomplisht Cooke* the number fell to about 3 per cent. Authors after Robert May included even fewer in their books. This is not to say that they faded away altogether, but rather that they faded into the background and began to change in texture.

Have a good look at Mrs Beeton's *Book of Household Management*, assembled in the middle of the nineteenth century. You can find faint echoes of medieval food, but they do tend to be rather wet and sloppy echoes. A puree of peas survived, for example, as a green pea soup, where one quart of peas was prepared in four quarts of liquid. But every type of beans was free-boiled in water, even where they were subsequently fried. Her gruel was so watery that she recommended serving it in a tumbler to invalids! And almost all of her 'thickened' sauces were made to be poured over drained ingredients that have been first boiled in water or thin broth.

Fashion versus tradition

Another, rather powerful reason for the change – and the one most usually cited as the explanation for the change in texture – was fashion, particularly the rising prominence of French cookery. There is good reason to follow this line of thought. By 1617 Fynes Moryson was describing differences between the cuisine of Britain and France by referring to the French preference for boiling over roasting: 'The French are commended and said to excel others in boyled meats, sawces, and made dishes'. The groundbreaking cookery book written by François Pierre de La Varenne, who is generally called the founder of modern French haute cuisine, appeared in 1651. It was translated into English and published in London just two years later under the title *The French Cook*. La Varenne's approach was decidedly lacking in thick puree dishes.

The French style had already begun to have an impact upon fashionable English cooking several decades earlier. In 1615, Gervase Markham, in *The English Hus-Wife*, began the cookery section of his guide for 'the inward and outward vertues which ought to be in a compleat woman' with 'fricasees and quelquechoses', giving a brief explanation of these foreign terms. He described them as 'dishes of many compositions and ingredients, as flesh, fish, eggs, herbs, and many other things, all being prepared and made ready in a frying pan'. His boiled dishes were not presented as being in any way foreign, but they were all wet rather than thick-textured. Even his ordinary pottage ('of use in every Goodman's House') used half as much oatmeal as 'herbs', a term that then included vegetables. It may have been less the boiling and wetness that characterized French cooking than the complication and mixing of multiple ingredients. Gilly Lehmann, in her study of changing food styles as revealed by recipe books, focused upon flavour mixes as the definitive difference, charting the embrace of a more French taste over the decades, where sweet and savoury were separated, and intense meat and fish 'essences' were given prominence.

Yet another recipe book from 1615, *A New Booke of Cookerie* by John Murrell, is particularly revealing about the differences between French cookery and what he termed 'London' cookery during this time of evolution in the kitchen. He set out his stall quite specifically upon the frontispiece, promising 'the newest and most commendable Fashion' and to this 'is added the most exquisite London Cookerie all set forth to the now, new English and French fashion'. He also claimed firsthand knowledge of French food as 'a Traveller'. The French dishes were clustered at the front in a block, before the book moved on to a section on baked meats, salads and puddings that were not marked out as anything special. The final part of the book was labelled 'London Cookery'. This makes it easy to compare what Murrell considered to be French cookery, ordinary English cookery and London – and thus specifically, coal – cookery.

His French cookery was certainly 'wet'. The thickenings, in the few cases where there were any, seem to be light. To one dish of boiled capon, 'a little' oatmeal was added, and a 'small' crust of toasted bread was used to thicken the liquid for a boiled flounder. But then in truth, the same could be said of the London recipes. Nowhere in the book do we find the thick purees and frumenties that appear in Robert May's manuscript. It would seem that while French fashion was pulling the top end of society towards more savoury flavours and lighter, wetter boiled foods, the practicalities of cooking on coal were giving it a quiet push in much the same direction. Wetter foods were both more fashionable and easier to cook on coal, which probably had something to do with ousting frumenty and starch-rich stews from the country's tables, high and low.

These thick, sticky dishes receded from the recipe books long before they receded from regional cooking because recipe books were not really national in character. They were written for the London market, where both fashion and coal had a strong influence. Some medieval dishes, such as mushy peas, somehow hung on despite disappearing from the printed record; there were no mushy peas in *Mrs Beeton's*, for example. They managed to enjoy a resurgence once coal was replaced by gas and electricity, whose steady, gentle heats made them convenient to cook once again.

If you trawl through the recipe books assembled by those who began to collect local and traditional dishes and methods in the nineteenth and early twentieth centuries, you will notice many of these thick, sticky and hearty boiled foods, particularly in outlying areas that for a long while escaped the domestic spread of coal. In Scotland, for example, large areas retained peat-burning traditions into the modern era, and the dishes of 'kail' and 'knockit corn', recorded in the Shetlands at the beginning of the twentieth century, are almost indistinguishable from the frumenty of the Middle Ages. Here, the local grain, an early form of barley known as bere, was dried, then moistened with a little warm water and beaten to remove the husks. It was then boiled in fresh water until soft. Chopped kale was added and the pot was brought back to the boil, then moved off the fire for the last of the liquid to be absorbed by the grain. The Scottish dish 'tart-an-purry', often shortened to 'tartan' or even 'dragon', is

This satirical engraving from 1811, entitled 'Scotch Training for a Milling Match', features a pot of 'crowdy' – a very thick porridge – cooking over a peat fire, with bags of barley and haggis, leaves of kale, bowls of Scotch broth and gruel, stacks of oatcakes and bannocks, and a crate of that essential ingredient – oatmeal – scattered around the room.

much the same but uses coarsely ground oatmeal instead of whole barley grains. While first London and then much of England went over to more watery soups, grain-thickened pottages like Scotch broth and 'hairst bree' (sometimes called harvest broth, or 'hotch potch') kept their place within upland homes down the centuries.

Vegetable and pulse purees continued to be made in the Highlands and Islands, although in the twentieth century the word 'mash' tended to take over from 'purry' when naming the dishes. It is hard to think of a Scottish main meal that doesn't come with mashed neeps, a term used to cover all root vegetables but most commonly that which is known in England as swede. And of course there was that simple staple, porridge.

Wales offers further examples. The 1896 report of the Royal Commission on Land in Wales and Monmouthshire noted that 'llymru', 'uwd' and 'brwes' were still being eaten in mountainous rural districts (where coal supplies arrived late in history). Llymru is often rendered into English as 'flummery'; the first to do so was Gervase Markham, who in *The English Hus-Wife* described this dish particularly favoured 'in the west': 'From this small Oat-meale, by oft steeping it in water and clensing it, and then boyling it to a thicke and stiffe jelly ... which they call Wash-brew, and in Chesheire and Lankasheire they call it Flamerie or Flumerie.' Other descriptions of llymru, dating back to the eighteenth century, speak of soured buttermilk rather than water as the boiling liquid. Uwd was occasionally said to be the same thing as llymru, the name changing according to whether you were in the north or south of Wales, but some people claimed it was in fact a slightly different dish, more akin to porridge using coarser ground oats and fresh milk. Brwes consisted of crushed oatcakes with hot beef stock poured over. (The term is pronounced in much the same way as the Gaelic word 'brose', which refers to the dish produced in Scotland by pouring boiling water over raw oatmeal.)

That other great staple of the Welsh diet, 'cawl', was traditionally described as a meat broth, flavoured with herbs and vegetables and thickened with whole grains that swell in the broth. The cawl served in homes and businesses across Wales today tends to resemble a thinnish lamb and vegetable soup with a few grains of pearl barley, but earlier recipes suggest there used to be a lot more grain and a lot less liquid. In North Wales and Liverpool, they have another meat broth with vegetables and grain called 'lobscows'. Again most modern versions retain the broth and vegetables and grain is rarely included. Nineteenth-century Liverpudlian sailors used 'hard tack', or ship's biscuits, to thicken it, but the old Welsh way was to add whole or simply crushed oat grains, or crushed oatcakes.

In 1811, an Irish woman explained cooking what was basically a frumenty over a peat fire: 'I let the water boil before I stir in e'er a grain; and when once it boils fast, I put in handful after handful, till I think there is near enough, stirring it well all the time; then I lift the pot a hook or two higher, and cover it up for a good share of half an hour, very seldom stirring it.' This was the old way of cooking.

Poor man's pottage?

Every now and again, we catch glimpses of the thick/wet divide where older styles of cookery hung on in more remote, wood-burning areas of England until they were finally swept away with the arrival of the railways and loads of cheap coal. William Ellis farmed at Little Gaddesden in North Hertfordshire, on the edge of the Chiltern Hills, but he made part of his living as a writer upon agricultural matters. In 1750, he published *The Country Housewife's Family Companion*, for which he took a journalistic approach to the subject of food and cookery. Rather than writing out recipes, he recorded the advice and practices of individuals from differing social classes and regions around the country. It is one of the earliest documents presenting ordinary people's domestic behaviours, if not quite in their own words, at least from a report of them. His section on dairy, for example, included 'The exact Method of preparing Scalded Cream for making it into Butter the Devonshire Way, by a Correspondent at Stowford, near Ivy-bridge, Feb. 25, 1746–7'. This was followed by 'A Somersetshire Dairy-Maid's Account of making Butter with scalded Cream'. And based on his collected accounts (unlike the printed recipe books of the era), frumenty was alive and well.

His chapter upon the use of peas is especially interesting because almost all of his examples were drawn from his local contacts. The one exception came from a farmer's wife who lived just over the county border in Bedfordshire, near Dunstable, on a continuation of the Chiltern Hills ridge. This ridge, on both sides of the county border, was a heavily wooded area in the mid-eighteenth century. (It still is.) It was also very poorly served by inland waterways. In other words, it was about as far as you could get from either the sea or a coalfield in those days. So, despite being just 50 miles (80 km) from London, this was one of the last places in England to become a coal-burning district. People there had to wait for the coming of the railways for that.

The most popular cookery book of the day was Eliza Smith's *The Compleat Housewife* (1727), which in 1750 – the year of William Ellis's survey – was already in its eighth edition. Smith's book contained only one recipe for a traditional thick pease pottage but seven recipes for wet-boiled pea soups. Ellis, reporting from his wood-burning neighbourhood, collected one pease pudding recipe that incorporated a wet-boiling method, calling for the dried peas to be soaked, put into a pudding bag and boiled in clean water until three-quarters cooked, then withdrawn from the pot, beaten into a mash, returned to the cloth and the pot, and boiled for a little longer. In contrast, he offered a barrage of thick pease porridge recipes, three from the wives of farmers and one from 'A Poor Man's Family'. Their accounts were full of instructions 'for thickening it, and making it the more hearty'. One told the reader to cook 'till the porridge is almost as thick as pap' – 'pap' being the bread and milk mush generally fed to babies then. The first farmer's wife suggested various types of peas, with the blue, white or grey varieties to be boiled with the short ribs of a hog and a handful of mint. The second wife added milk and wheat meal to hers and preferred a leg of pork. The poor man's pease porridge made use of bacon or pickled pork rather than fresh meat, and added flour but not milk. If you separate the advice into recipes, Ellis provided his readers with eight distinct pease pottages. It seems some liked it plain – and some liked it with bread crumbled into it.

Ellis collected thoughts on food and cooking from less humble members of society too. His book included a set of five recipes 'made by a gentleman' under the much more fashionable title of 'pease-soup'. These recipes involved a much longer list of ingredients and produced thinner, wetter dishes. All seem to have been copied from printed recipe books, mostly from Nathan Bailey's *Dictionarium Domesticum*. It is possible to imagine a class divide in play, and to assume the defining difference between those who made pottage and those who made soup was entirely about money to the exclusion of the influence of fuel. However, Charles Elmé Francatelli's *Plain Cookery Book for the Working Classes*, first published in 1852, was deliberately marketed towards poorer, coal-burning members of society. In it, Francatelli outlined the sort of coal-burning ranges he thought poorer households should have. He also listed recipes. His 'peasoup' called for three pints of peas and a gallon of water and included a rather concerned reminder that, unusually among his selections, it 'must be stirred from the bottom of the pot now and then'. It resulted in much the thickest mixture in the book, but it was still quite wet by pease pottage standards. It really is a 'soup', as the title of the recipe said.

For those among the upper echelons of society, who could afford to have wood, faggots, furze, charcoal and coal on hand, as well as the equipment to cook with whichever fuel suited a recipe, the methods of coal cookery were in the repertoire, even in a place as remote from coal supplies as the Chiltern Hills. But new techniques and tastes had not driven out the old in anything like the same degree as was the case in coal-burning areas. In a wood-burning home, thick and sticky was still easy to achieve and comfortingly familiar. Wherever traditional fuels remained in use, traditional cookery flourished. Wherever coal conquered, the inconvenient styles of recipe faded away.

Coal required a new menu.

A NEW MENU

The British cookery that was to emerge from this trial by fire was distinctive, robust, full of variety, adaptable and hearty – but never posh. Those who looked for fashion and social status in their dining trailed behind European leaders in the kitchen, the French in particular. Foreign visitors, subjected to the food of hotels and restaurants, frequently commented on the pale lacklustre copies of French cuisine they were reduced to, and mistakenly took those experiences as indicative of British cookery generally. But as George Orwell, writing in 1946 at the very end of the coal-burning years, explained: 'the first thing to be noticed about British cookery is that it is best studied in private houses, and more particularly in the homes of the middle-class and working-class masses'. This new, democratic form of cookery developed over time, with new foods, recipes and techniques emerging to fill the gaps left by the abandonment of older traditions. Experimentation and innovation in the kitchen included great leaps in the understanding of and control over heat, airflow, smoke and the mechanics of combustion. Fresh ingredients were embraced and old ingredients were put to new uses. Informality and everyday enjoyment of food triumphed over elaborate show and fuss. Roasting, toasting and baking evolved and gave birth to a host of new traditions. Puddings appeared, as if from nowhere, to stand alone as a national pleasure.

But perhaps we should start with the basics. The simplest way of filling a hungry belly was a slice of bread or a boiled potato.

One's daily bread

A powerful consequence of the progression from thick to thin recipes was the rise of bread-eating and, beginning at the end of the eighteenth century, the widespread planting of potatoes, a food that seems almost to have been designed for cooking over coal in pots of rapidly boiling water.

Medieval Britain, like the rest of Western Europe, had long been a grain-based society. Oats, barley, rye and wheat dominated agricultural production across the country. Foodstuffs processed from these crops were supplemented with peas and beans, as well as fish and meat from livestock. Grains were cheap, abundant sources of nutrition and formed the staple of everyone's diet, rich and poor, but most particularly they formed the vast bulk of food consumed in poorer households. In the days before coal, however, working people did not necessarily eat oven-baked bread. Instead, frumenties, porridges and pottages were cheaper than bread since preparing them incurred no costs at the miller's or the baker's; the grain was simply thrown into the pot with boiling water or broth. These dishes also required less fuel to cook. And nearly anything could be added to the pot to cook as the grains boiled and swelled. This provided a bit of variety in the diets of a beleaguered, poorer population.

We might imagine baked bread was more prevalent than it really was because it appears so frequently in the written records kept by a range of individuals and institutions. Bread was often a commercial product. Millers, bakers and their businesses left behind leases for their premises. Laws were written to regulate the pricing of their products. Because (predominantly male) millers and bakers were considered to be craftsmen with a particular trade, these occupations turn up in everything from coroners' records to military muster lists, as well as a sizeable number of wills and inventories of their worldly goods at their death. (Frumenties and pottages were produced in the main by women within the home as part of their general duties, not as part of a separate 'occupation'.) At the same time, baked bread was the ideal format for institutional provision of cheap grain food. A range of charitable organizations, religious foundations and wealthy households conspicuously distributed bread to the poor in addition to providing their own people with generous bread allowances, and many written accounts of their activities have survived. Clearly, a lot of baked bread was eaten; otherwise, all those commercial bakers would have been unable to make a living, and all those charities would have stopped doling it out. But it wasn't automatically part of the daily diet of a large portion of the population.

So, while baked bread is very visible in the historical record, food produced within the homes of more ordinary people was far less well recorded. We know what ingredients they could buy in the local market, and what foodstuffs were subject to tithes and taxes, but what people did with those basic ingredients in the privacy of their own kitchens is largely a matter of conjecture. There are William Ellis's journalistic accounts of housewifery in 1750 in his wood-burning area of the Chiltern Hills, where a rich variety of grain dishes held. Ellis described how his own maid prepared milk porridge. There were numerous recipes for 'water gruel' (made with oats) and frumenty (made with wheat and barley). 'Loblolly', another dish of oats and water, was taken from 'one of my day labourers' wives, having four children, [who] is often necessitated to find out the cheapest and best way to make the daily shilling go furthest'. But grain use was mixed. Ellis also included bread recipes followed in his own house as well as those of his neighbours.

Remnants of this pattern of mixed use were brought home to me during a conversation I had with a woman brought up in Glasgow in the mid-twentieth century. Her mother had been a Highlands girl and maintained many of the old cooking traditions. Every Monday morning she cooked up a large pot of plain oats and water porridge. Although some was eaten hot that morning, the rest was poured into a wooden tray – actually, the drawer of a dresser – and allowed to cool into a thick, solid slab. This was then cut into chunky squares and handed out as a portable breakfast or lunch over the next few days. Sometimes there was a bit of butter or dripping smeared on the slab; sometimes it was spread with jam. She was making porridge and treating it like bread.

Peas could be prepared and served in a similar way, as the words of the familiar nursery rhyme record: 'Pease pudding hot, pease pudding cold, pease pudding in the pot nine days' old.' It's a dish that I enjoy immensely. Dried peas are soaked and boiled until they break down into a thick starchy mass, like a medieval purry or the modern dish mushy peas. Allowed to cool in a bowl, they set into a fairly solid mass, which can be turned out and sliced. These slices make an excellent packed lunch, especially when well buttered.

Wood- and peat-burning, so perfect for making porridges, favoured this approach to grain cookery. Coal did not. As thick, sticky foods were removed from the repertoire, the gaps were filled first with baked bread.

Looking through local records noting the occupations of residents, we see the proportion of people listed as bakers rising rapidly during the eighteenth century. The baking and selling of bread appears to have become a growth industry just as domestic coal-burning spread across the British Isles. As households abandoned the old sticky, starchy mixes of the wood-fuelled past, they bought bread. With only the larger, more prosperous households being equipped with brick or stone ovens for baking bread at home, poorer people turned to the purchased takeaway option. Bread was respectable 'convenience food', considered to be a little posher than porridge, a little more desirable. So as the cheaper thick and sticky starch options became more difficult and unreliable to cook upon coal fires, many people increasingly chose the easy trip to a dependable baker's shop.

Meanwhile, potatoes had arrived in the British Isles from the Colony of Virginia in the 1580s. Initially, these root vegetables were seen as exotic treats and used as pie fillings, baked together with marrow, raisins and a sprinkle of sugar and spices. Some were even preserved and candied by comfit-makers. Soon enough, their potential as a daily starch was identified; in 1633 the Royal Society suggested planting them 'with the view of preventing famine'. They were not, however, either popular or quick to catch on in wood-burning rural regions. J. C. Loudon's *An Encyclopaedia of Agriculture* noted that, in the closing decades of the seventeenth century, potatoes 'were much used in Ireland and America as bread … and may be propagated with advantage in great quantities, for food for swine or other cattle'. But not, we might note, by the English for their own consumption. Tracing the uptake of potatoes into the daily diet is an interesting exercise that displays a considerable degree of confluence with the uptake of domestic coal, with urban areas leading the way. By the 1790s, for example, rural Essex had some 1,700 acres of potatoes under cultivation. Most of those potatoes were sold to Londoners. The early years of the nineteenth century saw potatoes forming a significant, perhaps the dominant, element of working-class diets in Manchester, Birmingham, Liverpool and other industrial cities – all coal-burning cities by that date – while potatoes rarely featured heavily in working-class rural diets until the end of the century, when railways finally brought cheap coal to the last wood-burning districts.

Cheap food requiring little fuss, whether bread from the bakers or, later on, potatoes for the pot, became the foundation of ordinary people's daily diet. These starches fulfilled the basic needs for those with little time or energy to spare. They had the harsh grind of trying to make a living to keep them occupied.

Proof is in the pudding

The meteoric rise of an altogether different type of recipe – the boiled pudding – also seemingly coincided with the rapid uptake of coal. The pudding owed nothing to French or other foreign influences, nor did it begin life as a commercial item or an exotic import from the colonies. It was, and quintessentially remains, a British type.

Like baked bread, the boiled pudding was a staple food of both rich and poor. For over three hundred years, until it began to fall out of favour almost exactly in sync with the departure of coal from the home, puddings were boiled in a pot hanging over the fire, whether they were filled with steak and kidney or a jam roly-poly, Bedfordshire clangers or a festive Christmas treat.

The first boiled pudding unambiguously appeared in print within the covers of John Murrell's *New Booke of Cookerie* (1615). Between his listings for French and London cookery, there was a dish described rather interestingly as a 'Cambridge' pudding – a city that converted to coal only very shortly after London by way of the barges carrying Newcastle coal up the Cam. Breadcrumbs, flour, suet, milk and eggs formed the pudding dough, which was flavoured with sugar, spice and dried fruit. A large knob of butter was tucked into the centre of the mass, from which it would melt and run out like a sauce once the cooked pud was cut. To cook it, the whole thing was 'tyed in a faire cloth' and dropped in rapidly boiling water – thence the term 'bag pudding'.

A woman pulls a steaming bag pudding out of boiling water.

While this was the earliest published recipe for a boiled pudding, older manuscripts reveal that the dish had been around for at least a decade. Quite a few handwritten personal or family recipe books survive from the decades around 1600, so many that it seems to have been fairly standard practice for gentlewomen to collect and copy out a wide range of household recipes. A significant number of the printed texts from the period claimed to be transcriptions of such elite family manuscripts as well. An interest in cookery and medicine was highly fashionable in this era, and most historians agree that it is in the handwritten manuscripts that we first see changing food fashions and innovations.

The recipes in both handwritten and printed books were often bunched together by theme or source, as if copied out from a series of loose leaves and smaller collections. Many were attributed to particular individuals. *The Complete Receipt Book of Ladie Elynor Fetiplace* was largely copied out in one go in 1604 by Anthony Bridges, working as her secretary, although a series of annotations and a few additions appear at the end in other hands, including that of Lady Fettiplace herself. She was quite the well-connected lady, counting among her contributions a salve for old sores attributed to one 'Mrs Panesfot' and 'Tobacco water by Sr W;R; [sic]', referring to Sir Walter Raleigh.

Most of Lady Fettiplace's book was concerned with medical recipes and sugar work, both of which were considered appropriate interests for a highborn woman, utilizing, as they did, very expensive ingredients, unusual skills and often elaborate equipment. Cookery as such also attracted elite attention, but not quite to the same degree, since much of it was actually handled by servants and based upon widely known skills. Nonetheless, among Lady Fettiplace's five hundred or so recipes were several dozen kitchen recipes, including 'a bagge pudding' and another simply called 'a pudding'.

She certainly knew her puddings. These two recipes contained most of the essential elements of the British boiled pudding tradition. The bag pudding was a rich, savoury but rather delicate pudding that called for eggs and cream to be mixed with breadcrumbs and flour. This batter was flavoured with fresh herbs and seasoned with a pinch of salt, nutmeg and sugar. The cook was told to 'wett your bagge in cold water' before dropping it into rapidly boiling water, and warned that 'yt must not bee boyled with meate but alone in fayre water'. This method produced a light, fluffy herb dumpling – delicious served alone with melted butter or as part of a meaty broth or stew. The second pudding was perhaps plainer but also heavier, calling for flour, suet, eggs and cream and a pinch of nutmeg.

But these were not the only puddings in her collection. She also featured a larger selection of boiled pudding recipes that seem to predate the adoption of the cloth bag. These puddings instead used 'guts', that is, sausage skins, as the cooking container, which (like the cloth bag) could be removed before serving. One of her puddings boiled in gut was made up of bread, suet and eggs flavoured with currants, dates and spices – a very familiar mix – but I think it is her almond pudding that I like best of all: breadcrumbs and ground almonds mixed with suet, egg yolk, rosewater, sugar and a little spice.

The development of such boiled puddings can be traced through the recipe books of the late sixteenth century, and these suggest the changes to the menu came quickly. There were no pudding recipes mentioned in the *Boke of Cokery* published by Pynson in 1500. Nor were there any in the *Proper Newe Booke of Cokerye*, a compilation from 1545 that signalled the first substantial move away from the medieval kitchen traditions. By the time *The Good Hous-Wives Treasurie or Book of Cookrye* was published in 1588, however, a whole host of puddings were given a separate section all their own. Every one of these puddings was savoury, stuffed into an eclectic mix of edible casings before being boiled. 'Black puddings' (blood and oatmeal) and 'white puddings' (milk and oatmeal, sometimes with a little liver) were listed first, followed by meat puddings. Then came a pudding in a hollowed-out turnip containing apple, currants, spice and hard-boiled egg yolk, and another where a stuffing was made of hard-boiled egg, spice and 'beetes boyled' (perhaps cooked beet leaves or chard, since elsewhere in the same book spinach was given as an alternative). There were also puddings in a carrot, a cucumber or the belly of a tench, a freshwater fish. The only thing these had in common were being flavoured stuffings in some form of casing that were cooked by being dropped into a pot of rapidly boiling liquid. So it was clearly the cooking method that defined the category of 'pudding'.

Once the pudding got going, it was seemingly unstoppable. *The Queen's Closet Opened*, which purported to be a 1655 transcription of Queen Henrietta Maria's handwritten recipe book, included a green herb pudding, an almond pudding and a 'quaking pudding', which resembled a cross between a custard and a soufflé and was accompanied with a special instruction to butter the cooking cloth before boiling. It was, as the name suggests, a wobbly pud, even when cooked. In 1660, Robert May had eighteen savoury boiled puddings and twelve sweet ones boiled in cloths, including the now classic Cambridge pudding with melted butter in the middle, in his *Accomplisht Cooke.*

A pudding, whether packed in sausage skins, a cloth bag or a ceramic pudding basin, is the easiest thing in the world to cook over a coal fire. It is also possible to cook it over wood (or even, at a push, over peat), but there is definitely far more faff involved. Keeping a pot at a steady, permanent boil over wood requires close attention. Recall that wood fires often provide cyclical heat, with the temperature falling as the wood burns away and rising again as the fuel is replenished and catches. The same sort of cycle occurs with coal, but it transpires over a much longer time period and the temperatures are steadier.

Pudding was a style of cooking that not only suited coal fires but became much easier over coal. It could even be accomplished quite successfully using the simple basket grates available in the seventeenth century. Of course the cookery books of the coal era were stuffed with them for the next three hundred years.

The art of roasting

The arrival of coal seems, if anything, to have initially prodded people to gain greater expertise in the art of roasting. A process of adaptation was embraced, and the roast became the centrepiece of the high table as never before. But when a more convenient technology solution arises, old traditions also vanish, almost without comment.

As people began to use coal grates regularly, they tried to improve them, seeking ways to continue cooking the foods they were most accustomed to. In the homes of the better-off, that meant working out how to roast with coal. When in 1617 Fynes Moryson characterized the best French cookery in terms of boiling, he went on to say that English excellence lay in roasting. The secrets of good roasting, wrote Gervase Markham, involved maintaining properly clean equipment, fastening the meat firmly and evenly onto the spit and then 'to know the temperatures of fires for every meat, and which must have a slow fire, yet a good one, taking leisure in roasting, as chines of beef … which indeed would lie long at the fire and soak well in the roasting; and which would have a quick and sharp fire without scorching'. The cook also needed to appreciate which meats should be roasted until just done and which should be well done, keeping some meats pale when cooked and others being allowed to take a high colour. During the roasting the meat would be basted, usually with one of a range of fats flavoured with spices. There were, however, 'some that will baste only with water and salt and nothing else', according to Markham.

Basting still occasionally turns up in modern recipe books, but in the seventeenth and eighteenth centuries, it was a frequent practice. Cooks also 'dredged' their roasts, scattering on dry ingredients at intervals throughout the cooking process. Markham considered the best dredging to be 'either white breadcrumbs well grated, or else a little fine white meal'. Basting and dredging were undertaken in alternation, gradually building up a flavoured crust around the joint. Lastly, it was essential to ascertain 'when meat is roasted enough', Markham wrote, 'for as too much rareness is unwholesome, so too much dryness is not nourishing'. He suggested watching for steam, smoke or shrinkage of the meat upon the spit, and pointed out where on each type of meat the cook should insert a knife or skewer to see if the juices were running clear – a sign that the meat was cooked sufficiently. He offered a detailed description of the signs to look out for when roasting a young piglet, but left his readers to make their own observations and judgements for most other roasts. Experience was the key. Good roasting technique was the mark of what most people of this time considered to be a skilled cook or chef.

Markham's emphasis upon different temperatures of fire was an essential consideration when roasting. However, he didn't describe what shape the fire should take. This was something so universally known about roasting that he simply didn't think of mentioning it. But if you do any open roasting, you quickly realize that it is as fundamental as the level of heat.

Roasting, for a start, never happens 'over' a fire. The food is always placed in front of the fire, ideally over a dripping tray of some sort. If you suspend meat directly over your fire, the fat will drip onto your fuel, catch and flare up, scorching your food. Such a flame-grilled effect can be tasty when thin, quickly cooked meats are involved. Burgers, as any barbeque enthusiast knows, can be quite good when grilled in this manner. The surface of a larger piece of meat, however, becomes unpleasantly scorched and burnt long before it is cooked through. Roasting in front of the fire permits you to oversee a much more controlled and even cooking process.

Countless images from the sixteenth and seventeenth centuries depicted joints or whole animals suspended upon spits in front of either a sheet of flame or a wall of burning coals. The sheet of flame was a sign of the old wood-burning methods holding sway, while the wall of coals was the new technique.

In the days of wood, the fuel had been held in place using andirons, allowing billets to be laid across and then stacked up leaning against the uprights at the front of the hearth. Generally, a second pair of andirons, often called cobirons, supported the spit. This arrangement created a long, thin and high fire, with flame around 18 inches (46 cm) high for most large joints. The same dynamics that cause the flame from a round or square

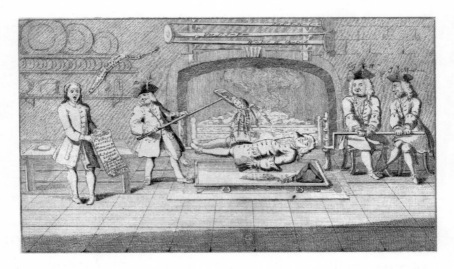

A cartoon from 1745 shows Sir Watkin Williams Wynn MP being roasted and basted on a spit before a fire, just like any good joint of meat. The wall of fire created by coals is visible behind him.

wood fire to pull together into a pyramid shape will produce a merged sheet of flame when burnt like this. The food held upon the second pair of irons can be moved closer or further away from the fire to help with temperature control. It could also be adjusted up or down by laying the spit across different pairs of supporting hooks.

Coal behaves differently. Its flames are small and many. The heat radiates more within the immediate vicinity of the combusting fuel. To cook in a similar manner with a basket grate, you need a grate tall enough to produce a wall of burning coals. Only the coal burning at the front of the basket will roast your meat; any coals more than a few inches back in the basket were entirely superfluous. So it made sense for those intending to do a lot of roasting to ask the ironmonger to procure them rather thin, tall grates. These grates also needed to be fairly wide to allow a large joint to be roasted at both ends as well as in the middle. Some extra brick- or stonework was a useful addition to the set-up. From around 1600, a new word enters the kitchen: the 'range'.

Later, this term would come to mean a cast-iron, coal-fired cooking stove, but at the beginning it referred to the combination of brick, stone and iron that permitted people to roast with coal as their fuel.

Ashley House was constructed between 1602 and 1605 near Walton-on-Thames for Lady Jane Berkeley. The agent employed to make payments and oversee the building work, Richard Mason, kept a careful set of accounts, detailing all of the materials and workmen involved. When it came time to fit out the kitchen, he sought out '1 anker of Iron for the chimney' and 'a dogge of iron with the staples and broads', which together cost 12s 4d. In contrast, a 'grate for a sinke' in the kitchen cost a mere one shilling, so clearly these other kitchen furnishings were substantial items. There were more irons in the kitchen too: '2 irons for the kitchen range', bought for 6s 10½d, and a 'barre for the potthangers' for 8s 4d. Ashley House was a grand edifice, built of brick in the latest style for a member of the aristocracy, and its kitchen fittings would have been entirely modern. It is hard, though, to work out exactly how all those iron pieces were employed. I think this may have been a kitchen with two hearths, one for boiling (thus, the bar for pot hangers) and one for roasting (employing the anchorage and dogge with its staples and broads – which may be a mistranscription of the word 'broaches', meaning spits) and the range.

A clue to the nature of these early ranges can be found in a reference to 'a range' marked upon one of Ralph Treswell's surveys of London in the early 1600s. The feature was housed within a building close to the corner of Giltspur Street and Cock Lane known as 'pye corner' (this survey is reproduced in Chapter 4). This property was rented out to a man called Robert Hollier who was clearly in the catering trade. On the ground floor were four rooms, a yard and two staircases; the floor above had six rooms, with a small garret above that. Two of the ground-floor rooms contained large ovens, and there was a well in the yard.

But the room of particular interest was the one labelled 'the shop', where the words 'a range' were noted by the drawing of two small, square sections of brick standing about 6 feet (1.8 m) apart on the back wall. A range at the very beginning of the seventeenth century would seem therefore to consist of two brick piers built against a back wall, perhaps protected by an iron fireback, into and between which were almost certainly set horizontal iron bars or grates. Such a structure would have been all but useless with a wood fire but highly effective with coal and suitable for roasting. The roasting hearth at Ashley House may well have had one of these partly brick, partly iron ranges, over which was fixed the roasting apparatus, the iron dogge.

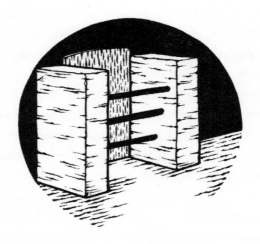

What Ralph Treswell probably meant by 'a range'.

Something that was a little bit more basket grate than range can still be seen in situ at Haddon Hall in Derbyshire. As you enter the kitchen, a fireplace stands upon your left. It is large and was originally a simple, wide-open space such as you would need for a wood fire. At some fairly early date (there is no record of exactly when, but the house was shut up in 1700 and left unused until the 1920s), the fireplace was converted to coal-burning. A large lump of masonry was added into the fireplace, taking up about half its depth, with a backwards-sloping front face. Into this masonry was set an iron grate. It was ideally proportioned for coal-roasting large pieces of meat, probably several at once. It was made of wrought iron, not cast, and has seen a lot of use.

Roasting in front of a range like this was mostly a matter of very generous coal provision. It took a lot of coal to fill such a grate, even if it was narrow. And it did need to be fully filled, during the whole cooking period, to achieve the constant wall of heat. Jonathan Swift's advice for servants spoke a great deal about economizing upon the use of fuel use: 'when you roast a long joint of meat, be careful only about the middle,' he wrote caustically, 'and leave the extreme parts raw, which may serve another time, and will save fireing'. Later in the text he admonished:

> Always keep a large fire in the kitchen when there is a small dinner, or the family are abroad; that the neighbours, seeing the smoak, may commend your master's housekeeping; but when much company is invited, then be as sparing as possible of your coals, because a great deal of the meat, being half raw, will be saved, and serve next day.

Now, it is possible to carefully regulate the size of your fire so that it perfectly matches the size of your roast, minimizing the amount of fuel you consume, by creating a smaller contained area within a large grate. Bricks and stones can be employed to pack out the sides of the grate, which works very well in my experience. But it is interesting to see that almost as soon as ranges and thin roasting grates appear, a less makeshift adaptation accompanied them.

Iron fireplates and 'cheeks' were listed in inventories from the early seventeenth century onwards. These movable metal plates could be loosely slotted into the grate or, in more elaborate versions, wound in or out, to adjust the size of the fire, giving cooks a great deal more flexibility in fire management. A coal-fuelled roasting fire was a very hungry beast, and such measures were clearly worth the effort.

An iron grate with 'cheeks'.

The consumption of huge quantities of coal was very common in coal cookery. Everything goes much easier when you pile it high and burn it hot. The only thing you need to do to keep it going is shovel more coal on, in a fairly random fashion. Getting the fire up to heat in the first place is trickier, however.

Henri Misson de Valbourg's *Mémoires et observations faites par in voyageur en Angleterre* described English and Scottish life in the late 1690s to a French audience. Domestic coal-burning was one of the subjects he felt needed explanation. After mentioning the superior burning qualities of more expensive scotch coal, he presented his review of the variety from Newcastle: 'the common Coal is not so combustable, but once when it is lighted, and there is sufficient Quantity of it, it burns very well.' Getting a large pile ablaze was the key to stress-free cooking. He continued:

> To make a coal fire, they put into the chimney certain
> iron stoves about half a foot high with a Plate of iron
> behind and beneath. Before and on each side are
> bars, placed and feathered like the wires of a cage, all

of iron. This they fill with coal, small or great as they run, and in the middle they put a handful of small coal which they set fire to with a piece of linen or paper. As soon as this small coal begins to burn they make use of the bellows.

He said it took two minutes of bellowing to get this first bit of coal to light, and just a few more minutes for the fire to spread to the larger mass beyond.

Personally, I don't think Misson had a lot of practical experience with the procedure. Getting coal to catch straight from a bit of burning paper is little short of a miracle. Most people with any coal fire experience will tell you that you need some wood. A piece of paper or charred linen is sufficient to light a few small twigs or shavings of wood, which will light some larger sticks, and this nice, hot little fire of sticks will set fire to your coal.

What Misson probably observed was the rekindling of a coal fire rather than the lighting of a new one. Wherever there were sufficient resources to keep a fire burning, people generally chose to do so. Servants had every reason to favour this option as they were the ones who would have the labour and trouble of lighting the fire, and bore none of the extra fuel costs. Naturally, masters and mistresses saw it rather differently, but they were not always the last ones to go to bed or the ones up at the crack of dawn, when fires were stirred back into life. It was common practice to pile on fuel last thing at night and then restrict the oxygen supply in some way. With Newcastle coal, it was possible to use a poker or shovel to pack down and compress the coals, then lay crushed coal dust over the top and splash a bit of water on top to form a sort of crust, much like blacksmiths did. The enclosed ranges of the late nineteenth century also had slides that could be pulled to block the airflow across the flue.

With plenty of fuel but restricted oxygen supplies, a coal fire burns very slowly – slow enough that a few embers are usually still alight in the morning. Revitalizing a fire is both easier and quicker than starting from scratch. Even if you cannot see a burning ember, it is generally possible to poke a piece of paper into the warmest spot, bellow for a few moments and watch the paper burst into flame. You then scrape the surrounding bits of partly burnt coal around the flame. If your coal is in a simple basket grate, it takes a full half hour longer to bring a single kettle of water to the boil if you have to light a fire from scratch rather than revitalizing a few embers. On a large cast-iron range such as those commonly used in the Edwardian period, the difference is even more pronounced since all that cold metal sucks up the early heat. Upon the two late Victorian and Edwardian ranges that I have used most, it took between forty-five minutes and an hour longer to bring a kettle to boil with a new versus a revitalized fire.

A nation of roast beef eaters

The effects of coal upon British food and diet were quiet but insistent. It was perfectly possible to roast without a dedicated roasting hearth. Various ad hoc arrangements with bricks, stones and string could be pressed into service. I have, for example, jammed a branding iron across the front of a tiny bedroom fire grate and built up a deep bed of burning coal behind it, suspending a joint of meat from a string secured at the top by a nail in the mantelpiece, twisting the string so that the meat turned in front of my blaze. But in general, roasting calls for investment in more complicated and more expensive grates or ranges. It's also fuel-hungry. A wood fire uses roughly twice as much fuel to roast than to boil a joint of meat, while a coal fire uses about four times as much. Once they'd made the switch to coal, those who could afford to still wanted to roast their meat, and they were willing to invest in the equipment needed to do so.

Take, for example, the area around Telford and the Severn Gorge. By the latter half of the seventeenth century, this was coal-burning country. A local supply at cheap rates, plus good waterborne transport links and the forces of fashion, had established coal as the main fuel throughout the region. And we can see iron grates and roasting equipment in almost all of the local probate inventories. Richard Darwall, who died in 1666, was farming in the parish of Dawley on a fairly modest scale. He had lived in a three-room house where, in addition to the 'two grats' that he had 'for the fyer' and his cast-iron fireback, he owned a pair of cobirons, two spits and three dripping pans for roasting.

Over time, roasting became more specialized. In the same parish, the carpenter John Duddell, who died in 1728, had an iron grate complete with 'niggards' – additional grates placed above the main base of the grate which helped to sift out larger, usable cinders – as well as three spits, two dripping pans, a tin baster and a brass basting spoon. He also had a jack chain and cord, although not the actual 'clockwork' jack used to turn the spit mechanically. John Harris, a wealthier yeoman who passed away in 1746, had amassed an iron grate with cheeks. He also possessed a 'hanging plate' (probably an iron baking stone that hung above the fire) and a 'purgatory plate' (rather like a trivet attached to the side of the grate with a hinge, so that it could be moved on and off the fire), as well as two spits and a dripping pan.

Throughout the eighteenth century, patriotic and propagandist literature placed heavy emphasis upon roast meat as a quintessentially English meal, as opposed to fancy, Frenchified food. The personification of the Englishman, John Bull, was frequently portrayed as a roast beef eater. A roast was good, solid traditional festival and party fare. It was aspirational cuisine – not among the very top echelons of society, who looked increasingly to the French for the next thing à la mode, but among the butchers, bakers and

'Mr and Mrs Bull giving Buonaparte a Christmas treat!'
in a popular etching from 1803.

candlestick-makers. And the yeoman farmers. Because it was such an icon of British cookery, it held on, despite the extra cost in fuel and new, nastier taste.

Meat roasted in front of coal does not taste as good as meat roasted in front of wood. Any form of cooking where fat comes into contact with smoke will result in the smoke flavouring the food. Open roasting is particularly prone to this. Wood smoke is generally considered to impart a pleasant taste, and certain woods are used for this very purpose. To this day, people consume oak-smoked this and applewood-smoked that. Indeed, one of the subtleties of good roasting technique in the old, wood-burning days had been the active selection of different woods for the roasting fire. In contrast, very few people think coal smoke tastes good. Just like the smell, the taste of coal smoke is acrid and sulphurous. It doesn't go well with any sort of meat. You can get used to it, of course, and you can minimize the taint by ensuring that your fire burns very hot and bright with minimal smoke – another reason to maintain a towering inferno. Basting with water rather than fat can help too, as the smoke will not bind to water as it would to a fat. You can also try flavouring your baste and dredge to mask the smoky coal tang.

The best instructions for using a coal fire to roast on are to be found in Anne Cobbett's *The English Housekeeper*, first published in 1835. She started by reminding her readers not to skimp on coal: 'as far as my observation has gone, meat cannot be roasted unless before a good fire.' After advising upon meat quality she turned to placing the coals:

> the thing of most consequence is preparing the fire, which ought to be made up (of the size required by the length and breadth of the joint) half an hour before the meat is put down … Let there be a backing of wetted cinders or small coals; this tends to throw the heat in front; lay large coals on the top, smaller ones between the bars, give the fire time to draw, and it will be clear. Before you put down the meat, stir the fire, clear it at the bottom, and see that it be free from smoke in front.

When I first read these instructions, I was rather surprised by the idea of wetting the small coal at the back of the fire. So I gave it a go. She was right: it does help to concentrate the heat to the front of the fire.

The birth of the baked joint

Separate iron ovens had been around since the early 1750s. Dr Richard Pococke, on a visit to Holyhead in June 1751, wrote: 'At the ironworks here, I saw octagon ovens of cast-iron from three to four feet long and about eighteen inches diameter to be put at the back of kitchen chimneys.' This octagonal ironwork created a shape around which a mass of brick and stone could be mortared. Installing such an oven required much less care, time and skill than building an oven entirely of brick or stone.

It had another advantage too. The old brick and stone ovens common in large houses and commercial baker's shops since the medieval period were heated by building a fire inside the cooking space. This fire, you may recall, was used to heat the stone or brick before being extinguished, and once the burnt material was swept out, food was placed on the hot stones to cook it. In a large and well-built oven, the residual heat could be used for a sequence of oven batches. To start, the temperature was high, suitable for bread baking. Once a batch of bread was cooked, the next batch of baking, something suitable for cooking at a mid-range heat such as biscuits or small pies, went in. When that batch had cooked, the oven temperature would have fallen to a level suitable for setting custards or perhaps meringues. If the baker wanted to bake more bread, it was necessary to light another fire inside the oven and wait for it to heat up. The iron ovens had iron floors set over a small fireplace. This meant the fire could be kept ticking over continuously, keeping a constant temperature and allowing the baking of batch after batch of bread or pies without a break – bestowing the equipment with the name 'perpetual oven'.

For late eighteenth-century commercial bakers and large households alike, perpetual ovens were attractive propositions. But such large, separate ovens were beyond the financial reach of most. Moreover, as built-in fixtures, they were the responsibility of the landlord rather than the tenant. For the majority of the population living in rented accommodation, perpetual ovens were simply unattainable.

A new type of range debuted around 1780. 'At one side of the fire is the oven and the other is made to wind up with a cheek.

The top bar in front is made to fall down occasionally to a level with the second bar, the moving cheek is made with a socket in it to receive a swinging trivet,' wrote Thomas Robinson of the advertisement for his new model. 'The oven is made of cast iron, nearly square front, the door with hinges and fastened with a handle and a turn buckle and the oven is provided with fillets for the shelves to rest upon. The oven must be enclosed with bricks and mortar.' Here, Robinson claimed to have invented the concept of the integral oven, with the oven and the main cooking area combined within one appliance. The image that appeared in his adverts is thought to be the earliest depiction of such an arrangement (although keeping brick piers short, and adding a plate of cast iron on top of one or both of them, had been happening in kitchens for quite some time already). Iron is very good at conducting heat, so with a good, strong blaze within the grate, the two plates of iron gradually warmed up, providing a useful flat surface upon which to stand pots not currently over the fire. This surface was generally warm enough to warm plates through and keep food hot enough, but not hot enough to cook it.

Turning one side of a kitchen grate into an iron box rather than an iron-topped brick pier was not particularly difficult nor especially expensive. Any landlord wishing to refurbish a kitchen or kitting out a new building could incorporate one of Robinson's ranges or a similar set-up for no more cost than fitting a simple, old-fashioned grate. The earliest of these appliances offered more flexibility in the kitchen, even if initially they were not all that good. Cooking successfully within the oven required frequently turning the food within while simultaneously maintaining a towering inferno in the grate itself. It was fiddly work, to be honest. Yet these ranges offered the first chance for many families to have an oven in their own home.

An iron oven beside the grate quickly became standard domestic equipment. When Thomas Robinson took out his patent for a grate and oven combination in 1780, he was far from alone in experimenting. Three years later, Joseph Langmead took out another for a range that incorporated an oven and a boiler to supply nearly continuous hot water. According to the engineer and patent agent John Farey Jr, writing in rural Derbyshire in 1813:

> About the year 1778 cast-iron ovens began to be made at the Griffen Foundry, now Messrs Ebenezer Smith and Company, and to be set by the sides of the grate at public houses and some farm houses, so as to be heated by the fire in the grate when a small damper in the flue is drawn and about ten years after, square iron boilers with lids were introduced to be set at the end of a fire grate and these have spread so amazingly that there is scarce a house without these, even of cottages of the first class.

Despite Farey's enthusiasm, it is worth noting that he was seeing such ranges only in 'some' of the farmhouses and 'even' the better class of cottage. Still, these conveniences were spreading. Foundries the length and breadth of Britain were starting to design, make and sell their own versions. The more sophisticated models had internal flues that channelled the fire's smoke and waste gases around the back and top of the oven to the chimney.

It was these improved built-in iron ovens that finally sounded the death knell for open roasting. With a coal-fired oven that was heated from more than one direction, baking became much more reliable. In very short order, all the difficulties, complexities and acrid tastes of open coal-roasted meat were swapped for the ease and cleanliness of the baked joint.

Writing in 1860, Isabella Beeton paid plenty of attention to traditional roasting: 'Roast beef has long been a national dish in

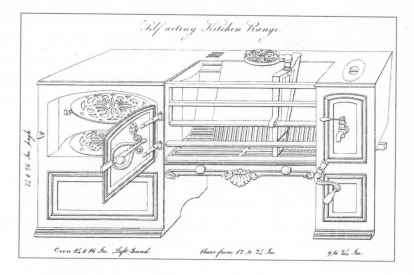

An early nineteenth-century catalogue of the Coalbrookdale
Company, in Shropshire, offered this 'self-acting kitchen range'.
This model featured an oven on the left and a boiler on the right,
with a single cheek in the fire grate.

England. In most of our patriotic songs it is contrasted with the
fricasseed frogs, popularly supposed to be the exclusive diet of
Frenchmen.' She too gave the usual advice that 'management of
the fire is a point of primary importance in roasting. A radiant fire
throughout the operation is absolutely necessary to insure a good
result.' She offered recipes explaining which dredges and bastes
to use, and when to move the joint further from the fire. And yet,
perhaps rather reluctantly, she also admitted:

> There are some dishes which, it may be said, are at
> least equally well cooked in the oven as by the roaster;
> thus a shoulder of mutton and baked potatoes, a fillet
> or breast of veal, a sucking pig, a hare, well basted,
> will be received by connoisseurs as well, when baked,
> as if they had been roasted. Indeed the baker's oven,
> or the family oven may often, as has been said, be

substituted for the cook and the spit with greater economy and convenience.

Mrs Beeton's open roasting recipes had probably already missed the boat.

A few years earlier Charles Francatelli, one-time chef to Queen Victoria, published his *Plain Cookery Book for the Working Classes*. He had become passionately interested in the plight of the poorer members of society and hoped his book would offer practical help in improving their diet. *Plain Cookery* provided recipes for a baked pig's head, baked goose, baked suckling pig, baked duck, three varieties of baked fish and baked potatoes and apples. The recipe for a dish of roast pork began: 'Let us suppose, or rather hope, that you may sometimes have a leg of pork ...'. Once the leg of pork was stuffed and the rind scotched, he told his readers, place it 'upon a trivet in a baking dish' surrounded by potatoes and apples with a splash of water and some seasoning. Then, he wrote, 'it will require about two hours to bake it'. The word 'roasting' had already become synonymous with baking in an oven.

In truth, I wonder a little about Mrs Beeton's recipes for roasting. In many ways they seem much like the older roasting recipes of Anne Cobbett and Eliza Smith, and were probably derived from them, but they had a habit of mentioning dredging only in the preparation part of the recipe, before the meat was set before the fire. Oven baking makes basting and dredging not just awkward but unhelpful. If you keep opening the door to get at the meat, you lose a great deal of heat, extending your cooking time. Starting your meat off with a dredge of flour and a baste and then largely leaving it alone sounds to me rather like a compromise that you might make if you wanted to hang on to as much of the traditional procedure and flavour as possible, but were in fact just bunging the joint into one of the new integral ovens.

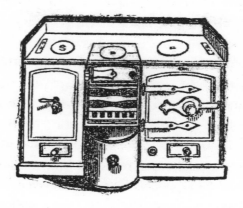

Mrs Beeton's exemplar of a closed range (1861).

Perhaps Mrs Beeton included the roast recipes simply for their status and tradition – dishes honoured in the breach and rarely cooked even by this date. By the 1930s, open roasting was a long-lost art. Elizabeth Craig, in *Cookery Illustrated and Household Management* (1936), wrote: 'Baking, as applied to meats, is the modern equivalent of roasting, by which joints, birds etc., were hung on a spit in front of or over a clear fire, and were turned from time to time during cooking.' Note how she was unsure of whether you roast in front of or over a fire. Here we have a professional cookery writer who didn't even understand the basic procedure of open roasting.

We should perhaps view the years of open roasting with coal not as a continuation of a traditional form of cookery but as a noble attempt to make a meal of privilege available to all. Never the cheapest or easiest of cooking techniques, open roasting had always been a special method for preparing food. Looking back at the daily kitchen records of sixteenth-century aristocratic households, we see a pattern: a small number of portions of roast meat were prepared for the top table, with a large number of portions of boiled meats served to the rest of the family and the servants.

For example, the kitchen accounts of the Petre family at Ingatestone Hall, in Essex, noted all the beef eaten on a daily basis in two separate entries, one for pieces of boiling beef and one for pieces of roasting beef. A fairly typical week in October 1592 listed 8 pieces of boiling beef against 1½ pieces of roasting beef upon the Sunday; 6 boiling and 1 roasting on Monday; and 7 boiling and 1 roasting on both Tuesday and Thursday. Wednesdays, Fridays and Saturdays were 'fish days', when no meat was served. The 'pieces' were not individual portions but 'messes', which were shared between four people. So while four people were served roast beef, around twenty-eight people got their beef boiled.

Roasted meat enjoyed a distinct social cachet, being generally reserved for those at the top. But on high days and holidays, the provision of roasted meat was extended to a larger group as a form of special treat. So the Petre family's kitchen accounts at Christmas displayed a very different balance, with almost as much roast beef as boiled beef being prepared for staff members. For the festive season the family themselves seem to have abandoned beef and mutton almost completely in favour of poultry and game.

When coal took over in the kitchen, roasting was widely considered to be a luxury. With coal, it became more expensive and tricky – and more desirable. It's a bit like sticking a designer label upon a handbag; the label shows that the owner can afford the additional cost. A kitchen equipped for roasting, and supplied with sufficient fuel to sustain a large campaign of roasting, spoke volumes about a household's finances and social standing. One equipped to do so with coal was still better off. Roasted meat – which had been actually roasted – was a status symbol.

Baking meat was both easier and much cheaper in terms of fuel use. Naturally, this made it more available to those upon the lower rungs of the social ladder, which helped to make the 'roast dinner' a once-a-week tradition. Those who previously could have only afforded a boiled joint of beef could now enjoy the more luxurious pleasure of a baked one. The roasts of Christmas, parties and feasts became the Sunday 'roast', produced in a domestic oven by lone housewives or the cooks in small establishments, under pressure to present food that pleased with minimal labour.

When electric and gas ovens came onto the scene at the beginning of the twentieth century, there were no serious attempts to find new ways to roast meat with these new fuels. The switch to baked meat was so complete and well-established that it wasn't worth the time and money to develop the techniques or equipment. Britons were totally satisfied with baked joints, although they liked to hang on to the word 'roast' – so much so that few people today are fully aware they are sitting down to baked beef and potatoes for their Sunday lunch.

Home-baking

Many European nations pride themselves upon the quality and variety of their sweet baked foods. The Viennese have a particularly long and illustrious tradition of pastries, and the French often consider themselves to have elevated bakery to an art form. But these elaborate pastries and confections were the work of professional bakers, developed in aristocratic kitchens by formally trained men before becoming the speciality of shops catering to the aspirations of the gentry and merchant classes of seventeenth-century Europe.

In Britain, professional bakers provided a narrower and simpler range – baked bread of course, but also relatively modest buns, cakes and biscuits. British innovation in baking took place instead in domestic kitchens, where an amateur baking tradition, led by women, was born. With its antecedents reaching back to the medicinal and sugar cookery of the sixteenth-century aristocracy, this non-professional feminine style of baking truly took off once the first integral ovens arrived. Coal made what had once been a country house convention into a national institution.

Towards the end of the sixteenth century, day-to-day medical provision in the homes of the wealthy was not solely provided by professional male apothecaries. Another authority held sway: the household's 'still room' (a name derived from the word 'distillation'). Here, the lady of the house, assisted by her gentlewomen, made distilled herb, spice and flower waters as well as a host of fairly simple medicines. Among favoured ingredients were 'electuaries', based upon honey, and 'suckets', based upon sugar.

Initially, honey and sugar were purely medicinal, their use no more prominent than, say, that of rosemary or feverfew. And in all but the wealthiest households, they may have been used quite sparingly, particularly given how fearfully expensive sugar could be. At the same time, they were prescribed for fairly common complaints. Considered to be both warm and dry in nature, honey and sugar were used to combat health problems associated with wet and cold conditions. They were used to 'dry up' coughs and colds and to encourage and speed up digestion after heavy meals.

Although they were a medically approved digestif, no one could fail to notice they were also very pleasurable to taste, and so the still room's production of sweet products expanded rapidly. By 1600 cooking with sugar was all the rage, done in still rooms by aristocratic ladies themselves, not by the staff in the kitchens of their grand houses. Recipe books of the era, both printed and handwritten, contained a high proportion of sugar cookery recipes, frequently outstripping the savoury elements by a large margin, as was the case in Lady Eleanor Fettiplace's book. A distinct social occasion was devoted to consuming the produce of the still room: the banquet.

Today, we generally apply the word 'banquet' to any large, formal meal for many guests. But in the late sixteenth and early seventeenth centuries, a banquet was a select gathering of only the most honoured and highest status individuals, who withdrew from the main hall to a separate, more exclusive place, perhaps in the garden or upon the rooftop, where a sort of sweet buffet was laid out. Merchant families aspiring to improve their position in society were keen to learn about this new upper-class diversion.

Gervase Markham's instructions to the upwardly mobile housewife of 1615 instructed her to lay an iced marzipan confection in the centre of her banqueting table and surround it with sweets: preserved fruits – some candied, some in syrup – fruit pastes, candied flowers and spices, fresh fruits and wafers. His recipes for banquets included several different gingerbreads and 'jumbles' (a type of biscuit), Banbury cakes (with lots of currants, a bit like an Eccles cake) and numerous biscuit breads that varied in nature from langue de chat to flavoured meringues.

By the 1670s the production of such sweet things was within the reach of those a little further down the social scale. No longer the fashionable activity of the lady of the house, sugar cookery had primarily become the domain of the gentlewoman or senior female servant within the household. Hannah Woolley's *Gentlewomans Companion* (1675), made this point: 'If you desire to be a waiting Gentlewoman, it will be expected that you can Dress well; Preserve well; and Write well a legible hand … If you would be a House-keeper … you must Preserve well, making Cakes, all manner of spoonmeats, and the like.' Chambermaids were also expected to be able to turn their hands to most forms of cookery, although they were 'not often required' to get involved with meat and fish, their work being more likely to involve pastry.

Over time, this division of labour became more pronounced in elite households. Housekeepers, assisted by chambermaids, provided the jams, marmalades, pickles, preserves, cakes, buns and biscuits distinct from the work of the kitchen. Housekeepers' pantries were increasingly equipped with small fireplaces and ovens to facilitate this independent production. A large proportion of the surviving handwritten recipe books of the nineteenth and early twentieth centuries owe their existence to this separate jam- and cake-making tradition.

The frontispiece of Hannah Woolley's *The Queene-Like Closet; or, Rich Cabinet* (1670) depicted scenes from a great kitchen and still room. In the upper right panel, a housekeeper or chambermaid stirs a pot over a chafing dish; flowers for distilling sit on the table behind her. In the middle left panel, the housekeeper seals bottles of her potions in her still room, with the distilling apparatus over a small stove.

Cooks and cook maids (generally known as kitchen maids in later years) generally memorized the recipes they used, but girls working as chambermaids under the housekeeper's eye were expected to be more literate and write down their recipes. Their career plan was aimed at becoming a housekeeper, and this necessitated the ability to keep accounts and write letters. Little notebooks full of cake recipes thus functioned as both practical memory aids and status symbols. Being a housekeeper was considered to be the more genteel route through domestic service. The gentility of home-baking and preserving was also evident in smaller households where the mistress did a share of this work.

The lighter, tidier and cleaner share of housework, as well as what Mrs Beeton called the 'higher department of cooking', was the province of the mistress of the household, while the hired help did the laundry, the cleaning of fireplaces and the basic cooking, tending to the meat, fish and vegetables.

Coal did a good deal to support this division of labour and ensure its spread down through the social classes. Brick-built, wood-fired ovens encouraged the production of large, uniform batches of baking. Each load, for efficiency's sake, should fill the floor of the oven. Successive batches ideally were uniform in size as well as type; the best results were obtained when everything in the oven required exactly the same amount of heat and time to bake. Try to bake a cake that needs forty-five minutes with a tart that needs just half an hour, and things had a tendency to go awry. Opening the door released a huge amount of heat from the brickwork, and there was no method of boosting the temperature back up. In a large household, this set-up was fine. Each firing of the oven produced a large batch of bread and possibly a second large batch of pies, which would see the household through until the next firing.

This was not, however, such a perfect arrangement for producing a small selection of luxury, sugar-based baked foods. While many households might need twelve loaves of bread to see them through the week, far fewer needed twelve fruit cakes all at once – even if they could have afforded all that sugar, spice and dried fruit. Small batches of baked goods were simply not practical, even in the great houses, until coal-fired perpetual ovens appeared around 1750.

When they first appeared, perpetual ovens were not especially cheap. They required setting aside a chimney exclusively for their use, and the work of a good mason or bricklayer. They also were not particularly useful as a replacement for the traditional wood-fired bread oven as they simply couldn't handle the necessary volume of baking without burning an extortionate amount of fuel. As a result, they were better suited to a wealthier household with aspirations towards fancy baking and rarely installed elsewhere. Neat, small and self-contained – the technical properties of cast iron dictated that these ovens rarely exceeded 18 inches (46 cm) across – these coal-fired ovens fit rather well within the concept of a separate, more genteel cooking space often found in grander households. They could be added into a housekeeper's still room without causing major disruption to the kitchen, and permitted an ever expanding array of cakes, biscuits and pastries to be pursued there.

Across the rest of Europe wood-burning ovens encouraged experiments with fancy cakes and pastries to remain within the purview of professional male chefs, who had the means to bake large batches of sweet luxury goods. Patisserie shops could sell a dozen fine apple tarts from a single firing, as well as the thirty small custard tarts that followed them into the oven. In Britain, the market for patisseries never really developed. Those with the spare cash to buy fine pastries were producing their own small batches at home in a coal-burning oven.

Coal also influenced baking recipes. Wood-fired ovens are especially good at producing crispy textures. Think of how different a thin-crust pizza cooked in a wood-burning oven is from one baked in a conventional electric model. Like the enclosed boxes of modern electric and gas appliances, coal-fired ovens held more steam around the food, producing baked goods with a moister texture. That which we call 'cake' – a mixture with an almost equal amount of butter, eggs, sugar and flour – bakes especially well in a cast-iron, coal-fired oven; it's rarely successful when attempted in a wood-fired oven. Meanwhile, the light crispy texture of puff or flaky pastry is more successfully achieved in a wood-fired oven. Flaky pastry cooked in a coal oven can often be disappointingly soggy. Because of coal, British baking slowly diverged from continental styles.

By 1850, a century after perpetual ovens first made their appearance, more and more ovens were routinely incorporated at the side of the grate as part of the range, or 'kitchener' as it was called in early adverts. Prices for these appliances were dropping rapidly too. Home-baking became accessible to more people, and it was meat, potatoes and cakes they were primarily baking, not bread.

Throughout the nineteenth century, well-meaning people were scolding poorer housewives that they should be baking their own bread, now that they had the equipment to do so at home. The advocates ranged from political philosopher William Cobbett, who argued that home-baking was more economical and conducive to an independent and self-reliant lifestyle, to health food pioneer Dr Thomas Allinson, who saw home-baking as an opportunity to produce wholemeal, unadulterated bread. But soaring commercial bread sales suggest very few people took them up on their advice. Had these (frequently male and well-off) commentators ever done much baking with a cast-iron, coal-fired domestic oven, they would have known its drawbacks as a bread-baking vehicle. Their small capacity, as mentioned earlier, made them uneconomical for baking on a large scale in terms of fuel use. It also made for a very time-consuming process, with the baker required to be on hand, turning the loaves so that they cooked evenly. Such time and fuel expenditures were all very well for the occasional cake or batch of biscuits, but not really viable as part of a general domestic routine.

Thus, the coal-fired domestic oven gave the working people of Britain not an up-to-date method of putting the basic baked goods on their table but instead a new means of producing what had once been luxury, party foods. Alongside baked meats mimicking ancient roasts, coal-fired ovens spread cake-baking and cake-eating far and wide. And this coal cookery tradition shows no sign of abating today. Indeed, certain TV series indicate that, if anything, home-baked cakes and other sweets are a growing obsession.

An unlimited supply of toast

With the adoption of coal, toast became almost as much of an icon of the British diet as did the roast. But toast did not arrive out of nowhere. It had a long history. All sorts of meat and fish had been served upon toasted bread in the medieval period. Recall the sippets and sops used to soak up gravy and sauces. In the sixteenth and seventeenth centuries, many a vegetable was added to the list of foods that might be piled upon toasted bread. For example, Thomas Dawson, in *The Second Part of the Good Hus-wives Jewell* (1597), offered a recipe for spinach on toast which I have to say is rather good. And toasted cheese was already established as the national dish of Wales.

Yet in the eighteenth century, when prepared in front of a coal fire, toast took on a different role. No longer just another dish at dinner, toast became a snack food for informal and private dining. Indeed, around this time it largely slipped out of the recipe books – and if these were the only sources of information about diet in the historical period, we would probably read them as a tale of decline. Luckily, an enormous number of toasting devices, as well as diaries, letters, stories and images of toast and toasting have survived, connecting the modern British love affair with toast to the switch to coal-burning.

A coal fire in an iron grate is a fantastic thing for toasting, so fit for purpose it seems to have been specifically designed for the task. Only the electric toaster can beat it for ease and convenience, and then only just. Toasting over a coal fire beats toasting over wood, hands down, and toasting over peat is particularly rubbish, as the fire rarely reaches a sufficient heat to sear or toast bread. Plus, the usual disadvantages of coal cookery simply do not apply to toasting. Since the butter is spread on the toast after it has been taken from the fire, toasting bread is an entirely fat-free enterprise, giving the noxious coal smoke nothing to bind with. There is no danger of the taint of coal smoke ruining toasted bread, buns, crumpets or muffins.

Coal fire equipment is also particularly well-suited to the task. Toasting on wood works best if you employ a gridiron over a raked bed of burning coals spread out to one side of the hearth, which is absolutely doable if you have a large hearth. If you only have a small hearth, you will be hard-pressed to make the operation work without sacrificing your main fire. You can hold your bread upon a fork or stick close to the dancing open flames of a brisk wood fire instead, but you have to get the bread very close to the flame to garner enough heat to toast it, which means keeping a close eye lest the flame should move or waver and spread a layer of soot over the bread's surface.

There is no need, however, to spread out coals beneath a separate gridiron when toasting with coal in a grate. The configuration of the grate throws the higher heat of the burning coal sideways into the room, while the flames move up and back towards the draw of the chimney, radiating heat past the bars of the grate's front without any danger of licks of flame smearing unpleasant soot upon your bread. A coal fire also holds steady in a way that the open flames of a wood fire does not. Suspending a slice of bread on a stick in front of a coal grate is just much easier and more reliable. The higher temperature of a coal fire also allows toasting to take place with the bread held much further away from the combusting material, further safeguarding the cleanliness and taste of the finished food. Toasting in front of coal is practically foolproof.

One of the great advantages of toasting was its simplicity and, specifically, its need for very little equipment. Wherever a fire was lit for the purpose of heating a room, toast could be made by anyone armed with a stick, poker or toasting fork. While main meals were generally produced in the kitchen, a bit of toast could be rustled up in other coal-burning spaces. And as coal-burning spread throughout the country, more and more people were in a position to enliven a piece of (possibly stale) bread rather quickly, without investing much in the way of additional capital or skill.

The eighteenth century was awash with pictures of people, up and down the social ladder, who had taken to toasting a range of muffins, crumpets, buns, teacakes and plain old bread in their chambers. One satirical print of the king and queen made a scene out of such slightly down-at-heel, homely gentility. Among the upper and middle classes, the experience of living in lodgings at the mercy of the landlady's cooking fuelled a slightly surreptitious toasting boom. Tiny bedroom fires of coal were pressed into service to warm and hearten the lives of bachelor clerks, lawyers and brokers. Faded spinster ladies managing on small annuities in a couple of rooms within someone else's house could cheaply entertain their friends with tea and toast without bothering the servants (who expected payment). The fashionable people packed into remarkably small spaces during the season at Bath, removed from the more substantial households of their main country seat, took to toasting their own small supper when not entertaining.

The royal couple 'Frying Sprats, Toasting Muffins'
by James Gillray (1791).

Basic grates set between two short brick piers were often termed 'Bath grates' because they were so popular in the spa town. And then there were the travellers holed up in country inns and looking for something warm and reliably edible after a numbing stagecoach trip. Lower down the social scale, the smallest coal fire could turn an endless diet of bread into something more appetizing.

As the eighteenth century gave way to the nineteenth, toasting became more widespread, particularly as coal grates became common in even the humblest of cottages. The Victorian chef Alexis Soyer, a flamboyant personality who believed that everyone, no matter their station in life, deserved instruction in the art of cookery, included quite precise instructions for making the perfect toast in *A Shilling Cookery for the People*:

> How to Toast Bread. – Procure a nice square loaf that has been baked one or two days previously, then with a sharp knife cut off the bottom crust evenly, and then as many slices you require, about a quarter of an inch in thickness. Contrive to have a clear fire: place a slice of the bread upon a toasting-fork, about an inch from one of the sides, hold it a minute before the fire, then turn it, hold it another minute, by which time the bread will be thoroughly hot, then begin to move it gradually to and fro until the whole surface has assumed a yellowish-brown colour, then turn it again, toasting the other side in the same manner; lay it then upon a hot plate, have some fresh or salt butter (which must not be too hard, as pressing it upon the toast would make it heavy), spread a piece, rather less than an ounce, over, and cut the toast into four or six pieces ... You will then have toast made to perfection.

Toast was a food of the people. It found its home not in posh dining rooms or grand kitchens but in spa towns, university lodgings, garrets and other chambers. Many of the most famous and long-lasting British food creations of the eighteenth century owe their origins to the toasting phenomenon. Bath buns and Sally Lunn cakes, crumpets, pikelets, muffins and teacakes all date to the days of the coal fire and the iron grate. Jam and marmalade, newly made affordable with the arrival of cheap sugar from slave-worked plantations in America and the Caribbean, rose in popularity, as a new way of eating the preserves, spread upon toast, became commonplace.

In earlier accounts, toast was mostly a food of afternoon tea and supper, a way for the ladies and leisured classes to entertain on the cheap within their rooms, or for bachelors to make their own supper. But fairly quickly, toast began to appear at breakfast too. Even in homes where the rest of breakfast was prepared by servants down in the kitchen, sliced bread was laid out for family members to toast themselves in front of the breakfast room fire. With the advent of coal, toast was the most democratic of foods.

Adaptations abroad

This then was the cuisine of coal: boiled or steamed puddings both sweet and savoury, roast meats which are in fact baked meats served with 'roast' potatoes and all the trimmings, Victoria sponge cakes and hot buttered toast with jam. It is a familiar menu, a nostalgic, romantic and old-fashioned form of cookery for which Britain is known around the globe. The dishes might be a bit bland or stodgy in the hands of a stressed or inexperienced cook, but done well they are warming, hearty and delicious, a comforting celebration of simple ingredients.

This style of cookery arose in large part as a response to the practicalities of a coal-burning kitchen, where bringing a fire up to heat can be a rather slow process, but once the fire is burning vigorously, it can be maintained at high heat with relatively little effort. It also favours foods that respond well to that other coal-based technological innovation: the small domestic oven.

The cuisine of coal is also the food of empire. When British colonists moved out across the seas, coal cookery went with them. The very earliest of such settlers, leaving Britain in the early seventeenth century for America, hailed more from the wood-burning regions of Britain rather than the coal-burning metropolis of London, and finding themselves on a wood-burning continent and encountering new sorts of food, quickly reverted to their old practices. Later settlers from Britain, more versed in the ways of coal than their forebears, may have struggled more, but they were living alongside peoples from many different backgrounds – European, Indigenous, African and later Asian – most of whom came from strong wood-burning cultures of their own. So although elements of coal cookery can be seen in the contemporary food of the US and Canada – particularly in the fondness for toast – these regions of early British colonization owe less to coal than more recently settled places.

Australia and New Zealand, colonized in the late eighteenth and nineteenth centuries, were more strongly marked by coal's influence. The male explorers and merchants of early expeditions may well have adapted to the local diet, but when families began to set up home in the Antipodes, they thought their homes should produce familiar British food. A large percentage of these British settlers had been brought up in a coal-burning world, eating coal-cookery food. On a new continent far from home, they stuck with what they knew, though until the great coal reserves of the two countries began to be unlocked, many of them had to manage coal cookery over wood fires. Here the baked meats known as 'roasts' remain popular, despite the climate and great influx of Asian cooking styles.

British colonists across Africa and Asia behaved in a similar manner, attempting to stick to the coal ways they had grown up with. They did so often in the face of hugely different and vibrant local food cultures as well as completely unsuitable fuel. If you want your pudding to be light and fluffy rather than stodgy, damp and slimy, you need to have a very good supply and selection of firewood at hand and remain at the fire throughout the hours of cooking time. It can be done of course – if you have the time, wood supplies and relevant skill – but it is neither convenient nor easy. That which had been a simple, basic dish back home, well within the skills of any cook or housewife accustomed to coal, frequently went disastrously wrong when attempted over wood in some distant corner of the British Empire. The mistress had scant experience of cooking over wood, and her local servants had no experience of the dishes and methods she was asking them to re-create. Indeed, they were being asked to do something technically awkward, and their chances of success were slim.

Many people, in search of the taste of home-cooking halfway around the world, went to the enormous expense of hauling familiar cooking equipment to their new homes. Cast-iron ranges began to show up on the African savannahs and the Indian plains. *The Indian Cookery Book: A Practical Handbook to the Kitchen in India* (1869) instructed readers: 'Coal should be used for all purposes of cooking.' Chief among the list of essential kitchen equipment was 'an iron stove'. Similarly, in her book *The 'Colonial Household Guide'*, Mrs A. R. Barnes gave advice to those setting up home in South Africa in 1890, declaring that 'a stove, which is the most economical and cleanly apparatus for a small household' must be purchased when fitting out a kitchen. She helpfully suggested several suitable models of cast-iron range by name. Once these large, heavy iron contraptions were in place, however, they generally had to be fired with wood since coal was scarce.

Among the cast-iron coal-burning ovens marketed to colonists was the 'Gem' portable range, manufactured by Brown & Green (1884).

Some coal and coke was often available in port towns where the refuelling of steamships was a major consideration. Railway lines across those lands controlled by European powers might also deliver coal for domestic stoves, but the supplies were never quite as dependable or ubiquitous as they were in Britain. *Hilda's Diary of a Cape Housekeeper* pointed out the fuelling challenges, which persisted into the early years of the twentieth century: 'I find coke and wood the most economic fuel. Paraffin stoves are a great boon.' Colonial homes often had to make do with a rather ad hoc mixture of fuels as both supply and price fluctuated. It is important to note that the particular iron stoves recommended by Mrs Barnes were chosen, she said, because they were 'suitable for wood also'.

While it is perfectly possible to heat an iron range with wood and cook upon it – and thousands upon thousands of people did so for decades – significant technical challenges and adjustments must be made. Because cast-iron ranges are designed for coal usage, the fire spaces are small and contained. Wood burnt within them has to be well seasoned and chopped into quite small sections, and the fire needs frequent feeding. Because wood burns at a lower temperature, bringing that whole big mass of iron up to temperature for cooking a meal is a very slow process, much slower than when the same range is fired by coal.

The exported foods of the British Empire – beef stew and dumplings, spotted dick, toad in the hole, rice pudding, boiled beef and carrots, apple crumble or a festive dinner of roast turkey and Christmas pudding – all relied on the long, rolling boil of a pot on top of a cast-iron range, or the red-hot iron oven at its side. The range had to be really hot to provide this sort of cooking, and it needed to stay hot for a long period. Anyone trying to fire one with wood had to start it up much earlier and work a lot harder to achieve the required temperatures in good time. It was also imperative to have far more fuel to hand. In addition to the outlay on the range itself, this was a very expensive approach to everyday cooking. No wonder that many of those who first encountered 'British' food in far-flung climes were unimpressed by the results, or that many British people adapted their diet and cooking techniques to something closer to those of their new home.

Indeed, in Europe, British cookery was viewed throughout much of this period with a degree of bewilderment. Every other nation was able to maintain a certain continuity with the menus of the past. Fashions in food certainly changed, and regional specialities and styles developed, but the heart of the kitchen was constant, with the same old wood-burning techniques holding sway. Some fancy work, particularly in the French tradition, was done over charcoal, while the vast majority of day-to-day cooking was conducted over wood well into the nineteenth century.

When domestic coal-burning finally came to continental Europe and North America, many of the early technical problems had either been solved or mitigated by updated chimney designs and endless experimentation with cast-iron bars, plates and ranges. The British had done the hard work of taming coal in the kitchen. The change from wood to coal as a cooking fuel had a much less dramatic effect among these late adopters. Nor was it so complete. Rural wood-burning continued across both Europe and America, despite industrialization and the conversion of urban homes to coal. For most of the world, domestic coal-burning was a fairly brief interlude between centuries of wood-burning and the dawn of electricity. Even in those areas that might be called heavily industrialized coal-burners in the nineteenth century, such as Belgium, northern Germany and the east coast of the US, domestic coal-burning barely lasted a century, and the practice was more usually counted in a handful of decades. London, by contrast, cooked on coal for over 350 years. Around three quarters of England's population burnt coal for 250 years, and in the final century of coal-burning, a full 95 per cent of the population were coal consumers.

The ingenuity of the British kitchen

Coal cookery was essentially a British phenomenon. Within Britain, the fundamental difference of fuel was acknowledged, but the influence of fuel on food has been overlooked. The British cookery tradition has been ascribed more to class and national character than to economic and technical pressures. These issues were, after all, well hidden from sight. Fashions in food and dining were very much in evidence from the writing left behind by the vocal, largely male elite. Production of food was the preserve of those on the other side of the green baize door. Even the mistresses of wealthy houses engaged more in the planning of menus and the accountancy of supply than in fire management and the juggling of pans and pots.

Well-equipped and abundantly staffed kitchens could afford the extra time, labour and technology required to mimic fashionable French cookery, developed with wood and charcoal fires, when they started cooking upon coal. Families with just a maid-of-all-work, or no hired help at all, were in an entirely different position. For them, a little additional convenience was a powerful persuader. When there was just one woman available to change the baby's nappies, bring in the coal, haul the water, fit in as much housework as possible and cook the dinner, then a dinner that didn't need watching as it cooked was a godsend. The freedom to bank up the fire with a mass of coal, stick a bacon and onion pudding wrapped in a cloth into a pot of boiling water and leave it untended for half an hour at a time was an irresistible option. Of course, middling and poorer households had much stronger reasons for adapting their menu to take advantage of coal's useful properties, just as they had the strongest reasons for sidestepping areas where coal's performance was weaker. The amount of labour involved in preparing a meal, coupled with the risk of spoiling precious ingredients, constrained the cookery of the vast majority of British society.

The richest and most influential could afford to eat meals devised with wood-burning in mind, even once they had installed the latest coal-burning equipment in their grand homes. Yet even the wealthiest in Britain grew up on coal cookery, eating it in the nursery and at school.

A new fuel had driven the development of a whole new way of cooking and a radically different diet. A menu based upon boiling and baking, with a side order of toast, was the cuisine that accompanied industrialization; cause and effect were intricately linked in a fossil fuel-burning age. Cooking on coal helped to develop the coal industry, and the iron industry too. Innovations within the iron industry permitted ongoing adaptation and experimentation with iron fire equipment.

Meanwhile, the cooks of the day invented newly effective ways of feeding the growing population of workers, inventors and entrepreneurs with their patented stoves, grates and ovens. Together, cooks and coal produced a set of recipes that cut down on the amount of attention and attendance that cooking demanded, and families of all social classes came to expect homes equipped with ovens and hobs. Steamed puddings and baked meats gave women a little more time and flexibility in one aspect of their domestic chores – a great help for the new millworkers juggling family responsibilities with a factory shift. Generations of women cooked breakfast then banked up the coal fire, stuck a pot in the oven and went off to work.

CLEANING-UP

The changes in food and diet that came with coal cookery are perhaps not that surprising. But coal also changed the British approach to housework. New cooking methods required new cleaning methods, and as it evolved, it caused a myriad of ripples in the larger pond of progress.

This seismic coal-generated shift in how we handled all things clean and dirty has often gone unnoticed in part because the earliest texts commenting upon such matters were written much later. Mrs Beeton, as we know, outlined household management in the firmly coal-burning era of the mid-nineteenth century, but so too did Susanna Whatman, who started penning her housekeeping book in 1776. Whatman included several pieces on coal fire management in the kitchen with no hint that anything but coal was in use domestically. Turning back the clock generation by generation, in 1760 we find small snippets of advice for a coal-burning home in Hannah Glasse's *Servant's Directory*; and the satirical *Directions to Servants* given by Jonathan Swift, published in 1745, was clearly intended for a household exclusively burning coal. Only back in the early 1600s, with Gervase Markham's *The English Hus-Wife*, do we find discussion of housework in the context of wood use. But in truth, there was very little about what might be termed housework in the modern sense within Markham's book of household management. There were plenty of good instructions upon subjects such as brewing, baking, the bleaching of cloth and the mixing of medical potions, but vital tasks such as laundry, scrubbing pots and cleaning floors did not appear within its pages. Still earlier texts contained the occasional tiny reference to household practices, such as a recipe for a powder to deter moths, but there was nothing approaching a wood-burning version of the coal-burning domestic routines of Mrs Beeton or her ilk.

A search for information on historic cleaning practices almost certainly directs you to practices associated with the era of coal. So strong is this focus that very few people, even within organizations that pride themselves upon historic housekeeping, such as the National Trust, are aware that another, completely different system of household management existed before coal. Indeed, historic houses, farms, dairies and other buildings throughout Britain are presented, and sometimes maintained, with coal-inspired cleaning techniques. For example, fourteenth-century timber-framed houses at the heart of traditional wood-burning regions have been subjected to soap and water – or else attract little speeches about how everyone and everywhere was filthy and smelly back in those days.

But back in those days, people did clean and they did care about cleanliness. The indispensable element of pre-coal domestic order was not soap, however, but wood ash.

Free from dirt

Free and readily available in wood-burning homes, wood ash formed the basis of food, laundry and household hygiene regimes.

When dry, it is easily removed with a brush; when wet, it is an effective cleaning agent in its own right. In contrast, coal ash is essentially dirt – and a pretty sticky and rather difficult dirt to clean up, requiring quite a bit of elbow grease and usually some soap for it to be removed.

I admit to being rather shocked the first time I found myself managing a Victorian coal-burning house. I was used to wood, and expert in dealing with the various types of filth that can accumulate in an active Tudor space. Over many years, I had worked out how to cope without the benefits of modern washing-up liquid, vacuum cleaners or biological washing powder. With each tiny scrap of historical information I put into practice, I was pleasantly surprised by the efficacy of ancient cleaning methods. So, standing in my coal-fired kitchen for the first time, I was feeling confident. Surely, I thought, the Victorian regime would be somewhere halfway between the Tudor and the modern. Dirt was just dirt, after all, and sweeping was just sweeping, even if the style of brushes had changed a little in the course of five hundred years. Washing-up with soap was not so very different from washing-up with liquid detergent, and adding soap and hot water to the old laundry method of bashing the living daylights out of clothes must, I imagined, make it a little easier, dissolving dirt and stains all that much quicker. How wrong could I have been.

Well, it turned out that the methods and technologies necessary for cleaning a coal-burning home were fundamentally different from those for a wood-burning one. Foremost, the volume of work – and the intensity of that work – were much, much greater. Yet, as I staggered under the weight of the housework, I could find barely any reference to how coal had transformed domestic life into one that needed nonstop cleaning.

As usual, there was very little comment in the historical record, largely because the people responsible for this aspect of the home were almost exclusively of lower social status and female. As a group they had low levels of literacy, and their opinions and experiences were least likely to be taken seriously by those who were literate enough to record and comment on the practices of the day. Unlike in the realm of cookery, there was little interest among the elite for a debate over fashionable brooms and washcloths. Recipes for removing stains from rare and expensive fabrics did circulate at the top end of society, but that was pretty much it. Housework was considered to be unskilled work, a matter of no intellectual interest.

Our old friend, the probate inventories, also hold very few clues. Household cleaning tools and substances were of very low financial value, so were rarely mentioned in these documents. A sermon preached by Thomas Gataker at the funeral of Mistress Joice Featly in 1638 gave another reason for the overwhelming silence: 'Is there any man so vile, and void of shame, as that he dare presume solemnly to bequeath to some honourable person some greasie dish – clout, or some durtie shoo clout.' Cloths used for dirty work were not fit subjects for official documents. In practice, the cleaning cloths of a grieving household probably did pass on to new hands, if simply because housework still needed doing, but the transfer did not merit any written reckoning.

Large households, keeping house on a grand scale, often made extensive records of even the most mundane supplies, however. In November 1648, the household of the Countess of Bath were finishing off several months' work overhauling her London town house. Over the summer, the kitchen chimney had been repaired by a bricklayer and then swept. The pump for supplying water was mended and a broken part replaced. A cooper had been employed to overhaul the tubs, buckets and barrels. A prodigious quantity of 'wax and tallow' was purchased 'to colour the rooms', and a carpenter was busy at something for a considerable length of time, since his bill came to over £6, which, even if the bill covered both materials and wages, was a considerable sum that spoke of a string of jobs being done. Once the work was completed, the staff had bought twelve loads of sea coal, a load of scotch coal, eight loads of billets and four loads of faggots in readiness for the winter. November was an expensive time of year to lay in large stocks of fuel. Those with the room to store coal and wood could obtain much cheaper supplies in summer, which suggests that while it was undergoing repair, the town house was not ready to accommodate these stocks.

With the fabric of the building sorted out, November also saw the purchase of a wide range of cleaning supplies. Sand and ashes were bought 'to scour with' and vinegar in substantial quantities was acquired, again 'to scour'. In addition, stocks of Flanders' tile (in later accounts, this is often replaced by brick dust) and whiting (essentially powdered chalk), again 'to scour with', had been purchased at the end of October. Three mops and numerous brooms were already in use. These were joined by another fourteen birch brooms and '2 wings to sweep'. A major campaign of intensive housework was being planned.

Cleaning supplies like these don't appear very often in the surviving accounts of this particular household. Ordinary daily purchases and provisions were generally recorded in other ways. As a result, we cannot get a sense for how this set of one-off purchases compared to the everyday provision of cleaning supplies. We don't know, for example, how long ten pence worth of ashes was supposed to last, or whether Flanders' tile was used once every couple of years or once every week. Regardless, nowhere in the accounts was there any soap. This was no oversight or accident; it reflected common custom. Cleaning aids and methods were primarily based on mechanical actions rather than chemical solutions.

Some surviving household records from the first half of the seventeenth century did show regular purchases of soap, but these were made in the context of laundry, and posh specialized laundry at that. Even where the use was not specified, a large proportion of soap references were listed immediately before or after an entry for starch or laundry blue (the optical brightener of the day). Once in a while, they were accompanied by saffron, the parts of the crocus sometimes used to colour ruffs. For the most part, household cleaning supplies were sand, ashes, whiting and brooms, like the ones purchased for the Countess of Bath's London house.

There were a few exceptions to this typical list of cleaning supplies. The home of the Reynolds family at Forde, in Devon, included purchases of materials 'for scouring' in their repertoire of cleaning equipment. They didn't, however, list sand among their provisions, probably because the house was situated right on the coast, where good sand could easily be had for free. Similarly, the home of Sir Thomas Puckering was somewhat unique in its day for making regular purchases of wax for 'rubbing' the floors of his and his wife's chambers.

Sand and brooms, in particular, were often bought in bulk. The Reynolds family appear to have got through somewhere in the region of sixty-eight brooms in a year, generally bought in batches once a month. This was a sizeable household, but by no means among the largest, with twelve permanent members of domestic staff. The Earl of Salisbury's kitchen account, kept on his behalf by the clerk of the kitchen, spent 6*d* every week on sand, always on a Friday. But the accounts did not note whether the sand was for house cleaning.

How then were such ingredients and tools used and why did coal necessitate a change?

What it means to wash-up

I'd like to start with the history of doing the dishes, since this subject was my inspiration when I first began my own investigations into living history. Way back in the 1980s, a lot of historical re-enactment – whether in Britain, Europe or America – involved battles and marching about with weaponry. (A lot of it still does.) This part of history never appealed to me, and I still feel rather uneasy about these activities, which to my mind seem to carry a sense of glorifying war and violence. Since I did not wish to take a place on fake battlefields, I often found myself left to keep an eye on the children, cook the dinner and wash-up afterwards. Perhaps there were some who saw this as second best, but I didn't think so. These areas of life were as fundamental to the experience of our forebears as they are to ours, and I soon became fascinated with how they managed it.

Getting hold of period recipe books proved fairly straightforward. I had a bit of camping experience, so I was able to cobble up something that at least vaguely resembled period food, and I managed to hunt down historically appropriate pots, techniques and ingredients. The more I learnt, the more I wanted my meals to reflect the region, social class and situation being portrayed. And so I worked out, step by step, how to adapt my modern 'Scouts' style of cooking to create meals closer to the original. But in my quest to replace supposition with realities, there was a big gaping hole in my knowledge: washing-up.

Numerous books and people could help me identify the right shape of cauldron; the metallurgy involved in frying pans; the varieties of wheat or apples being grown; and the official rations provided for soldiers, servants and labourers. There was period advice about roasting and baking, and archaeological evidence of bake houses and breweries. Historians had written about the cultural meanings of various foods, and economists had opined on the supply, demand and production of various crops. Period cookery books were very keen upon one using 'a clean dish' or a pot that was 'well scoured', but they never told you how to achieve these objectives. Modern histories were even less helpful, skipping over nearly all of the practical aspects of food preparation and domestic practice in the kitchen, or anywhere else within the home. While cooking did receive some attention, mostly at the aristocratic end of the scale, cleaning of any sort was almost totally absent from scholarly works. The notable and noble exception was Caroline Davidson's marvellous book *A Woman's Work is Never Done*, which I wish I had encountered much earlier in my endeavours. Sadly, however, it too contained very little about washing-up.

Finding the weekly mention of 6*d* worth of sand among the accounts of the Earl of Salisbury's kitchen was a eureka moment, as was the payment to Goodwife Weston 'for scoweringe the brasse & pewter att Quickwood, before the houshould came'. References to 'dish clouts' were also a clue. Scurrilous ballads were rich with them. 'Cucking of a Scould', recorded in a text dated 1615, satirized a scolding wife for making an enormous public fuss because 'A neighbours maid had taken halfe, Her dish-clout from the hedge'.

Thomas Tusser's expanded edition of *Five Hundred Points of Good Husbandry*, published in 1580, offered this proverb on the last jobs of the day: 'Wash dishes, lay leavens, save fire and away, Lock doors and to bed, a good huswife will say.' If nothing else, here was simple confirmation that people did do the washing-up as a matter of course. Mind you, Tusser was also keen that his readers should not overdo it, and wear out their pots: 'No scouring for pride, Spare kettle whole side, Though scouring be needful, yet scouring too much, Is pride without profit, and robbeth thine hutch.' Even in the sixteenth century, it seems, some people were too house proud.

It was quite a delight to discover that two different plants have carried the name 'scourwort' in Britain. One, *Saponaria officinalis*, is more commonly known as soapwort or bouncing bet and is still used as an ingredient in particularly mild and gentle detergents. Its sap contains a natural, soap-like substance. The other, *Equisetum*, is known as horsetail or scouring rush. Rather than being selected for its soapiness, it was prized for its abrasiveness. Silicates in the plant act as a biodegradable scouring pad, particularly effective on

The plant horsetail was used as a natural scouring brush, according to John Gerard's *Herball or Generall Historie of Plantes* (1597).

metal pots and pans. John Gerard, a barber surgeon whose book, *The Herball or Generall Historie of Plantes* (1597), was the standard work of botany in England for a century, called it 'shave-grasse', and said it was 'not unknown to women, who scour their pewter and wooden things of the kitchen therwith'.

Finally, there were clues to washing-up in servants' job descriptions. Great households considered the task to be important enough to have a male employee dedicated to it. This was in part because of the cash value of the household's dishes, which typically included substantial amounts of silver- and pewterware. In *Some Rules and Orders for the Government of the House of an Earle*, the 'office of the yeoman and groome of the squillery' was primarily described in terms of keeping tabs on the silver and pewter: counting the pieces after every meal and securely locking them away when not in use. However, it also instructed the scullion to scour and wash the plates on their journey from table back to cupboard. A similar set of rules was set down in 1595 by the Viscount Montagu (or someone within his household). A 'scullerye man' was to deliver the silver and pewter 'cleane scowered, and well ordered' to the yeoman of the cellar in the evening for safekeeping overnight. His duties covered processing 'all other things brought unto his office', which were to be dealt with 'decently and cleanly'.

In the wealthiest households, the scullion was often supported by a number of assistants. In summer 1587, Robert Dudley's house boasted five scullions: Peter Daniell, John Mason, Robert Holland, Rafe Powell and Thomas Tanner. The Earl of Leicester maintained a very large household – he was, after all, the Queen's favourite – but five full-time servants can get through an awful lot of washing-up and polishing. A late seventeenth-century portrait of a scullion employed at Christ Church, Oxford, painted by John Riley, showed the man carrying a large pewter charger under his arm. He wore a pair of leather palm gloves that left his fingers and thumbs free, offering some protection for hands that must have scoured many a dish in their day.

The inventory of the scullery at Ingatestone Hall, in Essex, taken in 1606 was exceptionally detailed. It began by listing two lockable pieces of furniture intended to provide secure storage for the silverware. Next came 'two great Booles to washe vessell in', which were accompanied by a plain wooden plank 'to skower upon'. There was a pail for fetching water and a 'flat copper kettle' that could be used to heat water to scald dishes with. A 'dust baskett' was provided for waste; fixed to the wall was a 'Rack to hange wypers on', along with six 'wypers' for silverware and seven for the pewter. The scullions also had some wooden stools to sit on while they scoured. 'Two longe boxes with handles to put skowering dust' completed the list.

Disgust towards badly washed dishes was also evident. The ballad 'Seldome Cleanely' from the mid-seventeenth century captured popular sentiments vividly. Following verses that described a housewife who left dung on her shoes for six months at a time, who employed straining cloths so foul and rank they turned the milk as it passed through, who wore clothes shiny with grease and who had such poor personal hygiene that 'flies blew up her smock', the ballad turned to her washing-up practices: 'If otherwise she had, But of a dishclout fail, She would set a dish to the Dog to lick. And wipe it with his tayle.' The song finished with a stomach-churning account of the woman using 'the droppings of her nose' to bind the fillings of her puddings.

The idea of dogs licking pots and dishes clean was a common joke and slander. It even turned up on inn signs, with one well-known example being The Dog and Pot, just outside the city of London on the road to Oxford. Another period ballad, 'The Description of a Bad Housewife', rehearsed the theme: 'It is (methinks) a cleanly care, My Dish-clout in this sort to spare, While Dog you see doth lick the Pot, His Tail for Dish-clout I have got.' A printed sheet of the ballad was complemented by a woodcut of the scene. Dogs licking pots made regular appearances in genre paintings of the period. In the Netherlands, the image represented moral as well as housekeeping laxity.

Washing-up, encompassing both washing and scouring, was deemed to be an essential task in homes up and down the social ladder.

How to wash-up

Using sand to scour dishes, for which there is ample evidence, brought practical considerations. Firstly, it demands a cloth. If you try to rub sand across a dirty pot solely with your hand, you will soon have no skin left – yet most if not all of the dirt will still be stuck to the pot. Sand applied and moved around with a brush of some sort will spare your hands, but it will also have very little impact upon the dirt. However, take a damp linen cloth, dip it into sand so that some of it adheres and use that to scrub with, and you have an effective cleaning method. The dish 'clouts' mentioned in this period were such cloths, as well as what we might call a tea towel, or drying cloth. 'Wypers' may have been intended for the drying up. Ingatestone Hall's record of its rack for wipers suggested these cloths were reserved for use with silver or pewter. The inventory of household linens at Petworth, the country residence of Henry Percy, in 1592 included seven 'wypers for the pantry' and five 'wypers for the scullerie'.

Secondly, the effectiveness of sand-scouring in the kitchen depends on having pots and dishes made of certain materials. If you attempt to clean a glazed pottery vessel or dish with a sand-covered damp cloth, you will be sadly disappointed in the results. You may achieve a reasonable level of cleanliness, but this will be accompanied by scratches and chips where in the future food may stick, rendering your vessels unhygienic as well as unsightly. A damp sandy cloth used upon a wooden bowl, followed by a quick rinse of water, is entirely satisfactory, and in my experience, it does the job much more effectively than a mixture of hot water, scrubbing brush and modern detergent. A sandy cloth is particularly good for scrubbing between and along the grain of wooden utensils. It not only dislodges food particles but also gently sands down the surface, as if you had used sandpaper. A wooden bowl scoured in this way is very hygienic indeed, in essence presenting a newly exposed and thus sterile surface. The same might be said of metal pots and pans. Sand-scouring can shift even the most burnt-on residue, and it also removes a microscopic layer of metal (hence Thomas Tusser's warning about the vanity of over-scrubbing). The brass and bronze pots that were so very prevalent during the fifteenth, sixteenth and seventeenth centuries were particularly suited to sand-scouring.

Brass and bronze are alloys based upon copper, a rather problematic metal in conjunction with food. Copper is a cumulative poison when ingested. When the metal comes into contact with acetic acid, it is corroded, creating copper salts, known in the sixteenth and seventeenth centuries as *verdigris*, for their bluish-green colour. Acetic acid is present in fruit and onions; it's especially strong in wine and vinegar. For this reason, it is imperative that these foods are not stored within brass pots and that any suspicious bluish-green trace deposits are assiduously removed. Sand-scouring wears away this potentially toxic patina. (Jams can be made in copper pots because sugar prevents the formation of the copper salts. It is dangerous to put fruit in a copper pot before sugar has been added to it.)

Thirdly, sand-scouring seems to work as well in cold water as it does with hot. I am in truth not quite sure why this should be so, but I invariably get *better* results when my washing-up water is cool or cold. Perhaps my hands are simply more comfortable in cold water, and thus I tend to do a more thorough job. Whatever the reason, there is definitely no benefit in heating up your water when using sand.

It is easy to see the benefits of sand-scouring in a world where there was little pottery but a lot of wood and copper alloys to be cleaned. Few inventories from the wood-burning era recorded earthenware vessels in the departed's household, and where they did, these vessels were often being used in specialist areas such as still rooms and dairies, where people were handling medicines and milk, both of which have a habit of impregnating wood in a way that can taint subsequent batches.

John Myll, of Ufcolm parish near Salisbury, was entirely typical. His executors in 1582 listed his goods as including 'crok brasses' valued at 20s, 'panne brass' at 28s, pewter vessels at 9s and 10s of wooden vessels (known as 'treen' or, in this case, 'treyng') – but no earthenware or pottery of any kind. One of Myll's neighbours, however, exhibited the sort of specialist use of earthenware that is the exception to the rule: when he died, farmer William Read had eight milking cows, a 'chisewringe and chiserakes', and 3s of

'Erthing vessells' in addition to the more usual domestic provision of brass pots and dishes of pewter and wood.

Cleaning with sand, a small cloth and some cold water was a particularly cheap option. Many people, not just those living along the Devon coast, would have been able to procure sand free of charge. For those who were forced to purchase supplies, they were not expensive. A cleaning method that required no hot water must also have been a real boon. It not only freed people from the time and labour of heating water, it was also cheaper in terms of fuel. In addition, pots and bowls could be scoured out in the yard, out of the way of the cook, and in a space that was itself easy to clean at the end of a messy operation.

But what about grease? Sand and cold water alone could not always shift it. That was what the wood ash was for.

In honesty, the vast majority of grease can be removed from wooden and metal vessels by sand-scouring, as the grease sticks to the sand particles, which are rinsed away. Any tiny residue of fatty acids that remains within a wooden bowl often is absorbed by the wood, seasoning and feeding it, and in quantities small enough to be counteracted by wood's natural antibacterial properties. A thin veneer of grease is also helpful upon brass, and especially iron, pots. It acts as a waterproof seal that helps to prevent the formation of rust and verdigris. But when there is too much grease, or grease that you are having difficulty dislodging, a handful of wood ash from the fire generally solves the problem.

All types of wood ash contain a proportion of potassium hydroxide, a chemical that is very alkaline in nature and prone to combining with fatty acids. Historically, wood ash was called 'pot ash', a name derived from its source, the cooking fire. The chemical reaction between pot ash and grease produces a new substance generically known as 'soap'. If you take a look at 'backwoods living' articles on the internet, you will find a plethora of sites that describe washing-up with wood ash. Most of these sites are written by people from the US, where domestic wood-burning remained the norm in many areas until the arrival of electricity. Because coal never had the same domestic impact upon America as it did in Britain, wood ash knowledge survived there well into living memory.

Used cold, a handful of wood ash rubbed around a greasy frying pan combines very inefficiently. Only a small percentage of the potential conversion to soap takes place. But in a wood-burning household, wood ash is free, abundant and convenient, so such wastage is of very little matter. You can readily improve the conversion rate by adding just a little heat. With a metal vessel all you have to do is pop it back on the fire for a minute or two, then take it off and rub ash over it with a greasy cloth. For wooden vessels, it is better to heat a small quantity of water with a good handful of ash stirred in. After you let the ash settle for a moment or two, you simply dip your greasy wooden spoons and bowls into the hot liquid before drying them with a clean cloth.

If you are short of a dishcloth, there is no need to resort to the tongue and tail of a dog. Handfuls of straw from a variety of plants perform well and can be used as something of a disposable cloth that needs no laundering. We have mentioned the scouring properties of horsetail, but for most ordinary washing-up, almost any dry or dryish plant material will do. Even fresh green plants can be pressed into service, but they will tend to leave a sap residue. Dry stalks of hay or straw – taken from wheat or barley crops, pea plants, turnip tops or meadow grass – are much cleaner and more effective. (Naturally, it is vital to steer clear of toxic plants such as monkshood and foxglove.) Scrunched up into a clump, the straw will absorb a little water; when dipped into a bowl of ash, the ash will adhere to it, turning your straw into something of a pre-soaped scouring pad. When you are finished with it, you chuck it onto your kitchen midden or compost heap to decompose with time.

Cleaning pewter tableware is a slightly more difficult matter, as pewter is a very soft metal. Sand-scouring will cover the plates in deep, unsightly and unhygienic scratches. Even horsetail is too harsh. A softer, finer abrasive is required. In the past, 'washing' pewter often meant wiping it with water and a cloth, perhaps with a dip into hot ash water to remove stubborn grease. An alternative, recommended in a letter between two members of the Verney family in the seventeenth century, was to use bran:

> For your plaites if they be well washed every meal with water and bran so hot as their hands can indure it, then well rinsed in faire water; and soe sett one by one before the fire, as they may drie quick, I am confident that they will drie without spots, for I never knew any sawce staine soe except it be pickled rabbits, which stand upon the plaite awile so they will staine them filethyly.

Both mildly abrasive and absorbent, bran is particularly good at absorbing hot fats. Mixing bran in hot water produces a paste that can be rubbed around greasy dishes, dislodging the fatty acids and gathering them into the paste. And once it has done its job in the scullery, bran paste can be used as a super-enriched feed for pigs and poultry; there is no soap or other chemical detergent present that would make it unsuitable for this purpose.

Bran was widely available in the more prosperous homes of the Tudor era. When grain was milled, the householder or the miller could sift the meal, separating out the flour (the starch within the grain) from the bran (the grain's outer coating). If they chose not to sift the meal, the bread baked from it would be dark, coarse and filling, and understandably, this was generally what the poorest did. If they instead removed the bran, their bread would be white, light and softer (as well as rather smaller). Wealthier families preferred whiter breads, leaving them with surplus bran. The Verney household seems to have had ample access to bran for their scullery.

It is hard to tell from the letter whether bran was their usual washing-up material or a special treatment specifically employed on damaged pewter- and silverware. The word 'plaite' was used at this time to delineate metal dishes of all shapes and sizes; it did not apply to wood or pottery. The staining of 'pickled rabbits' was evidence of the action of food acids upon metal dishes. Pickled foods can eat right through a pewter plate. Silver is a little more resistant, but unsightly black marks can quickly develop where lemon or vinegar has come into contact with the metal.

In some of the aristocratic households, there were regular purchases of chalk and oil 'for scouring'. The Reynolds family at Forde was fond of these substances, which were most likely applied to their pewter. Always purchased as a pair, when mixed together chalk and oil become a sort of putty or paste that, with the help of a small cloth, can be rubbed onto pewter to remove dirt as well as tarnish where the metal alloy has oxidized. If you put a great deal of work into this rubbing, you can burnish your pewter to a bright polish that resembles silver. After you wipe the plate clean with your cloth, a thin coating of oil remains, protecting the surface from further oxidization.

I seriously doubt anyone in the small farming households of Ufcolm, where John Myll lived, had the resources to regularly polish their few pieces of pewter up to such a brilliant shine. But in the houses of the great, with their abundance of servants, a perfect mirror finish was de rigueur. The vast majority of the antique pewter you see in country houses and museums these days has been woefully neglected, permitted to weather down to a dull grey. Next time you visit, try to imagine it brought back to its original shine.

Ready-made soap

When the people of London converted to coal-burning, they lost their access to free wood ash. Yes, sand-scouring still worked fine, and pewter could still be brought up to a shine with a cloth, but some cooking and foods simply engendered a lot of grease. A dip in very hot water would help, as this melted the fats and made them easier to wipe away, but a large batch of greasy plates would quickly foul both water and cloths. With no free ash to hand, it is possible that some households began to buy in wood ash. It was for sale.

In addition to domestic usage, wood ash was a central ingredient in industrial processes such as glassmaking and the preparation of woollen cloth, and commercial ash burners operated in several parts of the country. For example, Celia Fiennes recorded that those around Cannock Wood in Staffordshire, for example, burnt bracken and, from the ash, manufactured balls that were sold for use in scouring and laundry.

But ready-made soap was also for sale, and perhaps more available than was wood ash. The city of Bristol had a long-standing tradition of soap manufacture and its soap was sold widely. London also had its own soap industry, although John Stow, in his 1598 survey of the city, considered it to be a relatively recent development, noting: 'I have not read or heard of soap-making in this city till within this fourscore years.' He reported that around 1510, John Lame was said to have set up a boiling house in Grasse Street to produce 'black soap'. 'White soap' in hard cakes or bars was imported, Stow said, but also available. Most people called it 'castle soap', a linguistic corruption of its place of origin, Castile, in Spain, although by the end of the sixteenth century much of this variety was actually being produced in southern France. Bristol's product was 'grey soap, speckled with white, very sweet and good'. London's black soap was the cheapest, selling for halfpenny a pound. The better Bristol soap fetched between a penny and a penny farthing ($1\frac{1}{4}d$) per pound. The best soap – the castle soap – sold for $6d$ a pound.

Black soap was not sold in cakes or bars. It was a liquid soap, or one of jelly-like consistency, and while not truly black in colour, it was dark. Every batch that I have made has turned out a sort of middling brown.

This cheaper style of commercially produced soap was essentially the same as that produced in the kitchen when a handful of wood ash was rubbed around a greasy frying pan. Potassium hydroxide was paired with available fats and heat was applied to facilitate and speed the chemical reaction. The differences were mainly ones of scale, and the level of refining of the basic ingredients. Sieving the ash removed any small lumps of charcoal or unburnt matter. Water was passed through the ash, dissolving the useful potassium hydroxide and filtering out most of the other constituent parts. Hot water did a quicker and more thorough job of leaching out the useful alkali or 'lye', as it was more usually called. Boiling this liquid, so that some of the water evaporated off, resulted in a much more concentrated solution, better for combining with the fats. The traditional way by which people knew their lye was sufficiently concentrated to combine well with fats involved placing a fresh egg into a bowl of cold lye. If the egg floated, the lye was ready.

Animal fats were the cheapest of all the fat options. William Harrison in 1587 called the product 'refuse soap' and complained about the smell. He was referring specifically to soap made from the fat scraps of butchers and tanners. Such fat could be quite rancid. The easiest method of cleaning and purifying such refuse was to chuck it in a big pot with plenty of water and boil it for hours until all the fats melted and floated free. The vat was then allowed to go cold, so the liquid fats would rise to the surface and gradually solidify into a layer on the top. This layer was skimmed out of the pot, leaving the majority of the skin, bone, gristle and other unwanted matter in the waste water. Repeating the process several times removed more and more impurities. It was a stinky, messy business, but at the end, the renderer had a fairly clean and pure tallow that could be used for making both soap and the cheaper sort of candles (beeswax was largely reserved for aristocratic and church use). The process could be performed at home, and some people probably did make their own soap. But on a small domestic scale it is not very efficient in terms of time or fuel.

There is some suggestion in old soap boilers' records that tallow had traditionally been the fat used for soap-making. But from the Elizabethan era onwards, from which time more records have survived, it is clear that tallow was falling out of favour in commercial soap manufacture. These entrepreneurs sought to raise the quality of British-made soap and establish a reputation that would allow them to compete successfully with foreign imports. As the population rose there was also a growing demand for tallow for candles. Within a generation of John Stow's dismissive review of London's soap-boiling industry, commentators had a rather different take upon their subject. An updated survey of the city, compiled by John Strype in 1633, noted that grey soap – the sort that Stow said came from Bristol – had been made of tallow and, as such, had been banned by the Common Council of London: 'The reason was, it would so waste, in short Time, the Tallow of the Realm. That the poverty would have no Candles ... and besides it smelt worse than the soap with train oil.'

Commercial soap boilers turned to two other fats in place of tallow: train oil and olive oil. 'Train oil' are marine oils derived from the bodies of species of fish such as cod as well as the bodies of a range of whales. Mostly, in Britain's case, it was derived from bowhead whales, which were hunted in the waters between Greenland and Spitsbergen. Bigger, more robust and reliable ships had allowed whalers to travel further out to sea, where mariners noticed the regular presence of large numbers of whales in the Greenland Sea and set about exploiting this resource in earnest starting around 1610. Small quantities of train oil had arrived in Bristol and other ports before then, mostly from Basque-country whalers, and been found to be ideal for the manufacture of black soap, but from 1615, the quantities were much greater, and they arrived predominantly in British vessels. The 1633 survey of London reported that the most common soap

Some version of Field's 'Genuine Spermaceti Soap' was
manufactured in Lambeth Marshes, on the south bank of
the Thames, from 1642.

in London was made of train oil and 'danske' ashes (imported
from Denmark). Train oil remained a key ingredient in mass-
market soaps until the international whaling moratorium came
into force in the 1980s.

The other important soap fat, olive oil, was also more
available. With bigger ships carrying larger cargoes and sailing
all year round, the prices of most Mediterranean goods dropped
significantly. An Italian soap recipe from 1560 probably described
how the Bristol soap-boilers were taking advantage of increased
olive oil imports:

> To make black Sope for clothes, with all the signes
> and tokens that it giueth and maketh in beiling …
> Use 3 pounds of egg bearing lye to 1 pound of oil,
> pour the oil in and stir and mix well. Do this in the
> evening so that the infusion can stand overnight. In
> the morning start to simmer it, for seven to eight

hours; if it is over 100 pounds simmer ten hours or more ... When it has boiled until the right time you shall see it become thick, and make long and thick bubbles when simmering.

Olive oil soap was still relatively expensive, however, so it was not the first choice for making washing-up detergents when wood ash was not available.

It is hard to imagine any household with free wood ash in the hearth paying good money for something else to cut the grease on their dishes. But beginning around 1570, a significant proportion of Londoners lacked sufficient ash supplies, and by 1600, with the conversion to coal almost complete in the capital, ash was very hard to come by. Black soap, bought in pots and jars for a halfpenny a pound, was the next best thing, and it did the job so long as you dissolved it in hot water. Washing-up as we know it today had arrived.

To use black soap effectively, the cleaning water first had to be heated. The soap was added and stirred about, and then dishes were immersed in the hot soapy water and rubbed with a linen cloth or a handful of horsetail to dislodge stubborn dirt. Afterwards, the dishes were rinsed in clean cold water and dried with a clean dry dish cloth or wiper. As ashes were replaced with black soap in coal-burning districts, sand-scrubbing of pots and bowls gradually fell out of use too. What began as an emergency stopgap for one part of the process became the default approach.

And similar to how the idea of coal as being uniquely suitable for kitchen fires spread out among the population since it was associated in many people's minds with high-status households, so too did the idea of soap and water spread as being 'better' tools for washing-up than the old scouring regime. Over the course of the seventeenth century, purchases of household soap in aristocratic households rose, regardless of the type of fuel being used in the kitchen; at the same time, purchases of sand declined, particularly in the context of the accounts for kitchens and sculleries.

The embrace of full soap-and-water washing-up by the mid-nineteenth century can be inferred from *Mrs Beeton's Book of Household Management*, although elements of the regime were rather scattered around the text. The most comprehensive discussion can be found in her directions to housemaids and footmen. Silver was to be washed 'with a soapy flannel in one water, rinsed in another, and then wiped dry with a dry cloth'. Elsewhere mention was made of using only common yellow soap and boiling water for this job; in yet another section, she instructed that the plate must be brushed once it was dry. Then some hartshorn powder (powdered deer antler) was mixed with cold water to form a paste and smeared over the plate. Once the paste had dried, it was brushed off with a special soft brush. Finally, the silver was polished firmly with a dry chamois leather.

Knives were to be washed in warm but not hot water, and very thoroughly dried. Mrs Beeton included several exhortations to her readers to ensure that no grease remained on them, implying that this water was soapy, although it was not specified. Once free of grease and completely dry, the knives were placed into a patent knife-cleaning machine that in essence buffed them with emery paper and stiff-bristled brushes, removing traces of rust and staining and bringing them back to a shine. Forks and spoons were also washed in warm water before being dried and vigorously brushed with a small stiff-bristled brush resembling a nail-scrubbing brush, and then polished with leather.

Glassware was supposed to be washed separately in a wooden bowl or tub, where it would be less likely to chip if it came into contact with the sides of the vessel. Glasses were first to be washed in 'moderately hot' water and then rinsed in cold water. Turned upside down, they were to be laid upon a folded cloth for a minute or two to drain before being wiped and polished, by first a coarse cloth and then a much finer one. Once again, the use of soap was implied rather than specified – why else would you need to rinse?

Mrs Beeton gave no special instructions for crockery, pots or pans. This was considered to be general knowledge, and did not warrant description.

Instructions about methods for cleaning ordinary crockery appeared in some detail in Elizabeth Craig's book in 1936, however. She told her readers to sort the washing-up into separate piles and then fill a bowl or sink with 'very hot' water. She continued:

> A small quantity of soap is necessary, either in the form of soap flakes or powder, or part of a household bar. A good way of using up odds and ends of soap is to place them in a tin, such as a small mustard tin, the bottom of which has been well perforated with a nail, and to which a string handle has been attached. The tin can then be dipped in the basin until sufficient lather is produced, and afterwards hung up until the next occasion.

Washing-up with soap may have played a part in the rise of pottery within the home. We are generally told that the great surge in the use of crockery in the seventeenth and eighteenth centuries, when wooden and pewter platters and bowls were replaced en masse, was a result of fashion, a desire to emulate the technically innovative wares of the Rhineland and the maiolica of Italy, and then, from about 1600, the shockingly delicate and bright Chinese porcelain that began to arrive in English ports. How rapid would have been the take-up of pottery had Londoners not, by great happenstance, recently converted to a new method of washing-up, one that suited these new wares to perfection? It works the other way round too. Households that were acquiring more pottery were more likely to convert to soap. A feedback loop may have quickly developed, supporting the spread of both pottery and soap across the country.

Housework

Soap was not only making an appearance in the kitchen. Soon it was being used in the rest of the house. This was driven less by a lack of grease-cutting wood ash and more by a rise in coal-produced smuts.

With the exception of food preparation and laundry, a wood-fired home had very little need for grease removal. Mud, hair, fluff, cobwebs and dust responded very well to the ministrations of the various brooms and brushes listed in the household accounts of the wealthy, as well as in the cargoes of incoming ships and the inventories of shopkeepers. Traditional materials from the heathland, such as broom, ling and various rushes, were often called into service. Coarse brushes, called 'besoms', were made of birch or hazel twigs, ling or broom. There were also a wide range of brushes made with horse hair or pig bristle. The different materials used to make besoms, brooms and brushes were well suited to different types of dirt. Because the same household accounts usually mentioned purchasing all three at differing prices, it seems clear that people did not consider these terms to be interchangeable. Each had a very separate and specific cleaning purpose.

Besoms were simple bundles of stiff, small vegetation, tightly bound, into which a pole was firmly thrust as a handle. They were cheap items, sold several to the penny. Locally made, they sometimes show up in farm accounts, when the people producing them were paid, or in the stock records of shopkeepers, but they never appear in ships' cargoes; they were not imported. They

'Old Shoes for Some Brooms' by Marcellus Laroon, from
The Cryes of the City of London, Drawne after the Life (c. 1688).

were made out in the woods or upon the heaths, often by workers who were also employed to make faggots and coppice woodland.

Costing four or five times as much as a besom, brooms were made from broom or ling (as some besoms were), or from bull rushes, flag rushes or horse hair. They were more common in the accounts of town houses than those of farms. These were rather more complicated items to manufacture, using finer material that had to be bundled more carefully. The broom, ling, rushes or hair was generally tied into a series of small bundles before being combined into one large broom head and trimmed to an equal length. They were sometimes imported, the versions made of hair in particular.

As for brushes, they were mostly made of hair of one sort or another, horse hair being the most commonly mentioned, and sold for a halfpenny up to sixpence each. Lots of brushes were imported, especially from Germany (where many of the best quality hair and bristle brushes are made to this day). They came in all shapes and sizes, with prices varying accordingly. Nuremberg was especially well known for the quality range of its brush-making craftsmen. Hans Sachs and Jost Amman's *Das Ständebuch* ('The Book of Trades') from 1568 featured a woodcut of a brush-maker surrounded by his tools and products in his workshop, over a short verse that crudely translates as: 'The brush-maker manufactures brushes of all qualities for all purposes, from gold-mounted hairbrushes to brushes for scouring glasses.' Hanging on the extreme right of the scene are what appear to be glass-scouring brushes; pictured elsewhere are brushes that look as though they belong with a dust pan, as well as some resembling large paintbrushes. Several hand brushes were of the type suitable for caring for textiles. Although brush-

'Der Bürstenbinder' by Jost Amman, with accompanying verse by Hans Sachs, from *Das Ständebuch* (1568).

makers were frequently mentioned in this period, their products were never present in such profusion as brooms and besoms.

The coarse texture of a besom is particularly suited to moving and removing large volumes of loose matter on rougher surfaces. Some types, generally made of birch twigs, are still commercially produced, marketed to gardeners who wish to sweep leaves from their lawns, a task which besoms perform admirably. They are also good for moving straw from cobbles or general detritus from earth floors. Historically, however, not all besoms were made of birch twigs. The variety of materials used in besom-making reflects not just the local resources but also the purpose of these coarse brooms. Occasionally the same household used more than one type of besom. In 1714, for example, Lady Grisell Baillie bought twelve 'broom besoms' – besoms made of the broom plant – in addition to birch besoms. Often the general term 'besom' was listed in household accounts, with special mention of 'birch besoms' intended for use in the stables.

I have made and used my own besoms of broom, ling and butcher's broom and can attest that they behave very differently and would suit different areas of the home. Butcher's broom (*Ruscus aculeatus*) is a stiff, spiky plant that, turned into a besom, is particularly good at cleaning cobbled areas or loose-laid brick floors, as it can get into the various cracks and crannies and flick out the dirt. Broom (*Cytisus scoparius*) and ling (*Calluna vulgaris*) are much more closely packed, less scratchy articles. They can deal with the finer dust and fluff of indoor spaces and work much better on smoother surfaces, such as tiled floors or a beaten-earth floor, hardened with ox blood and lime, or milk and lime. These are the besoms you would choose for your great hall or parlour. I have found rush brooms to be particularly suitable for dealing with cobwebs high on walls and ceilings.

The large numbers of besoms, brooms and brushes regularly purchased by larger, wealthier households point to the importance of sweeping in maintaining domestic order. The rules and regulations laid out for several elite households give another hint of this. While the duties surrounding the serving of dinner tend to dominate these instructions, mention was made repeatedly of whose responsibility it was to sweep each area of the house. At Lord Montagu's house at Cowdray, for example, all 'lodgeinges, galleryes, greatchambers, dyneing rooms, parlours etc' were to be overseen by the gentleman-usher, who was to make sure the grooms did their jobs properly 'cleanely keeping' them. The great chamber was to be daily 'swepte, and kepte clean' and kept 'sweete with perfumes, flowers, herbs and bowes in their season'. The yeomen of the chamber were to 'ryse at a convenient hower to remove the pallets (if there be any) out of my said withdrawing chamber: to make ytt cleane ... and decently clensinge chamber pottes and the like'. The head of each small household department from the brewery to the wardrobe of beds was responsible for the cleaning of their own spaces, using their own brooms and besoms.

The household of Sarah Fell, in the Lake District, involved sweeping on a much smaller scale. In 1673 hers was primarily a peat-burning house, with whin and ling providing additional fuel for ovens and brewing vessels. Besoms, chalk and lea sand were regularly purchased, and the periodic labour of a woman called Pegg Dodgson appeared now and again, providing around twenty days of 'rubbing and scouring' each year.

Just what that rubbing and scouring entailed was nicely outlined in *Madam Johnson's Present*. Mary Johnson published her book in 1753, at the end of a long life as 'superintendent of a Lady of Quality's Family' in the city of York. Her instructions for housemaids boasted an excellent section on how to clean wooden floors. Her annual spring cleaning guidance explained that ingrained grease spots and stains could be removed from the boards by laying ox gall upon them overnight. In the morning the boards were scrubbed with strong wood-ash lye all over, using first a stiff-bristled brush and then cloths. Her general weekly cleaning routine was done almost entirely without water, however. Damp sand was to be flung across the floor. Then the maid was to get down on her knees and rub all over with a dry cloth. When this was done, the sand was swept outdoors.

By 1776, however, when Susanna Whatman wrote out a summary of the duties of her maids, things had completely changed. She was concerned that, unless specifically instructed otherwise and watched to ensure compliance, her maids would wash the rooms of the house with copious quantities of soap and water. In her very first instruction to the housemaid she wrote: 'To use as little soap as possible (if any) in scowering rooms. Fuller's earth and fine sand preserves the colour of the boards, and does not leave a white appearance as soap does. All the rooms to be dry scrubbed with white sand.' Later on, she warned against using soap upon oil cloths, recommending instead a wipe with a soft linen cloth dipped in milk and water. The reliance on soap was clearly an ongoing issue, since in a 1799 letter to her housekeeper, she reminded her to be 'careful that the carpets do not get any wet when they scower the rooms', once again requesting that the cleaning be done using the old dry methods, because soap and water were damaging her wooden floors and carpets.

Whatman repeatedly wrote out long descriptions of the dry-rubbing technique that she favoured, but she seems to have been fighting a losing battle. Maid after maid joining the staff was accustomed to the new methods and seemingly reluctant to abandon them. Soap and water had become the default. Indeed, as early as 1715, Lady Baillie was purchasing 'sope and sand to scour the house' when she moved down to London.

The accounts of Audley End, near Saffron Walden, Essex, provide another case in point. In 1764, a campaign of home improvement was under way there, encompassing an updating in terms of both architectural fashion and practical management. As part of a scheme to unite the house visually and accord with the latest style, a large new space was constructed above and adjacent to the great hall. On the first floor the space was dedicated as a picture gallery but above this, on the second floor, a new service area, designed to improve the efficiency of the household, was constructed. They called it the 'coal gallery', and it served as a central point for coal distribution throughout the building. A hoist was used to bring sacks of coal up to the gallery, where it was transferred into open bunkers or bins, enabling the maids to collect scuttles full of coal for fuelling the fires in the house's upper storeys. And from 1765 onwards, the household accounts for Audley End have survived, giving us an indication of the routines in a grand coal-burning home of the period.

In an analysis of the Audley End accounts, J. D. Williams found that alongside the soap purchases sat purchases of mops, brooms, flannels and clogs. Gone were the besoms and sand, the whiting and Flanders' tile, the brimstone and ash. Instead there were mops – a tool almost completely absent in earlier wood-

This 1829 caricature by William Heath shows a maid-of-all-work wielding a mop while wearing risers to lift her feet off the wet floor.

burning households – for use with soap and water. The same held for the flannels – these were woollen squares eminently suitable for washing walls and furniture with soap and water. Even the clogs, with their high, water-resistant soles, spoke of housework conducted on wet floors.

A French visitor to England in 1720 reported upon the locals' wet approach to cleaning with an obvious sense of surprise: 'Not a week passes but well kept houses are washed twice in the seven days and that from top to bottom; and even every morning most kitchens, staircases and entrances are scrubbed.' French wood-fired homes received nothing like this much attention. Apart from any cultural differences, without coal smuts, they simply didn't need it.

A major reason for the turn to soap were the black, greasy smuts floating up from the coal fires of London. They settled on every surface. Walls, ceilings, floors and furnishings acquired a sticky black coating when coal fires burnt day in and day out. John Evelyn, writing in his 1661 treatise *Fumifugium*, moaned that coal smoke was 'superinducing a sooty Crust or Furr upon all that it lights, spoyling the moveables, tarnishing the Plate, Gildings and Furniture, and corroding the very Iron-bars and hardest Stones with those piercing and acrimonious Spirits which accompany its Sulphure'.

Of course, wood ash also flies up and out into the room, but it is not sticky and tends to fall out of the air and settle quickly. It is easy to dust and sweep away. A brush or a broom can deal with the dirt of a wood fire in a fairly quick and simple operation. If you try the same methods with coal smuts, you will do little more than smear the stuff about. A good chimney that draws well and reliably can significantly reduce this cleaning problem, but efficient chimney design was a long time in development. The precise set of curves, sizes and distances that provide for a clean burning experience were not really understood until the early twentieth century, and even to this day, mistakes and miscalculations occur. Those who hark back to the days of domestic coal-burning with fondness are frequently calling upon experiences with twentieth-century chimneys. The chimneys of the seventeenth and eighteenth centuries, although a vast improvement on smoke hoods and open hearths, were far from perfect in drawing the coal smoke away from a home's interior.

Smuts were a fact of life in coal-burning homes. In urban areas where coal-burning was the norm, such as London from 1600 onwards, smuts floated in the air outdoors, to a degree that even homes without fires got their share of the black sticky coating. Victorian housekeeping advice sometimes advocated keeping windows shut as much as possible to preserve the cleanliness of rooms. Isabella Beeton, for example, made a number of distinctions between the cleaning methods adequate in country houses, where the air was relatively free of smuts, and the more intensive, soap-based regime necessary for smut-laden town houses. Bedroom floors only needed tending to once a week in the country, in her opinion, but in town, they needed to be cleaned a little every day, in addition to the weekly cleaning. 'In the country,' she advised, 'cold soft water, a clean scrubbing brush, and a willing arm are all that are required.' In town, soap and soda were required, together with some hot water, to lift all the dirt. Soap was necessary, despite it being 'liable to give the boards a black appearance'.

Paint the town black

The shift to soap and water nudged people towards choosing interior surfaces that could handle these new tools for domestic maintenance. The tipping point, however, came with the Great Fire of 1666. With a huge swathe of the capital being rebuilt from scratch, and countless other dwellings requiring major repair, an opportunity arose to instal interiors that suited the new realities of coal-burning. Older housing stock, dating back to the middle of the sixteenth century, sometimes even earlier, had prominently featured raw wood throughout. Window frames, beams, floorboards and panelling were generally either left plain or painted with designs executed in distemper paint. Such paint was produced using a pigment and an animal skin glue or gelatinous substance (called 'size'), which allowed the pigment to stick to a surface. Limewash, which was generally used on building exteriors, consisted of a thin, watery mixture of slaked lime (the same stuff used to make mortar). It was naturally white, but could be coloured by stirring in a pigment such as red or yellow ochre. Both distemper and limewash had a dusty finish, and could rub off if you tried to wash them with soap and water.

Smoky chimneys were an annoying hazard, spreading dirty, sticky smuts over all your surfaces, as seen in this 1790 engraving entitled 'The Comforts of Matrimony – A Smoky House & Scolding Wife'.

Where wood-smoke stains had been kept at bay with regular use of a soft broom, coal smoke permanently spoilt the old paint designs in very short order. Further, tired home decoration schemes, painted in distemper and stained with wood smoke, were easy to paint over, requiring no more than a brushing down before repainting. In contrast, the sticky, greasy nature of coal smuts resisted fresh coats of glue- and size-based paint. Bare wood areas could be kept clean with some sand-scrubbing in the days of wood fires, but needed soap and water to remove coal smuts. Sealing wooden surfaces with either an oil-based paint or a wax coating helped to stop the smuts from sticking.

You may recall the avant-garde use of wax upon the floors of Sir Thomas Puckering's chamber when he lodged in London in the 1620s. The household accounts noted that this was a special treatment, carried out by his wife's personal maid, in just the two chambers occupied by the heads of the household. The wax was bought only when the family was in town. With their wax polished floors, these two private chambers could be maintained with a periodic wipe with a damp, soapy cloth. Moreover, they could be kept scrupulously clean without the soap staining the boards – something that was universally considered to be unsightly.

Applying oil paint to window frames and doors may have signalled a similar evolution in cleaning tactics. Most architectural historians imagine that it was the rise in the use of softwoods that triggered this change. Traditionally, British homes had employed oak and other hardwoods – woods that could stand up to the vagaries of the climate – for the structure as well as window frames and doors. Cheaper pine window frames were much more prone to rot unless they were protected from the elements in some manner, and several coats of oil-based paint did the job very well. Inside the house, however, where weatherproofing was of little value, people were discovering that the same protective layer was ideal for surfaces that needed regular cleaning with soap and water.

One indication of the domesticity of this development comes in the form of the era's DIY guides. The 1758 edition of Eliza Smith's cookery book *The Compleat Housewife* contained the usual mix of food and medical recipes, but these were supplemented by a small section entitled 'Directions for painting rooms or pales' ('pales' meaning fences). She began by outlining the cost of materials: red lead, white lead, linseed oil and a touch of turpentine. She then led her readers through the process of mixing paints, priming surfaces, filling holes with putty and applying top coats. One recipe was for coloured 'wainscot' paint, which, she said, was the most fashionable finish. Another two recipes were for varnish, to be used upon wooden furniture and picture frames – a yellow varnish for dark-coloured items and a white varnish where a lighter look was required – many years before shellac and French polishing were in vogue. Doing it yourself (or at least instructing the servants to do it according to Eliza Smith's directions) was stated to be 'more clean and more durable than it can be perform'd by a house-painter, without you pay considerably more than the common rates'. The householder who understood the procedure could achieve higher quality finishes at little additional cost. The inclusion of such a section in a book of housewifery suggests the importance of well-painted surfaces in coal-burning home economics.

Her instructions for 'compleat' housewives were by no means the first house-painting instructions to be aimed at the general home-owning public. Almost a century earlier, John Smith had published *The Art of Painting; Wherein is Included the Whole Art of Vulgar Painting* – meaning the painting of ordinary people's things. The initial edition, published in 1676, lingered at some length on the art of painting sundials, but from the second edition, published in 1687, and onwards, he provided an enthusiastic introduction to the art of house-painting, presumably in response to a rising demand for such information. The frontispiece squarely proclaimed the author's intentions:

'The whole treatise being so complete, and so exactly fitted to the meanest capacity, that all persons may be able, by these directions, to paint in oil colours, all manner of timber work.' Painting woodwork in weather-resistant oil paint was evidently standard procedure. This early manual was aimed at the male householder, and thus focused on the exterior of the house, repeatedly emphasizing the benefits of oil paint in protection from the elements. Interiors were not wholly overlooked, however. He described various white paints suitable for indoor or outdoor use, with some forms being prone to yellowing when used indoors: 'but if you use white-lead alone within doors it is then best to mix it with drying nut oil, for linseed oil within doors, will turn yellow and spoil the beauty of it.'

Washable paint had, by the mid-seventeenth century, moved indoors. While we could assign such a move purely to fashion, it seems much more realistic to propose a mixture of motivations. Even in today's smoke-free homes, the grease of fingers and cooking fumes can be much more easily removed from painted windowsills and other paintwork than from raw, untreated wood. Those with the time and money to achieve a fashionable home probably also valued a clean home, one that showed off their fine taste and investment to best effect. Those who valued a practical approach to housekeeping probably also enjoyed having the cachet of purchasing the latest looks, which homely economy could afford them. Like the possible positive feedback loop between soap and pottery in the kitchen, there might have been a positive feedback loop between soap and oil-based paintwork and varnishes.

A tapestry of change

Seventeenth-century Londoners' homes differed from those of their forebears in other ways too, as fashion and practicality combined to oust the traditional coverings for walls and floors. For those who could afford it (and many of course could not), comfort and fashion up until the sixteenth century had called for textile wall hangings and rush floor matting, which kept out the chill and added a burst of colour – and an indication of social status. For the very richest, tapestries had held pride of place for centuries, but cheaper, plainer textiles were also available, and common.

Cloth hangings of one sort or another appear in somewhere between one quarter and one third of surviving probate inventories. Although far more inventories survived for wealthier members of society, the huge numbers of middle-ranking homes with cloth hangings cannot be ignored. People clearly wished to have these furnishings in their home, and they could realistically aspire to having them. Even quite humble husbandmen and craftsmen boasted one or two in their best room – men like Nicholas Wynn of Stockport, who worked as a 'shearman', a job which entailed providing a smooth finish upon woollen cloth. At the time of his death in 1604, Wynn was worth a grand total of £6 16s, a sum that included a debt owed to him by his son, all of his working tools and the full contents of his humble home. Among the goods listed, however, were the 'paynted clothes' that hung upon his walls, which were valued at eight pence.

Even the best wall coverings, tapestries, were made in a variety of types and qualities. The best were woven in silk and gold threads, the gold thread consisting of thin strips of gold foil wrapped around cores of yellow silk thread. Not only were the raw materials sufficient to make a wall-sized tapestry extortionately expensive, but the labour involved in weaving with these thin, fine materials was enormous. Such tapestries were rare even within royal households. Those woven in the main from wool, with silk and gold used in small areas of high detail such as faces or a coat of arms, were marginally more common. Still, the vast majority of tapestries were made solely with woollen threads. Even here there was a plethora of descending grades based upon the fineness of the threads, the complexity and uniqueness of the design, and the depth and range of the colours. Generic tapestries of 'verditure', or greenery, which displayed a small range of colour and were woven with coarse wools, cost a fraction of those that featured figures or complicated scenes.

Since tapestries were both very high value and remarkably sturdy, the secondhand market was brisk. Even the royal household was happy to buy and display used tapestries. A study of the tapestries of the court of Henry VIII made by Thomas P. Campbell revealed that some tapestries given by Philip the Bold to Richard II sometime before 1399 were still hanging at Windsor Castle in 1547, the year of Henry's death. The furnishing of the Manor of Beaulieu in 1516 involved James Chapell, one of the senior staff of the Great Wardrobe, travelling to Flanders where, over thirty-nine days, he purchased 108 tapestries.

Woollen hangings were more common in the homes of gentlemen and wealthy merchants. These were still woven from wool, but they were not woven with figurative designs. Some contained decorative elements, usually stripes, woven in, but they were essentially plain cloth that was sometimes painted, embroidered or decorated in some other fashion. Thomas Mill, a gentleman living in Southampton before his death in 1566, had hanging in his hall 'ane old clothe of a storye of Hercules' valued at 1s, as well as other hangings 'with a border of olde grene saye' worth 6s 8d. These contrast significantly with the value of two pieces of tapestry 'bothe of imagerye' that he had in his parlour; these were valued at £5. Upstairs, one of his chambers was furnished with alternating strips of blue and yellow woollen cloth, while two others had coloured linen canvas cloth hanging in them.

Surviving examples of these woollen hangings are supremely rare, probably due to the ease with which they could be cut up and turned into something else. There are a few such hangings at Hardwick Hall in Derbyshire, and a few more were said to have been worked on by Mary, Queen of Scots at Oxburgh Hall. The Hardwick hangings fall into two styles. In the first, separately worked areas of embroidery, complete in their own right and following a loose common theme and schemata, were sewn onto a backing. In the second, fabrics and braids were assembled and embroidered into a single, coherent design or scene, occasionally embellished with some painting or staining. These were works reflecting very high status and much labour, suitable for aristocratic settings. It is no wonder they survived while so many of their more modest cousins did not.

Rush matting was sometimes also used upon walls, but this was too expensive for most households. Instead, it tended to be employed in wealthy establishments, primarily in rooms of a secondary, or non-entertaining, nature, in areas where warmth rather than show was wanted. Sir Thomas Puckering's accounts, for example, listed rush matting being used for both floors and walls, 'for 44 yards [36 m] square of bull-rush-matt, where with hee matted the Hall-chamber'. This rush matting was firmly fitted, much like fitted carpets are laid today, with nails fixing the matting in place and heavy-duty thread stitching the pieces together.

This matting was particularly suitable in areas inclined towards damp. Rushes, as marsh plants, are very tolerant of damp conditions; in fact, they last better, retaining their spring and suppleness, if they do not dry out too much. Loosely laid or laid as a plaited and stitched mat, they had long been the treatment of choice for beaten-earth floors. Despite lying upon a slightly damp surface, they provided a completely dry and warm surface to live upon. The air trapped in their hollow stems offered extra insulation from the wet and the cold.

In other books, I have shared my own experiences of trying to live and work with loose rushes, so suffice it to say I have been impressed with the ease and cleanliness of the system, providing the rushes had been air-dried before use and laid to a suitable depth of two or more inches (at least 5 cm). A rush-covered earth floor is comfortable and warm, perfectly reasonable to sit and even sleep upon. To keep the flooring tolerably clean, fresh rushes are spread on top, creating a new, clean surface while the worst of the detritus of daily life filters down to a composting layer lower down. I experienced no nasty smells or unpleasant soggy patches, despite all the usual spillages and accidents. A periodic cleaning, where worn-out, crushed and broken rushes are carried to the garden compost, the earth floor is swept clear and fresh rushes are laid, is helpful too, but how often you need to do this probably depends on how much traffic the area receives, and how many rushes are available to you. In the past, larger, wealthier households could afford more regular changes; smaller, poorer households may well have stretched things out.

According to John Gerard in his guide to plants and herbs, the sharp rush (*Juncus acutus*) was 'fitter to straw houses and chambers than any of the rest, for the others are so soft and pithy that they turn to dust and filth with much treading, where contrariewise this rush is so hard it will last sound much longer'. 'Strewing herbs' could be laid down upon and among the rushes to deter insects and vermin, using a range of species well known at the time for that purpose – and which modern scientific analyses confirm as containing insecticides. Tansy (*Tanacetum vulgare*), wormwood (*Artemisia absinthium*) and rue (*Ruta graveolens*) are particularly powerful.

Wetlands both large and small were valued for producing these useful household furnishings. Even the ditches around an individual plot could furnish a small supply of rushes if carefully managed. Just as we saw with heathlands, fenlands and other fuel-producing landscapes, these areas of wetland were guarded and tended as long as they provided useful resources. When their usefulness faded, these lands were abandoned and repurposed.

Loose rushes do not work so well upon stone-flagged floors, having a tendency to skitter about underfoot. Nor do they last so

John Riley's 1686 portrait of Bridget Holmes, who was James II's 'necessary woman' – a sort of maid-of-all-work for the royal bedchamber – shows her, long-handled brush in hand, by one of the king's exquisite tapestries.

well: crushed against stone, they tend to break up more easily. So as wealthier homes upgraded to flagged floors and chimneys, loose rushes were replaced with rush-matted floors. The rushes, dried and held in five or seven small bundles, can be plaited into long, flat strips that can then be stitched together into mats of any size and shape. (An even number of bundles will not lie flat, instead twisting into a spiral.) Mats were more expensive than a layer of loose rushes, but they were tidy, controlled and versatile.

Matting upon the walls can be seen in a number of images from the period as well as appearing in written records. These mats generally covered the lower half of the wall, up to chest height, and were more often found in what might be termed offices – places of business where men sat all day at desks or awaited orders. They kept out draughts, and provided a warm and comfortable wall to lean back upon at a time when chair backs were uncommon and most people sat upon benches or stools.

The very cheapest sorts of wall hangings were coarse linen or hempen cloth painted with thinned distemper. They too provided a degree of insulation and draught-proofing; the painted designs added a splash of colour and interest to a room. Because tenterhooks were often purchased at the same time as these hangings, the textiles were probably stretched upon fixed batons an inch or so away from the wall surface. This lifted them free from damaging damp, while also trapping a layer of air between the wall and the hanging.

Caring for these wall-mounted textiles in wood-burning homes was a matter of regular brushing. Periodically the hangings were taken down, beaten and aired; occasionally they were washed. Soft but springy short-bristled brushes were best for tapestries and any sort of textured cloth hanging; the spring of the bristles helped to flick dirt up and out from between the fibres. Clothes brushes of this type continued in use well into the twentieth century for the care of men's wool suits and jackets before chemical dry-cleaning. For those not accustomed to seeing this method in practice, it can come as a surprise to discover just how good a finish can be achieved. It is slow work, but effective. You always work downwards along the grain of the fabric, holding the cloth either flat upon a table or draped over your hand to give a gentle curve that opens up the texture and allow the bristles to get deep inside the weaving.

The accounts of elite households frequently listed one-off payments to fullers for cleaning woollen hangings. Fullers cleaned woollen fabrics once they had been woven, removing the oil and grease that had protected the fibres during spinning and weaving and which permitted the yarns to slide over one another. Among their tools was fuller's earth – the dry fine clay that was worked into the fabric and then beaten or rinsed out – and wood ashes or soap, which was rinsed through the cloth.

Painted hangings could not be treated with fuller's earth, ashes or soap, so were simply brushed down. Rush mats could be taken up and beaten, or brushed in situ with a rush broom. Much of this work was done inside the house rather than sending out to the fuller's. In the largest households, an entire department of staff, that of the great wardrobe, performed the task. Unlike privy wardrobe staff, who were more likely to deal with clothing, the yeomen and grooms of the great wardrobe were responsible for putting up and taking down different sets of wall textiles as well as repairing and cleaning them.

The switch to coal-burning significantly raised the long-term costs involved in covering walls with textiles or rushes. Coal smuts did not simply brush off. They could not be reliably removed by beating, shaking or careful rinsing. They clung. A sticky coating formed over the textile, attracting and holding other dirt. In a coal-fired home, these expensive furnishings quickly became stained, greasy and foul. A tapestry that might have been expected to last for generations with a simple routine of brushing could be utterly ruined in just a decade around coal fires.

As early as 1512, people were expressing concerns about the damage. Henry Percy replaced the provision of sea coal for his Northumbrian residence, close to the Newcastle coalfield, with much more expensive charcoal for use at Christmas, when the best arras was hung upon the walls. Frequent soap-and-water washing did far more damage to woollen hangings than brushing and shaking them, so people had to choose to either put up with dirtier furnishings that were cleaned less often or replace them much more frequently. Unsurprisingly, more and more people turned their backs on wall textiles. The super-rich carried on with silk, but tended to use sheer and shiny textiles made of highly spun yarns that were tightly woven and which could in fact cope with an occasional, careful wipe-down with a damp cloth. But most people gave up on hangings, mats and textiles of any sort until paper began to offer a cheaper alternative.

Wallpaper had two advantages for the coal-burning household: it was cheaper than textiles to replace when it got dirty, and it created a much smoother wall surface, giving coal smuts less purchase in the first place. Early wallpapers were not cheap as such, but they were much less expensive than woven fabrics. They had also been around for quite a while. The oldest surviving fragments of wallpaper in situ in England, dated to 1509, were discovered covering the beams of the hall and dining room in the Master's Lodge at Christ's College, Cambridge. Another piece, found in a closet at the Dower House in Dinton, near Aylesbury, and dated to the early seventeenth century, turned out to be an exact match with paper found lining a charter box belonging to the Abbot's Hospital in Guildford. One rather wealthy tailor in Southampton, a man called John Lumberte, had 4*d* worth of 'olde paper hanginges' in one of the less prestigious upper chambers of his home when he died in 1570. At these early dates, however, these were more of an exception rather than the rule.

Wallpaper really began to take off a century later, in a largely rebuilt London that was already taking advantage of the new soap-and-water regime. Where the earlier wallpapers appear to have been produced in short runs alongside other forms of woodblock printing, a new breed of dedicated wallpaper businesses were appearing. By the 1680s, George Minnikin had established himself as a wallpaper specialist, advertising 'Japan and other colord paper hangings'. A rival firm, the Blue Paper Warehouse, had opened a 'large Japan warehouse' in Covent

Trade card, with engraving by John Sturt, for the Blue Paper Warehouse, London (c. 1715).

Garden by 1694. Their trade card, featuring a small vignette of the production process, was illuminating: long rolls of paper were block-printed or painted with colour washes using large soft brushes. Less than a decade later, in 1701, Jacob Hinde had set up a shop on King Street selling 'all sorts of Paper Hangings by the yard'. Abraham Price was advertising paper hangings that imitated wainscoting in 1706, and two years later a group of stationers and card makers were offering 'all sorts of Paper hangings for rooms' in addition to their other lines. Yet another new industry had been born.

In 1712, a new levy upon paper was introduced, which gives us a sense for the volume in trade. Some 197,000 yards (180,000 m) of wallpaper were taxed in that year. Clare Taylor, in her study of the development and use of wallpaper in the eighteenth century, traced how these upstart businesses recruited workers and investors from several different trades. As a new craft, it had no established lines of entry. Instead, it grew as people in related businesses saw an opportunity and rushed to take advantage of the demand.

By 1763, with more than 1½ million yards (1,371 km) taxed annually within Britain's shores, Thomas Mortimer expressed the opinion that wallpaper was good commerce as well as good art. 'The art of Painting and Staining Paper of various patterns and colours, for hanging of rooms, is lately become a very considerable branch of commerce in this country,' he wrote, 'for we annually export vast quantities of this admirable article; and home consumption is not less considerable, as it is not only a cheap, but an elegant part of furniture.'

Inside people's homes, coal was enforcing new regimes, a new modern way of life. It encouraged and supported a different range of products and practices, pushing out the age-old goods, styles and methods. And as London became a cultural and commercial centre of global rather than just national significance, the ways of doing things in this first coal city began to have a relevance and an influence upon the lives of people in the most surprising of places. In tandem, coal and soap had repercussions around the world, even where wood continued to be the preferred fuel.

THE DOMESTIC
BURDEN

However much soap was involved in washing-up and house cleaning during the coal-burning era, this volume was surpassed by the amount of soap employed in laundry. Once soap took over, a series of changes followed, with effects on the division of labour in the household, the organization of the soap industry and the role of cleanliness in societies, including places far from London.

The majority of laundry during the wood-burning era was undertaken using wood ash and cold water, while during the coal era it was utterly dominated by soap and hot water, but the swap was not made overnight. Some soap had been used for laundry for a very long time, particularly in caring for certain high-status and specialist items and as part of a battery of expensive stain-removal products, and soap manufacture in Britain dates back to around the twelfth century, with imports arriving even earlier. The volumes involved were tiny, however. There is some reason to believe the quantities of commercial soap began to rise in the late fifteenth century, but the evidence is patchy. It is not until the sixteenth century that a significant number of surviving customs dues books, guild records, probate inventories, medical texts, recipe collections and household accounts begin to provide a picture of how much soap was being used, and what it was being used for.

Port books from London in the 1560s logged fairly small amounts of soap arriving as part of mixed cargoes on an occasional basis from Antwerp and Amsterdam. Among these, just 1,500 hundredweight of Castile soap – the white bar soap considered to be of the finest quality – was recorded. Three other soap cargoes listed were specified as liquid soaps, or of Flemish origin. In 1559/60 a document was drawn up to show 'The particular valew of certayne necessary and unnecessary wares', including items not subject to tax in London because they had already been assessed at another English port, such as Bristol, a centre of the soap trade. According to this document, £9,725 15s of soap moved through the capital's docks in the year. That might sound like quite a lot of soap, but it matched almost exactly the value of prunes arriving from France that year. A partial list for the year 1565/6 recorded just £4,422 worth of soap passing through the port of London (with a commensurate drop in the value of prune sales too).

Records from Bristol show the trade in soap to have been fairly steady but very much secondary to other products. Wine, salt, raisins, oranges, lemons and oil – both olive oil and train oil – outstripped soap imports many times over. A 1537 document describing a disputed payment noted that one whole cargo weighed 20 tonnes plus a hogshead. Three 'bagges alum' and 7 'serons' of soap accompanied 487 'peces' of raisins. I am not sure quite how big bags of alum were, but a seron of soap was a small bale or parcel no bigger than that which could be wrapped in a single animal hide. The soap and alum were small fry compared with the cargo of raisins. Similarly, the 80-tonne ship the *Saviour* arrived at Bristol from Mallorca in 1599/1600 with 70 tonnes of oil, 16 barrels of capers, 3 bags of aniseed and 8 serons of Valencia soap, while the 130-tonne ship the *Unicorn* arrived from Toulon with 212 casks of oil, 12 bags of aniseed and 36 chests of white soap. Many vessels tied up at Bristol with no soap at all. While this random snapshot is not a proper analysis, it still suggests that the soap trade was relatively small. Oil imports, in particular, dwarfed soap, by a factor of at least ten to one.

Much of this imported oil, of course, went to Bristol's soap-boilers, who used it to make 'grey soap'. Pure white castle soap was an item in short supply in Britain – not because of the olive oil, but because of its other key ingredient: plant ashes. The soap-boilers of the Mediterranean had access to different varieties of plants than did those in northern climes, and these plants' ashes, known as 'barilla ash', produced a different chemical, sodium hydroxide, which formed a white soap that set into hard blocks or bars. The plants most frequently used in Mediterranean soap-making were *Salsola soda*, known in English as the barilla plant; *Salsola kali*, or prickly saltwort; and *Salsola sativa*, today called *Halogeton sativus*. Each are salt-tolerant plants that thrive in marshes. You can also derive sodium hydroxide from kelp, which is available at northern latitudes, but its yield is typically only one third of these marsh plants. To get castle soap, you had to import it.

Traditional laundry

Leonard Mascall's 1583 translation of the Dutch *Profitable Boke Declaring Divers Approved Remedies* was the source for most stain-removal advice in the late sixteenth and early seventeenth centuries. Milk and salt were recommended for wine and vinegar stains, and lemon juice was the cure for ink and general 'spotting'. Honey was employed to clean gold-thread embroidery, while velvets and the highest quality of scarlet cloth, which was dyed in the grain with the crushed bodies of *Kermes* beetles, was to be washed only with the juice of soapwort. Most linen and woollen cloth was to be washed with either ashes or white soap.

One recipe called for the ashes of the roots of the broom plant to be employed 'and with the ashes make a lie, and with the said lie, ye shal wash your spotty clothes'. Common ashes, mixed with alum and a drop of water to form a paste, were a 'good way to take spottes out of woollen'; for the best results, 'lay it upon the spottye places on the cloth, and when it is drie: doe sponge it off'. Ashes of grapevines were considered particularly effective upon linen. Another recipe combined soap and ashes in a belt and braces attempt to shift 'spottes of oyle and of grease'; 'scowering sope' was mixed with finely sifted vine ashes in equal quantities along with some powdered burnt alum and the dried lees of wine (cream of tartar). After being mixed together with a drop of water, the paste could be formed into small bricks or balls and easily stored.

Soap appeared without the extra boost of ashes in a recipe entitled 'a sope to take out all spottes in woollen cloth'. Linen is a particularly tough fibre that can survive a harsh battering and the use of powerful chemicals. Wool is less robust, so a gentler approach was sensible for these more expensive items of clothing. One milder concoction called for Venice soap, egg yolks and the juice of beets to be pounded together into a paste and formed into balls. Another recipe took a bit more of a risk, as it called for 'white sope' along with the gall bladder of an ox, a little alum, ashes and egg yolk – a harsher combination of ingredients. A third recipe used white soap, ox gall and the lye of ashes. Soap was milder in action to pure ash, although the intensity of both could vary a great deal.

Clearly, ash had a major role in laundry in this period, but the use of soap was also not unheard of. Knowing the right recipe for the job was a necessary skill of the launderer or laundress. Recipes mentioned both ashes and the lye of ashes, which allowed for a wide range of possible cleaning strengths. Because lye is produced by dripping water through a layer of ash, the strength of the lye can be altered in several ways: by the ratio of water to ash, by the number of times the lye is cycled through the ash or by the amount of time the lye is boiled, with how much water evaporates determining the concentration of the solution.

Soaps can also have different strengths, depending on the balance of lye and fat and the amount of time allowed for the chemical processes to work. Long, slow processes using a minimum of heat promote the production and retention of natural glycerines. Hotter, quicker processes tend to produce low glycerine levels and harsher soaps, but they are much easier to manage with unsophisticated equipment. And naturally, differences in the ashes and fats employed also play their part.

Fine linens and cloths embellished with embroidery, drawn-thread work or lace edgings are particularly delicate items for laundering. As items of dress they also tended to be the visible means of signalling status in this period. Collars, cuffs, caps, neckerchiefs, rails, veils, handkerchiefs, pinners and, above all, ruffs needed to be spotlessly clean. Greasy necks and hair, dropped morsels of food and runny noses combined with smuts in the air to befoul such linens. Social standing demanded they be kept clean, even when a blind eye might be turned to some mud around the hem of a skirt or a patch of horse hair adhered to a pair of breeches. Unfortunately, the sorts of chemicals that could be relied upon to shift greasy marks most efficiently were also most likely to damage these finer garments.

From around 1580, soap and starch started to appear together in the recipes used by ladies' maids in caring for delicate linens. Starch, as we are all aware, permitted these elaborate linens to hold an unwrinkled and smooth shape, often standing up in defiance of gravity. It also provided a protective coating over the fabric. When a starched ruff became soiled, the dirt barely touched the linen, instead sitting upon the starched surface. So long as it was promptly laundered, the soil dissolved away with the starch as soon as the item was immersed in hot water. The addition of a little soap to the hot water lifted any grease from the garment, so that it too was easily rinsed away. The combination of soap and starch minimized the need for harmful rubbing and scrubbing: soaking, gentle squeezing and careful rinsing in a small bowl or basin was enough, and quickly became the standard laundering method for delicates. In large households these were laundered separately from the rest of the wash and often handled by a different member of staff, with ladies' maids and valets put in charge of this specialist laundry for a good four hundred years. The rest of the laundry was treated with ash or, in a few cases, dung and urine.

Dung may perhaps be particularly surprising as a cleaning agent, but it does work. Somewhat obviously, you do not use the dung directly as it falls from the beast. Instead, you lay it in a bucket of water overnight and strain off the liquid the next day. This liquid both loosens grease and bleaches stains. Understandably, you must be very thorough in rinsing your laundry in clean water afterwards.

William Harrison in his *Description of England* (1587) mentioned the practice with noticeable distaste: 'In some places also women do scour and wet their clothes with their [pig] dung, as others do with hemlock and nettles, but such is the savor of the clothes touched withal that I cannot abide to wear them on my body, more than such as are scoured with refuse soap, than the which (in mine opinion) there is none more unkindly savor.' Washing in dung was worse than washing in cheap soap, he thought. More than a century later Joseph Taylor reported a very similar laundry regime in Edinburgh, where he saw women 'put their cloaths with a little cow dung into a large tubb of water, and then plucking up their petticoats up to their bellyes, get into the tubb, and dance about it to tread the cloaths'.

Aged urine was even more widely used. It is stronger than dung water, changing over time into ammonia. It is not the best of degreasing agents, but it is a very effective bleach. (Fulsome rinsing is again recommended after use.)

Wood ash was good at removing grease and other bodily wastes from linens, especially when used in conjunction with heat. The first step was to reduce the ash to a good strong clean lye, removing any charcoal particles that might mark or stain the cloth. Many medium to large households had a dedicated vessel for this purpose, called a 'buck tub'. It was generally an open-topped coopered tub with holes placed near the base to facilitate drainage, or 'driving the buck'. In smaller households with fewer resources, a brewing tub could, with a good cleaning, serve both functions.

First, the base of the tub was filled with a medium to act as a filter. This might be a layer of small pebbles or sand with straw or hay laid on top, or a thick, felted woollen cloth, or 'buck cloth', laid in the bottom. Wood ash was then added – the more the better – and water trickled through. The resulting liquid was collected in a jug or bowl as it dripped through the holes in the base of the tub before being poured through the ash again. Once there was enough lye of the needed strength, the tub was cleaned and the dirty laundry was loosely folded into it or a 'buck basket', such as the one featured in *The Merry Wives of Windsor* by (mostly) Shakespeare. (In the play, the rambunctious character Falstaff is told by the merry wives to hide within a buck basket full of the foulest of soiled linens. It must have been a very big basket indeed.)

Loosely folding the clothes allowed the lye to run wherever it was needed. Hot or cold lye was poured into the tub or basket, depending on the laundry. Lightly soiled articles, such as bed sheets, could be adequately cleaned with cold lye; babies' nappies benefited from the lye being hot. Lye that dripped out of the bottom of the tub or basket was poured through again, because very little of the lye converted into soap. It thus remained 'fat hungry' while being used many times over.

None of this was particularly strenuous work. Even if the lye was heated, laundry required a fairly small volume of liquid, which could be accommodated in an ordinary cooking vessel. The lye, whether hot or cold, was highly alkaline, killing bacteria at the same time as it worked upon grease (without much in the way of elbow grease). And although the process was often slow, large batches of laundry could be managed at once and fitted around a myriad of other jobs. A buck tub could sit for a full day or two, the lye collected and poured back through whenever it was convenient. For this reason, pouring hot lye repeatedly through dirty laundry remained common practice in wood-burning Spain well into living memory. There were even some small-scale commercial laundries operating in this manner into the 1970s.

Once the lye had done its work, however, the tougher part of the job came: beating the clothes in cold water to dislodge the dirt before rinsing it away. Ideally this was done in running water, and many communities had common washing places along the banks of rivers or streams where women took their lye-soaked laundry. I remember as a child on holiday in various regions of France in the 1980s seeing such spots still in daily use. In Britain, the common washing places (all long gone) were typically open-air, unimproved and fairly informal. For example, the 1561 Agas map of London showed Moorfields, when it was just a set of fields, covered with shirts laid out to dry. Small groups of women were depicted guarding their laundry, with a couple of men carrying a huge basket of laundry slung on a pole. It is an image of communal washing just before the big switch changed London laundry for ever.

This work was hard and cold. Lye-soaked linens were dropped into the water and pulled out onto a stool or suitable stone. They were then mounded up into a small pile and hit repeatedly with wooden bats, some no more than a foot long, others nearer 2 feet (about 60 cm). Some resembled a short cricket bat; others had a round profile, more like a rounder's bat, or were square, like a big meat tenderizer. After five or six strikes much of the water, along with some of the dirt, was driven out. The pile was dipped into the stream again, and the process repeated, until the laundry was clean.

Two Welsh women beating clothes with a battledore at a common washing site along the bank of a river, as captured for *The Costume of Great Britain* (1861).

A number of probate inventories from Ipswich list laundry equipment, although it was often not considered necessary to include such cheap household items. They provide a snapshot of a variation in laundering practices that may well have been more common within Britain. In these inventories the wooden laundry bats, generally known as 'battledores' or 'beetles', were occasionally accompanied by 'washing blocks', sturdy contraptions much like a chopping block or perhaps a butcher's block. Having a washing block in the yard permitted a household to do their laundry in a more private environment, but it did require carrying water, sometimes across a long distance, and disposing of it afterwards. If the yard had both a well and a drain, gutter or other area where water could be disposed of, this probably required less effort than a trip to a common riverside washing place. Sailor Edward Barnes, who died in 1590, had listed among his belongings 'a washinge blocke' and 'a batledor' that would have been used to wash several other items in the inventory, including eleven pairs of bed sheets, six pillowcases, a couple of shirts, a collar, a tablecloth, six napkins, six towels, a dozen diaper napkins, two small diaper tablecloths, a hand towel and a cloth to cover the cupboard. (There were probably linens for other members of the family, but these were not inventoried at the time of his death.) Someone in the household spent a good deal of time in his yard with aching arms and a damp skirt.

Modern laundry

By the beginning of the seventeenth century there were signs of a more modern approach to laundry in several accounts. For example, the laundry room at Ingatestone Hall, in Essex, was equipped to handle a lot of laundry, in a sensible and efficient manner.

The inventory for the room listed a low bench to stand bucking tubs on, along with a shallow tub to stand under the tub's tap, a sieve for ashes and bucking cloths – everything needed to manufacture a supply of lye. It had four bucking tubs – enough to allow several batches of laundry to be soaking at the same time. There were two washing blocks and two beetles, indicating that laundry work in this household was not a solitary occupation, and indoor drying racks, which meant the work could continue whatever the weather. Three herring lines (a type of thin, strong cord used by fishermen that does not stretch unduly when wet) were available for hanging the laundry outdoors on fine days. But alongside all of this paraphernalia for laundering using lye and beating, there was also equipment for washing with the room's box of soap. Two large copper pots were used for heating water on the laundry room's fireplace, and a large washing bowl was available for sloshing about the household's finer garments in hot water and soap.

By 1698, the tide of laundry had changed. Parisian Francis Maximilian Misson was surprised to find that 'At London, and in all other Parts of the Country where they do not burn wood, they do not make Lye. All their linen, coarse and fine, is wash'd with Soap. When you are in a Place where the Linen can be rinc'd in any large Water, the Stink of the Black Soap is almost all clear'd away.'

White or black, soap required hot water to do the laundry; it was no longer possible to do the main part of the job in cold water. Soap was also a lot milder than lye, and thus unable to dissolve and dislodge body grease with just a few jugs of water poured through a pile of linen, as was the case with lye and a buck tub. Now, articles of clothing had to be completely immersed in hot, soapy water and beaten, scrubbed and agitated within the laundry tub. Only the rinsing could be done in cold water, and even then the effects were not very good. If you really wanted to get rid of the dirt, you needed hot, clean water. All of which involved a lot more fire and a lot more moving of water.

It is interesting to note that Misson complained of the 'stink' of London's black soap. He was accustomed to clothing washed with lye, which is much less odorous. In Britain the smell of soap soon became ubiquitous – and, as we'll see, imbued with a positive set of associations and meanings, closely bound up with modernity, urban living and affluence.

Reading the household manuals of the day, it is evident how quickly and thoroughly soap and hot water were adopted as the 'right' method for laundry in coal-burning districts. Londoner Hannah Woolley's *Gentlewomans Companion*, published in 1675, offered some of the first snippets of ordinary laundry advice in print. Washing and starching 'Tiffanies, Lawns, Points and Laces' was the responsibility of the chambermaid. When Woolley turned her attention to the laundry maids of the great houses, she urged them to rise early, mend everything before they began the wash and to be 'sparing of your soap, fire and candle'. They were also to keep their tubs and coppers clean and in good repair. Soap had plainly taken over from lye for the main wash.

In *At Sandpit Gate* by Paul Sandby (1752), a woman is shown washing fine garments by hand in a small basin.

Eliza Fowler Haywood's set of instructions for laundry gives us the fullest description of eighteenth-century laundry methods. Probably born in London, Haywood had a long and successful career as an actor and author mostly within the city, spending but a few shorter spells in Dublin. In her book she provided a couple of stain-removal recipes, then set out the steps for preparing the laundry water. 'Some people are so inconsiderate as to wash with Water when it first comes in', she whinged, 'which being always thick, and very often yellow, gives the linen a muddy cast.' This was truly a Londoner's advice, since by the time she was writing in 1743, somewhere around half of the capital's properties were connected to a piped water supply, albeit a frequently intermittent one.

The water came – unfiltered and often a bit muddy, hence the need to let it stand and settle before use – via three main suppliers. The New River Company controlled an aqueduct that supplied nearly two thirds of the metropolis, particularly in the north and east of the city. This was supplemented by a series of water wheels, originally installed by Peter Morris below London Bridge, which pumped water out of the Thames to city-centre customers as well as works built by the Chelsea Waterworks Company, which brought water to Westminster and other higher areas that the New River Company could not reach because of the low pressure of its supply. Having access to piped water naturally made washing at home much more convenient, and probably sounded the death knell for London's common washing places, regardless of whether people found soap or ash to be more suitable for their laundry.

Haywood spent a good deal of her time discussing the subject of soap. 'Be careful in chusing the oldest Soap you can, for that which is new made not only spoils the colour of the Linen, but also does not go so far,' she warned. This was because of the propensity for the chemical reactions to continue for a considerable length of time after the soap had cooled. The free alkali in new soaps was harder on the skin, and it yellowed white linens. New soap was also softer, and often dissolved much faster in hot water, so a laundress might accidentally use rather more than she needed.

Anticipating that many of her readers would have to use the same pots for laundry as they used for cooking, she reminded them to clean the pot very thoroughly before filling it with water and putting it on the fire. While the first batch of water heated, dry clothing was laid upon a board or table where the laundress was to 'rub them all well over with Soap, especially those places where you find much dirt'. The soaped clothes were dropped into a wooden washing tub and hot water ladled on top of them. Everything was then sloshed and slapped about in the water, dissolving and activating the soap. Each article of clothing was next lifted out separately and rubbed against itself. There was no mention of any sort of washboard or dolly at this date; instead, the cloth was rubbed together by hand. Then, the dirty water was thrown away and the process began again, starting with the cleanest and finest clothes and working towards the coarsest and dirtiest. 'If it is not very dirty, two lathers will suffice, but if it has been worn long, you must give it three,' she explained.

Having rubbed everything individually at least twice in two changes of soapy water, it was time to boil the linen. A fresh lot of water was brought up to the boil and a small load was again soaped – although less soap was needed at this stage – and a small portion of blue dye was added. This dye was essential if you wished your laundry to appear white at the end of the process. Soap, unlike lye, always yellowed cottons and linens, even if it was old soap. The blue dye did not take away this yellowing, but instead disguised it. (To this day 'optical brighteners' are used in modern laundry products for much the same purpose, giving the illusion of whiter whites.) While this mixture of soap, water, laundry and dye boiled over the fire, it was stirred and beaten until it seemed to be done, then the contents were poured out

Mrs Grosvenor, Laundry-Woman to the Queen, adds blue dye to her tub of washing (*c*. 1750–1800).

into the wooden tub to cool. Finally, everything was rinsed out thoroughly 'taking care that not the least smear of Soap remains', then wrung and hung upon lines to dry.

This is monstrously hard work – long and slow and very damaging to the hands. A poem published in 1739 gives us some sense of this. Mary Collier spent her life labouring in other people's homes, working well into her sixties. One of her employers heard her recite her verses and encouraged her to publish them. In 'The Woman's Labour' she described arriving before dawn to find 'Heaps of fine Linen we before us view, Whereon to lay our strength and Patience too'. After hours of heavy work her mistress finally appeared – not to help, but to pass on words of wisdom gleaned from some household manual similar to that of Eliza Haywood's: 'And there most strictly does of us require, To Save her Soap and Sparing be of Fire'. The day wore on:

> *Untill with Heat and Work, t'is often known,*
> *Not only Sweat, but Blood runs trickling down,*
> *Our wrists and fingers; still our Work demands,*
> *The constant Action of our lab'ring hands.*

Women's labour, never done

I have, for various reasons, spent a considerable amount of time maintaining domestic spaces with both a wood- and a coal-burning regime. I have experimented with cooking, cleaning, baking, brewing, dairying and laundering with both fuels over the past thirty years. It was this experience that first stimulated my interest in the revolution that took place as households made the big switch from wood to coal. But this experience also raised an issue about which I have found nothing in the historical record:

the increased workload. I believe there is vastly more domestic work involved in running a coal home in comparison to running a wood one. Although this is a personal observation, I am unaware of any discussion of the subject in period sources – and I have looked for such accounts quite determinedly.

In this instance, an absence of evidence is not evidence of absence. Maid servants and working-class housewives were rarely in a position to record their experiences, and the few precious voices we do have tend to be interested in other subjects, in particular religious and spiritual matters. Time, place and chance also conspire against our gaze. Mary Collier's poetry is a rare insight into a washerwoman's life. Unfortunately she was not comparing two competing approaches to laundry but reflecting upon the burden of the established system. She could not compare the work of soap laundry to lye because she had only ever known soap. So few testimonies of domestic practicalities have survived from any period that it is little surprise that none coincides with a household's participation in the big switch, or relates differing practices from one maid-of-all-work's youth and her old age.

The magnitude of silence leaves room for the question: Did the change from wood to coal increase the weight of the domestic burden?

Take laundry. I have gone through the full process for laundry using wood ash and lye, beating it all clean in streams and rivers as well as within tubs at home. I have also laundered clothes with soap and hot water, following the system employed in the mid- to late nineteenth century (using washing dollies rather than rubbing everything with my hands). I have washed large loads and small loads, linens, cottons and woollens, clothing, sheets and other household textiles. The old cold-water process is hard work – and often bitterly chilling – while the newer soap process is hard work – and hot and steamy. Neither is easy or pleasant. But I have found there to be a lot less work involved in the old process based on using ashes, lye and cold water. Most of all, it just takes less time.

'How are you off for soap?' a young woman is asked in this satirical political print from 1816 by William Elmes. She has a coal fire burning to boil her linens, with two other tubs of washing and another batch of laundry drying outside.

The difference primarily comes down to the amount of lifting and shifting you must do. Soap and water laundering uses much more water, all of which has to be carried to the fire, poured into washing coppers and tubs, then carried back out and poured off when you are finished. You generally need at least two changes of water for soaping and another two changes for rinsing. Lye, in contrast, being a stronger chemical that rinses out easily, requires just one tub of water for washing and one for rinsing. In addition, soap-based laundry requires your water to be hot, so fuel has to be carried to the fire too. At the end of your day, the laundry fire has to be raked out and soap scum removed from your tubs and coppers; if you leave it in situ, it can turn quite nasty and spoil your next wash. These extra tasks are unnecessary with ash and lye-based laundry. Given a choice between the two systems, and with no other constraints, I would probably choose to cold wash with lye all summer and put up with the additional work of using soap with hot water in the depths of winter.

Of course, few in the past were likely to have had such a choice. The price and availability of laundering ingredients and fuel probably forced the hands of most poorer families, while the wealthy – who could pick and choose – were not much interested in the opinions of the servants who actually did the work.

I have also found that the sticky smuts of coal smoke, along with the coal dust of unburnt fuel, make a home much, much dirtier than the wood-burning equivalents, either as raw fuel or by-products. It is not merely that the smuts and dust of coal are dirty in themselves. Coal smuts weld themselves to all other forms of dirt. Flies and other insects get entrapped in it, as does fluff from clothing and hair from people and animals. To thoroughly clear a room of cobwebs, fluff, dust, hair and mud in a simply furnished wood-burning home is the work of half an hour; to do so in a coal-burning home – and achieve a similar standard of cleanliness – takes twice as long, even when armed with soap, flannels and mops.

Unless you are willing to try some of this out for yourself, you may well have to choose whether to believe me or not. I can offer little in the way of independent evidence. There is undoubtedly a major rise in the number of young women employed as purely domestic servants as the era of coal-burning dawns. Sixteenth-century servant girls were expected to carry out a wide range of activities, many of them agricultural or craft-based, in addition to their domestic chores. Nineteenth-century servant girls were much more likely to be employed exclusively within the home: cooking, cleaning, doing the laundry and caring for children.

Household manuals chart a similar journey when outlining female duties for both mistresses and maids, with women's tasks gradually narrowing down over time to those contained within the walls of the home. Fitzherbert's *Boke of Husbandrie* (1523), for instance, allotted a couple of pages to the work of a housewife, mostly in a list of jobs that she needed to know how to perform. In addition to cooking, cleaning, laundry and childcare, he included gardening, brewing, baking, dairying, raising poultry and pigs, milking cows, preparing flax, spinning thread – both flax and wool – taking grain to the miller, malting barley, winnowing wheat, making hay, doing the family shopping, selling on her dairy and poultry produce and sewing the family underwear. In between these tasks, she was to help her husband filling the muck wagon, driving the plough and reaping the corn. This is a daunting list, to be sure, but it also suggests that relatively little time in the average woman's day was devoted to activities encompassed by the modern concept of 'housework'. And much of the average housewife's work overlapped with her husband's.

By the eighteenth and nineteenth centuries, household manuals included far less agricultural work among the wife's responsibilities. For example, William Ellis, the agricultural journalist from the Chilterns, reported that the wives, daughters and servant maids of farmers and agricultural labourers did a good deal of dairy work and typically looked after the poultry yard. They also did the cooking, cleaning, laundry and needlework (and the childcare, although he barely noted this). However, work in the fields was not part of these women's daily routine. Plenty of agricultural work was, of course, being done by women – but as paid labour, not as part of the domestic role of wife or daughter.

This raises a question about the increasing emphasis upon women's place being within the home. Did the philosophy of 'separate spheres' for men and women, which defined much of life in the Victorian period, initially grow out of practical realities? There are many erudite historical gender studies that talk about elite and middle-class women 'retreating' into the home in this period, with a corresponding change in attitudes about the roles of men and women. And many historians discuss the social pressures on women to focus their attentions and energies upon a smaller range of domestic activities and duties. But I wonder if the additional demands

'Miseries of Human Life' clearly included cleaning a coal-fired home.
The woman responsible for the cleaning was up 'early in a cold gloomy
morning', the 'carpet tossed backward – floor newly washed', and
surrounded by brooms, brushes, mops, pails and fire furniture.

of running a coal-fired household might have also helped to push
the idea that a woman's place is within the home. If I am right
and there was significantly more work involved in maintaining
domestic cleanliness after the switch from wood to coal, then there
may well have been a practical pressure for women to prioritize
domestic tasks centred around the hearth at the expense of other
activities – be they in the garden, the poultry yard or further
from home.

Naturally, those at the bottom of the social structure had less
choice in the matter. The provision of food for the family always
took priority over a clean shirt or a sticky floor. If indeed the
domestic burden rose, then for many poorer people, the swap to
coal must have translated into dirtier living conditions. Perhaps
the divide between those who could meet the additional domestic
burdens and those who could not became wider and more marked,

dividing the population more visibly into a 'respectable' elite and 'the great unwashed'.

Cleanliness asserts itself as a powerful class marker throughout the eighteenth and nineteenth centuries. In the same period there was a rising division in labour between the sexes. Was the shift to coal the spur to both of these cultural phenomena? The historical record is not definitive, but the experience of cleaning was forever changed.

The cleaning industry

It is rather significant that soap manufacture entered the realm of politics in the early seventeenth century. Just at the moment when domestic demand began to seriously rise in the crucible of London, soap was a topic of controversy.

During their reigns, Queen Elizabeth and her successor, James I, enthusiastically granted protected monopolies to commercial concerns through letters patent. The common goal of these grants was to stimulate invention and raise cash for the Crown, but the details of each case varied enormously. Some arrangements exempted the patentee from certain laws; others granted the right to suppress similar commodities. Local guilds were often cut out of the negotiations in favour of the preferences of courtiers. In the case of soap industry, the grant-making process exposed a division in how people viewed the market potential for this new product.

When the soap monopoly was first proposed in 1623, it was the emerging market of household users that the prospective patentees had in mind, not the industrial usage. They claimed they had invented a new process that required only British pot ash to make a hard white soap. Companies that imported ash from Denmark and areas of the Baltic were offered large amounts of money to buy their acquiescence, but London's old soap-boilers resisted. In an attempt to sway the debate, one of the main backers of the scheme, Sir John Bourchier, staged a public trial of the new and old styles of soap – what might be considered the earliest laundry detergent trial. Bourchier's soap came out the victor and the Crown granted the monopoly in London, banning the old soap-making method of using train oil. When the patent failed to make enough profit, the new soap-boilers negotiated a deal whereby they – and only they – could use train oil to make soap. A long, confusing battle ensued, but eventually the old soap-boilers prevailed, regaining the monopoly. After that, they set out to drive their competition in Bristol out of business.

The fight over the use of train oil and the nature of the public trial reveal how the new household use of soap was to outstrip the old industrial use of soap and had in fact already done so within the minds of the governing elite. Bourchier and his fellow promoters of the new soap had observed the rise in soap usage in their own establishments. They were able to persuade the Crown to back them based upon laundry evidence – not industrial evidence – because so many royal and aristocratic households were using more soap too. To the eyes of the rich, powerful elite of London, soap was the future of good housekeeping.

The furore over London's soap monopoly was felt globally. For the first time, the dominance of the continental soap-making centres was truly challenged. The vigorous and expanding market for soap in Britain encouraged investment and experimentation with alternative ingredients. Throughout the seventeenth and eighteenth centuries, Britain was the site of an almost continuous procession of small adjustments, refinements, efficiencies and developments in the industry, with the country shifting from being a major importer of soap to be a major exporter of it. In quantity and in quality, home-grown manufacture was beginning to outstrip continental output, so that by the nineteenth century, Britain dominated the global soap-making industry.

From this point forward, many of the most significant scientific leaps in soap manufacture were put into production in Britain. The chemist Nicolas Leblanc, for example, devised a way of making the first non-organic supply of alkali, freeing the soap industry from the need to use ash of one plant or another. In Leblanc's method, salt reacted with strong sulphuric acid to produce sodium sulphate, which was then heated with coal and lime to create sodium carbonate. Unable to find suitable backing in his native France, he found business partners in Britain in 1823. An American called Hamilton Young Castner came to England in 1886 looking for backers for a process he had discovered that would help to push the soap industry yet another step ahead. Castner had found that placing a mercury cathode in brine caused salt water to split into caustic soda, chlorine and hydrogen. An Austrian by the name of Carl Kellner had patented a similar, though less efficient, process a few years before, and the two men went into business together in Runcorn, in the midst of Cheshire's ample rock salt reserves. These technical developments gave the soap industry an enormous boost by significantly reducing the cost of alkalis. In their first year in business, the Castner–Kellner Alkali Company were contracted to receive up to 10,000 gallons (45,000 litres) of brine per day to produce 6,300 tonnes of pure caustic soda and 13,500 tonnes of chlorine-based bleaching powder for soap production.

The large-scale production of these chemicals out of cheap and readily available raw materials was transformative to both the soap industry and the larger chemical industry in Britain. Once again, domestic practice inspired industrial progress.

'Soap is civilization'

As domestic coal-burning spread out from London across the country, soap followed, and alongside these two practical changes came a modern concept: urban, civilized living. We have already seen how coal-burning arrived in new locations outside London first in the homes of the wealthy and those with strong London connections. Early adopters outside the capital were swayed by considerations such as the lower price and easy storage, but also by positive, aspirational associations. They considered coal to be a modern solution to fuelling a modern home. London living was at the forefront of fashionable living, and London living meant coal and soap.

Soap, in particular, was beginning to be presented as an indicator of civilized living, upward mobility and industriousness. This mark of status was helped, of course, by the fact that soap was relatively expensive. Although increased international trade and technological breakthroughs did conspire to bring down the price of imported and locally produced soaps, British manufacturers increasingly aimed to raise the quality of their product and, in turn, raise their profits. The taxes imposed on imports of soap and related ingredients were also high. Soap had its price, and there were plenty of people who struggled to afford it as well as their food, rent and clothing.

Those at the bottom of the social heap were forced to make choices. A china cup upon the mantelpiece might represent a humbler family's interest in a genteel style of living, but it could also be dismissed as a one-off acquisition, made in a moment of fleeting prosperity. The regular smell of soap about the home or laundry spoke of a family who were consistently holding their heads above water over the medium or long term. Soap displayed social status and security.

In the late seventeenth and early eighteenth centuries, outward displays above your station in life, whether through your clothing or household goods, were often deemed to be an overturning of the natural social order – and a road to ruin. Consider the innumerable versions of the popular subject 'the high life below stairs', where servants made free with their master's goods. Their indulgence in tea and fancy clothing was depicted alongside sexual laxity, drunkenness and ugly poor health, moral failures commingled. A servant who used soap, however, received no such disapproving comment. Indeed, soap use was seen as virtuous and industrious.

Starting from the sixteenth century, the housekeeping guides written by elite mistresses were packed with precepts of good morals, order, behaviour, method and cleanliness, which the mistresses' maid servants were supposed to take up. Domestic service was often envisaged as a positive means of informing and improving the lives of the lower classes by allowing them to spend their formative years in the homes of their social 'betters'. Eliza Fowler Haywood's *Present for a Servant-Maid* (1743) and Mary Johnson's *Madam Johnson's Present* (1753) were dominated by moral guidance; the practical advice in both treatises accounted for less than 10 per cent of the content and was printed at the end of the text, almost as an afterthought. These were teaching aids. When former serving maids and aspiring tradespeople adopted the cleaning practices of the wealthy, it was seen as a proper upholding of the social order.

The link between clean linen shirts, smocks, cuffs and collars and a person's moral worth can be traced in literature back to the sixteenth century. By the eighteenth century it was the standard shorthand by which an author hoped to gain an upper-class audience's sympathy for lower-class characters. In *Moll Flanders* (1722), Daniel Defoe presented his central character, Moll, as an unusually clean young woman who bathes often and is scrupulous about the care and cleanliness of her clothing. Samuel Richardson's eponymous heroine in *Pamela* (1740) was described as being 'so neat, so clean, so pretty' and declared of herself that, 'tho' ordinary, I am as clean as a penny'. Both of these women were said to be from very humble backgrounds, finding their adventurous way through a moral morass, and yet for all their exotic beginnings and scandalous exploits their cleanliness reassured upper-class readers that they were part of 'our world'. The homes of 'good' characters might be damp and broken down, but they were always well-swept, and the laundry was always whiter than white. 'Bad' characters lived in filth and squalor. These novels naturally reflected the prevailing social attitudes and realisms, but they also helped to cultivate them. Soap, cleanliness, order and morality were more and more closely bound together in the culture and the marketplace.

Despite the high rate of tax, the price of soap eventually began to drop in real terms. In 1600 white Castile soap, you may remember, retailed at 6*d* a pound; in 1833, it was still selling at 6*d* a pound – even after taxes and two centuries' of general price inflation. In 1600 you could have bought six loaves of bread for the price of a pound of soap; in 1833 you would have got not much more than half a loaf.

When Robert Montgomery Martin published his political and economic discussion *Taxation of the British Empire* in 1833–4, he argued that soap was a commodity 'of essential importance to the cleanliness and comfort of the people'. He may well have been entirely unaware that there were effective alternatives for cleaning available and still in daily use in those remote pockets where the waterways and railways were not yet delivering cheap coal. In any case, his figures were certainly based upon the premise that everyone needed soap. He calculated that in 1811 sufficient hard white soap had been sold through legitimate, taxed means for every man, woman and child in Britain to have 132 ounces (3.75 kg) per year. Sales had risen threefold by 1822, but by 1831 they had fallen back to the 1811 level. Such wildly fluctuating figures he put down to widespread smuggling.

Since taxes typically made up more than two thirds of the overall price of a bar of soap, large-scale smuggling had become endemic. Martin believed that pretty much all existing forms of taxation ought to be abolished. He used the case of soap to bolster his argument, saying that soap provision in 1831 was less than what might be allotted to inmates of workhouses. People needed around four times this amount, he asserted, to keep their laundry and homes clean.

Neither Martin nor anyone else at this date thought soap was essential for body-washing. This was two decades before the widespread acceptance of the 'germ theory'. But as more and more people took on board the mounting evidence that disease was the result of tiny organisms invisible to the naked eye, soap use gained another rationale: it maintained good health.

Cleanliness had always been seen as a pathway to vim and vigour. Florence Nightingale's hugely influential work *Notes on Nursing* (1859), for example, was little more than a paean to the importance of cleanliness, based entirely upon old ideas of hygiene with no mention whatsoever of the discovery of 'germs'. Like those before her, she primarily viewed cleanliness as a method of banishing dangerous, disease-laden odours and airs. But just as her book hit the printer's, lay people were hearing all about germs, and they eagerly went to war against these tiny new creatures hiding in the corners, nooks and crannies of their homes. The traditional value of scrupulous cleanliness was given fresh validity.

While the housekeepers went to work, the medical profession, in the main, dithered for over half a century. Many ignored, denied or ridiculed the scientific evidence for the existence of bacteria and their role in causing sickness, since doing so was a direct attack upon their knowledge and authority. Housewives saw the same information, repackaged in mainstream publications, as a continuation of centuries of practical advice.

It is important here to note how inextricably soap and hygiene were linked up in the popular psyche. The truly big leaps forward in public health were the provision of clean water and the rapid separation of human waste from human living spaces. It's a story of the triumph of two great life savers – piped water and public drains – not of soap. But from the start, soap has piggy-backed its way into our ideas of sound hygiene. Of course, soap does make some difference to death rates within hospitals, where hand-washing has been accepted as an essential procedure; and hand-washing in ordinary life does reduce infection rates. But as we have seen, most forms of cleaning, including effective hand-washing, can be achieved with other substances and methods.

Fuller's earth and water (or olive oil, if you have very dry skin) mixed to a paste does a very good job of thoroughly cleaning the hands, especially if you add a drop of lemon juice. The paste removes grease and dirt down to a microscopic level, and the light acidity of the lemon juice makes life very difficult for many harmful bacteria. Laundry that has been soaked in lye, beaten in cold water and then dried out in the sunlight is just as hygienically clean as that which has been washed in hot water with soap, and lye's high pH can be more effective at sterilizing textiles than soap, which is more pH neutral. In fact, the new soap-laundering system relied upon boiling the wash to sterilize fabrics. To make laundry soap more hygienic, it is sometimes mixed with an antiseptic agent. From 1894 onwards, carbolic acid was added to Lifeguard soap for this reason, and tea tree oil is widely used today.

But by the time bacteria were recognized as agents of disease, soap had ceased to be seen as one option for cleanliness: it was the *only* option for cleanliness. For this reason, the fight against germs was waged in terms of soap. The message 'Health comes from cleanliness' poured forth from the scientific community; the message 'Cleanliness comes from soap' was the British addition – taken up far and wide.

'Lightening the white man's burden'

If the eighteenth century saw soap emerge as a cultural status symbol, a necessity for the productive and forward-thinking people of the new 'middle class', the nineteenth century saw concerted attempts to spread that same set of beliefs and practices ever wider. The most visible manifestation of this development can be seen in the advertising of the late Victorian era. One advert, published in Britain in the late 1880s and early 1890s,

Pears' Soap advertisement 'The Birth of Civilization', as it appeared in *The Graphic*, 30 April 1890.

carried the title 'The Birth of Civilization'. It depicted a crate, washed up on an exotic shore, that was broken open to reveal bars of Pears' Soap, the gentle, translucent body soap concocted by Andrew Pears eighty years earlier. A dark-skinned man of rather ambiguous racial background clutched a spear in one hand and a bar of Pears' Soap in the other, captioned by the mantra: 'The consumption of soap is a measure of the wealth, civilization, health and purity of the people'.

The advert was aimed squarely at increasing sales in the British market by encouraging those at the bottom of society to see themselves as part of a superior class of people. Soap use was now a signifier of not just modernity and upwards social mobility but also national and racial superiority. A soap user was a member of the global elite. Very soon similar advertising was being deployed across English-speaking parts of the world, as soap companies looked to expand in markets throughout the US, Canada, Australia and New Zealand, as well as among the English-speaking administrators, soldiers, traders and settlers in every corner of the British Empire. One Pears' advert from 1899 brashly set down the line of thought, declaring: 'The first step towards lightening The White Man's Burden is through teaching the virtues of cleanliness. Pears' Soap is a potent factor in brightening the dark corners of the earth as civilization advances, while amongst the cultured of all nations it holds the highest place.'

Pears' Soap was not the only offender. Brooke's Monkey Brand soap advertised along very similar lines once it was in the British ownership of the Lever Brothers, based at Port Sunlight, near Liverpool. (Initially an American company, it was taken over in 1899.) The company were not shy about using the soap's monkey logo as a demeaning stand-in for black people of all backgrounds. Other soap manufacturers may have been more subtle, but the central theme remained the same: those wishing to move 'forward' towards civilization and modernity were soap users.

An 1899 advertisement for Brooke's Monkey Brand soap included testimonials from *The Lancet* and the *British Medical Journal,* suggesting that soap was scientifically hygienic – though neither quote actually spoke of medical benefits.

Advice aimed at prospective missionaries exhorted them to introduce soap as part of their 'civilizing' endeavours. In 1913 a Canadian missionary called Murdoch Mackenzie reported back from China: 'Some houses are saturated with deadly germs and need the gospel of soap and water, light and fresh air. Cleanliness, as well as godliness, is profitable for the life that is now, in Honan as elsewhere.' China, like most of the world through the early twentieth century, continued to employ ash as a degreasing agent alongside a range of clays and beans (particularly *Gleditsia sinensis,* the honey locust plant), utilizing brooms, brushes, cloths to clean.

Soap – which appears to have been invented independently in China some time around AD 900 – was also in use, but it was a minor element. This was of course an ancient civilization, one that prized cleanliness for spiritual, cultural and practical purposes. But despite twenty-five years' living in China, Mackenzie seems to have been blinkered to this. The idea that soap was morally and physically superior to every other method of cleaning was firmly embedded in the Western mind. This signalled a total rejection of the efficacy of alternative cleanliness regimes that, only a few centuries earlier, had been the norm across Britain.

He was not alone in his beliefs, nor would he be alone now. The modern belief in soap remains very strong. Anyone questioning the necessity of soap in the West today is likely to get a scolding at some point. Cleaning with soap has become an article of faith – almost as Mackenzie phrased it, a 'gospel'. Science may well confirm that giving your chopping board a good scrub under a stream of scalding hot water is a highly effective method of killing bacteria as well as removing any matter that might permit further bacteria to multiply, but most people brought up in mainstream Western culture are extremely nervous if you suggest it is okay to skip the washing-up liquid.

As patronizing and disrespectful as these advertisements were, the message that soap routines were superior routines was received, loud and clear. Early accounts by journalists and Western travellers made passing neutral or positive references to the local use of various fats, oils and clays for cleaning, but these faded away from the record after the middle of the nineteenth century. Many scholars investigating issues of race and colonialism point to soap manufacturers' advertising as a central method through which colonizers asserted cultural domination over the colonized. For example, according to American sociologist Zine Magubane, little comment was made by the British about the 'dirtiness' of native South Africans before around 1870, with the association growing more frequent as soap adverts became widespread.

Similarly, Anandi Ramamurthy, reader in post-colonial studies at Sheffield Hallam University, sees soap adverts as 'a form of cultural production that permeates every aspect of ... lives', even being used as a form of justification for the occupation of colonies. Colonial masters increasingly argued that their conquest, control and governance benefited the people under their control. By bringing soap and civilization, they were improving the lot of the locals, even if the locals clearly didn't like it much. And in the late nineteenth century and early twentieth centuries, soap use was embraced in a wave of almost crusading zeal. Korean scholar Hye Ryoung Kil argues that in this period, in particular, soap was an effective weapon in the ideological struggle to define superiority based on race.

We live in a world cleaned according to methods and principles that were hammered out in the seventeenth century, by a generation of Londoners who made a largely economic decision to switch to coal as their daily fuel. Their coal use led to the rise of soap. Together, coal and soap forged a new way of living, with new patterns of domestic expectations, gender divisions and class prejudices. When Britain exported these ideas throughout the Empire, the concept of soap as a mark of social and societal superiority was seeded and planted around the globe. In some places, coal and soap followed conquest and colonization; in other places, the influence of a seemingly successful and confident nation was sufficient to alter people's perceptions and practices.

CONCLUSION

Our Past is Our Present

Those who look at our planet's biggest problems and seek to map out the future have been telling us for some time that the small individual choices we each make – about what to buy, what to throw away and which of the world's resources to consume and which to preserve – are important. Every plastic bag counts, they tell us; every puff of smoke, every burst of methane. Our daily living practices and domestic habits hold the power to transform the world.

We can look to history to see the truth in this. The households who in the late sixteenth century switched to domestic coal-burning did so for a variety of reasons. They were influenced by economic advantages, practical improvements and the quest for status. Few of them imagined that their switch from wood to coal would ripple in a myriad of directions across Britain's landscape and then the globe, bringing a series of technological and cultural changes with it. But their individual choices, in aggregate, did change life for centuries, and continue to do so.

The adoption of coal within the home was largely responsible for the decline in Britain's managed heathland, the near demise of wood pasture, the loss of many hedgerow trees and the draining of many fens. What had once been important and useful landscapes became 'waste'. As people stopped cutting the furze and ling, tree seedlings invaded and, growing unchecked, once open heathlands evolved into scrubby, dense woodland. Many areas were newly ploughed up as the demand for organic fuel fell and the pressure to supply food for cities grew. Ancient wood pasture all but vanished, surviving only in tiny fragments here and there, mostly within deer parks and stately, landscaped gardens. The nature of hedgerows changed almost overnight in those districts where coal arrived. Tenants with coal fires no longer had any need for the fuel-producing trees around their fields and came to view them as a nuisance drawing light, water and nutrients away from their crops. And out upon the moors and fens, the switch to coal put an end to most peat-digging for fuel. These lands suddenly offered a rather meagre return for landowners and tenants, and drainage schemes became far more attractive.

The medieval managed landscape was of course no more 'natural' than the modern one is. But the switch to coal altered the balance significantly, away from a wide mix of uses towards a more uniform, cash-crop agriculture. When certain plants were used for fuel as well as food and livestock grazing, a greater variety of plant communities were nurtured. Commoners valued their rights of access much less when those rights no longer provided their daily fuel, and they became more willing to accept deals in favour of eventual enclosure – taking cash and small parcels of 'better' land in exchange for their access to ancient shared resources.

Criss-crossing this new landscape were transport routes and supply lines that received much of their early boost from the bulk trade in coal for the home. Although often overlooked, the first great domestically driven expansion in coal haulage by land and by water, both inland and at sea, strengthened trade routes and encouraged investment in seventeenth-century Britain. Seamen trained upon the coal run from Newcastle to London provided skilled and semi-skilled labour for the rapidly expanding Royal Navy and the tougher mercantile routes across the Atlantic. The Newcastle run made ship-building more economically worthwhile, reducing the financial risks involved in a once volatile trade. Inland waterways became busier, with schemes to improve docks, dredge sections of river and introduce locks being discussed in earnest within a few decades of the domestic coal switch. Road improvements followed too.

Rising up in thin columns above this increasingly connected land was the smoke of coal fires channelled through thousands of custom-built chimneys. Urban pressures upon living space in sixteenth-century London had already stimulated the erection of some chimneys and the insertion of upper floors into smoke-free roof spaces, but coal fires accelerated the process. Within a generation, more modern-shaped, multi-roomed homes were appearing. Life within the four walls of these modern homes was changing as well. Cooking pots took on a new shape, and a larger range of iron fire furniture and utensils were developed to meet the unique challenges of coal fires. Rising demand for these domestic tools led to greater experimentation and innovation, spurring advances in bronze-, brass- and especially ironmaking. In discovering new methods for casting the iron pots suitable for a coal fire, the clever and ambitious entrepreneurs at Coalbrookdale unwittingly unlocked the key to massive industrial expansion: much cheaper iron made a whole host of other processes economically viable.

When owners and inventors in industry after industry began to see the potential for growth that came with coal, they did so in part because this fuel was much more visible and much more available than it had been a century earlier. Domestic use had raised coal's profile, as people learnt how to manage and exploit it in the home. Those who experimented with coal in furnaces, kilns, fireboxes and engines did so from a position of personal experience, the famous though probably apocryphal story of James Watt gaining inspiration for his steam engine from witnessing a kettle boil being a colourful example. Coal, as we have seen, was not an easy fuel to burn. It required coaxing. People knew they had to devise ways to harness its potential. Chimneys, flues, iron grates and plates were constantly tweaked and readjusted to maximize their efficiency and their ability to redirect heat and smoke. Everyone who dealt with coal – whether a cook juggling pots in a great house kitchen, an engineer hunkered over a patented machine or a bachelor shivering in rented lodgings – had learnt that coal responded in widely different ways to different handling, but if you did it right, it provided a hot and steady energy source. The domestic coal revolution was not the sole foundation of the Industrial Revolution, but it was a significant factor. It prepared the ground and greased the wheels.

British cuisine gradually adapted to the idiosyncrasies of coal. First boiled food and then baked dishes rose to prominence, ousting the older, more European styles of recipe. Porridges, pottages and frumenties retreated to the remote peat-burning fringes, where they held on as regional oddities. Spotted dick, steak and kidney pudding and boiled beef and carrots took their place as favourites. Roasted meats retained only their name as coal encouraged a shift towards baking meat and potatoes. And toast began its inexorable rise as the staple of informal cooking, with home-baking raised to a national virtue.

Throughout the rest of the home, coal was encouraging the adoption and proliferation of wipeable surfaces and cheaper, replaceable floor and wall coverings. Paints, varnishes, oilcloths and wallpapers replaced the tapestries, wall hangings and rushes of earlier times. Cleanliness could be maintained in a coal-burning home – but at the expense of old-fashioned insulative layers.

Soap's great rise as both an industry and a philosophy probably also owes its origins to the domestic switch to coal. The arrival of coal in the home deprived people of access to large quantities of the traditional grease-cutting chemicals found in wood ash, forcing them to turn to soap for this. Then coal created dirtier, stickier, greasier clothes and homes, which needed more soap to keep clean. To work well, soap needed hot water – heated over even more coal. It was an interdependent cycle.

With the switch to coal and soap happening first in London, and with early adopters among both the social elite and the poor, it is not surprising that from a very early date, soap and social status began to be intertwined. London was the centre of British society, no matter what class you came from; countless servant maids from great households left their coal-fired kitchens to set up households of their own. To their eyes, other methods looked outdated, provincial and inferior. The philosophy of soap proved to be both more powerful and more long-lasting than many a technological or economic surge, particularly once it was exported around the globe, from Nairobi to Mexico City, Singapore to Seattle.

A single generation or two of Londoners, living between 1570 and 1600, made the big switch. They surely gave little if any thought to the long-term consequences of this private, household decision. They didn't set out to be global soap supporters, or to invent a wallpaper industry. They didn't intend for the trees to be thinned from the hedgerows, or to create a nation of toast lovers. But they did. These changes were driven, bit by bit, by the 'hidden people' of history. The voiceless, the unregarded and uncelebrated, they have constituted a vast army of practical, unintentional radicals. Many of them were women, operating primarily within the domestic sphere. Together they laid the foundations of industrial expansion and shaped the nature of Britain's cultural impact worldwide.

Ordinary people's decisions have, through history, proved to be a powerful force. The demands of domestic life set into motion a range of new realities. As the cook down in the basement kitchen piled on the coal to form an easy-to-manage towering inferno in the grate, she not only increased the demand for coal but brought into being a new mindset that equated additional energy use with ever more ease. The lesson at every hearth was the same: burn more coal and life becomes softer, warmer, more predictable and more comfortable. Energy is there for the taking. Having more energy no longer means having less food. In a coal-powered home, the more fuel you used, the more modern and convenient your life was.

The domestic matters. It is the base unit upon which all else is built. The history of the domestic is the history of everything: how ordinary people choose to lead their lives dictates the future of mankind. Politicians come and go, ideologies wax and wane, but the practical details of how you warm your house or do your washing-up will, added up with the actions of your neighbours and their neighbours, reach into the longer term. Your heating and washing-up habits don't simply use a few resources or add a touch of pollution. Nor do they merely favour some industries over others. They also create a mindset that will touch future generations and shape their decisions.

The domestic past charts how we have changed the world before. The domestic present has the power to change it right now.

ACKNOWLEDGEMENTS

There are so many people who have helped in one way or another with this book, sharing a passion for fires, food, housework and history. Many more have put up with me spouting forth on these subjects for years. But I really owe a particular debt to Eleanor Lowe, Jacqueline Warren, Paul Hargreaves, Mark Goodman, Katherine Adams, Natalie Stewart, Karl Robinson, Joan Garlick, Shona Rutherford, Paul Binns, Jon Emmett, Adrian Braddock, James Biddlecombe, Cathy Flowerbond, Jo Briffet, Hannah Miller and the late Paula Senior who have tended fires, fermented urine, beaten the living daylights out of laundry, and searched through countless original records alongside me.

I owe a debt of thanks to the Weald and Downland Museum, who have allowed me to practise and experiment over many years in their fabulous buildings, gardens and woodlands and to their staff and volunteers who have donned their aprons and joined in the messy work. I am in debt too to Lord Manners for letting me loose upon the fires, ovens and service spaces at Haddon Hall, to the Mary Rose Trust, The National Trust, Sulgrave Manor, St Fagans National Museum of History, Avoncroft Museum of Buildings, Chiltern Open Air Museum, John Moore Museum, The Weaver's House Spon End, who have all given me the opportunity to cook and clean, make charcoal and chop wood in the historic structures under their care.

My thanks too to the staff at Cheshire, Buckinghamshire, Essex, Devon, Hertfordshire, Staffordshire and Derbyshire Record Offices who have been unfailingly helpful and patient.

I must also thank – and you should too – the wonderful team at Michael O'Mara books who have helped to haul my ungainly mess of writing into some sort of shape. If there are any good bits that seem to make sense and flow nicely that is all down to them, any remaining chaos is all my own fault. In particular I would like to thank Fiona Slater, Robin Dennis and Gabriella Nemeth for mammoth word wrestling, Aubrey Smith for his lovely illustrations and Judith Palmer for her invaluable picture research.

Finally I would like to thank Mark and Eve for many, many interesting and supportive conversations and Ben for putting up with them all.

LIST OF
ILLUSTRATIONS

Page 47 'Charcoal Burning', woodcut from *De la pirotechnia* by Vannoccio Biringuccio (1540). Courtesy of the Smithsonian Libraries

Page 49 How pollarding works. Illustration by Emma Jolly / Woodland Trust Media Library

Page 52 Figure 2.1, photo of hedge tree map, © Tom Williamson (2017), from *Trees of England* by Tom Williamson, Gerry Barnes and Toby Pillatt, (2007). Reproduced with permission of University of Hertfordshire Press and Norfolk Record Office

3. The Draw of Coal

Page 60 A simple basket grate. Illustration by Aubrey Smith

Page 61 Capel Garmon firedog. Photograph reproduced with permission of the National Museum of Wales

Page 70 Detail from *The River of Tyne Leading from the Sea*, etching by Wenceslaus Hollar (1651). Credit: © The Trustees of the British Museum. All rights reserved, Q,6.125

Page 74 Detail from Agas map, sheet 10, showing part of Southwark, London Bridge, River Thames, part of the City of London and the Tower of London (1561). Credit: Heritage Image Partnership Ltd / Alamy Stock Photo

Page 75 Photograph by Tom Kent of the kitchen at Kirbuster Farm, Birsay, Orkney (*c.* 1900). Reproduced with permission of the Orkney Library and Archives, Kirkwall, Orkney. Image negative: TK2227

Page 76 Interior of the Weaver's House, Spon End, Coventry. Illustration by Aubrey Smith

Page 78 A smoke hood. Illustration by Aubrey Smith

4. London, Transformed

Page 90 Detail from Treswell survey of Giltspur Street and Cock Lane, Christ's Hospital Evidence Book, 1611. Courtesy of Christ's Hospital. Credit: *The London Surveys of Ralph Treswell* by John Schofield (ed.), photos by Godfrey New, London Topographical Society (1987) and London Metropolitan Archives, City of London CLC/210/G/A/004/MS12805

Page 92 Detail from *Long View of London from Bankside*, Sheet VI, after the etching by Wenceslaus Hollar (1647). Credit: Yale Center for British Art, Paul Mellon Collection

Page 96 'Small Coale', engraving by Marcellus Laroon from *The Cryes*

5. The Spreading Blaze

6. Cooks' Tools

7. A New Menu

8. Cleaning-Up

9. The Domestic Burden

BIBLIOGRAPHY

Introduction

Cavert, William M. 2016. *The Smoke of London: Energy and Environment in the Early Modern City*. Cambridge: Cambridge University Press.

Hatcher, John. 1993. *The History of the British Coal Industry: Volume 1 – Before 1700*. Oxford: Oxford University Press.

Nef, John Ulric. 1932. *The Rise of the British Coal Industry*. London: George Routledge & Sons.

Wrigley, Edward Anthony. 2010. *Energy and the English Industrial Revolution*. Cambridge: Cambridge University Press.

1. Living off the Land

Bealer, Alex W. 1984. *The Art of Blacksmithing*, rev. ed. New York: Harper & Row.

Broadberry, Stephen, Bruce M. S. Campbell and Bas van Leeuwen. 2010. 'English Medieval Population: Reconciling Time Series and Cross Sectional Evidence'. Leverhulme Trust ref. F/00215AR.

Day, Anthony. 1999. *Fuel from the Fens: The Fenland Turf History*. Seaford: SB Publications.

Earl, Derek E. 1975. *Forest Energy and Economic Development*. Oxford: Clarendon Press.

Fiennes, Celia. 1949. *The Journeys of Celia Fiennes*, ed. by Christopher Morris. London: Cresset Press.

Lambert, Joyce M., Joseph Newell Jennings *et al.* 1960. *The Making of the Broads: A Reconsideration of their Origins in the Light of New Evidence*. London: John Murray.

Meriton, George. 1697. *A York-Shire Dialogue*. s.l.: s.n.

Moxon, Joseph. 1677. *Mechanick Exercises, or The Doctrine of Handy Works*. London: s.n.

Norden, John. 1607. *The Surveyors Dialogue*. London: s.n.

O'Sullivan, Humphrey. 1936. *The Diary of Humphrey O'Sullivan*, ed. and trans. by Michael McGrath. London: Simpkin, Marshall Ltd for the Irish Texts Society.

Piercy, Frederick Hawkins. 1853–5. *The Route from Liverpool to Great Salt Lake Valley*. Liverpool: Franklin D. Richards.

Rotherham, Ian D. 2011. *Peat and Peat Cutting*. London: Shire Publications.

Tusser, Thomas. 1580. *Five Hundred Points of Good Husbandry Together with a Book of Huswifery*. London: s.n.

Walker, Revd Dr John. 1803. 'An Essay on Peat', *Prize Essays and Transactions of the Highland Society of Scotland*, vol. 2.

Williamson, Tom. 1997. *The Norfolk Broads: A Landscape History*. Manchester: Manchester University Press.

2. Out of the Woods

Aberth, John. 2013. *An Environmental History of the Middle Ages: The Crucible of Nature*. Oxford: Routledge.

Bailey, Mark. 2010. *Medieval Suffolk: An Economic and Social History, 1200–1500*. Martlesham, Suffolk: Boydell & Brewer.

Blagrave, Joseph. 1675. *The Epitome of the Art of Husbandry*. London: Benjamin Billingsley.

Cleere, Henry, and David Crossley with Bernard Worssam *et al.* 1985. *The Iron Industry of the Weald*. Cardiff: Merton Priory Press.

Cook, Moses. 1676. *On the Manner of Raising, Ordering and Improving Forrest-Trees*. London: Peter Parker.

Evelyn, John. 1661. *Fumifugium, or The Inconvenience of the Aer and Smoak of London Dissipated*. London: s.n.

——. 1664. *Sylva, or A Discourse of Forest-Trees and the Propagation of Timber*. London: John Martyn for the Royal Society.

Fitzherbert, John [or Sir Anthony]. 1523. *Boke of Husbandrie*. London: s.n.

——. 1598. *This Ryghte Profytable Boke of Husbandry*. London: s.n.

Gray, Todd, ed. 1995. *Devon Household Accounts, 1627–59, Part I: Sir Richard and Lady Lucy Reynell of Forde House, 1627–43, John Willoughby of Leyhill, 1644–6, and Sir Edward Wise of Sydenham, 1656–9*. Exeter: Devon and Cornwall Record Society.

——. 1996. *Devon Household Accounts, 1627–59, Part II: Henry, Earl of Bath, and Rachel, Countess of Bath, of Tawstock and London, 1639–54*. Exeter: Devon and Cornwall Record Society.

Havinden, M. A., ed. 1965. *Household and Farm Inventories in Oxfordshire 1550–1590*. London: Her Majesty's Stationery Office.

Månsson, Peder. 1530. *Art of Glassmaking*. s.l.: s.n.

Marsden, Peter, ed. 2009. *Your Noblest Shippe: Anatomy of a Tudor Warship. The Archaeology of the* Mary Rose: *Volume 2*. Chapter 9 'The Galley'. Christopher Dobbs. Portsmouth: The Mary Rose Trust.

Moore, N. W. 1962. 'The Heaths of Dorset and Their Conservation'. *Journal of Ecology* 50(2): 369–91, doi: 10.2307/2257449.

Nicholas, J. G., ed. 1852. *Chronicle of the Grey Friars of London – Camden Society Old Series: Volume 53*. London: Camden Society.

Rackham, Oliver. 1986. *The History of the Countryside*. London: J. M. Dent.

Richardson, Catherine, and Mark Merry, eds. 2012. *The Household Account Book of Sir Thomas Puckering of Warwick, 1620: Living in London and the Midlands: With His Probate Inventory, 1637*. Stratford upon Avon: Dugdale Society.

Williamson, Tom, Gerry Barnes and Toby Pillatt. 2017. *Trees in England: Management and Disease Since 1600*. Hatfield: University of Hertfordshire Press.

3. The Draw of Coal

Chandler, John, ed. 1993. *John Leland's Itinerary: Travels in Tudor England*. Stroud: A. Sutton Publishing.

Evelyn, John. 1661. *Fumifugium, or The Inconvenience of the Aer and Smoak of London Dissipated*. London: s.n.

Galloway, James A., Derek Keene and Margaret Murphy. 1996. 'Fuelling the City: Production and Distribution of Firewood and Fuel in London's Region 1290–1400'. *Economic History Review* 49(3): 447–72, doi: 10.2307/2597759.

Harrison, William. 1577. *An Historical Description of the Island of Britain*. London: s.n.

Hatcher, John. 1993. *The History of the British Coal Industry: Volume 1 – Before 1700*. Oxford: Oxford University Press.

Owen, George. 1603. *The Description of Pembrokeshire*. London: s.n.

Pearson, Sarah. 1996. *The Medieval Houses of Kent: An Historical Analysis*. London: Royal Commission on Historical Monuments.

Prior, Mary. 1981. 'The Accounts of Thomas West of Wallingford, a Sixteenth-Century Trader on the Thames'. *Oxoniensia* 46: 73–93.

Quiney, Anthony. 1990. *The Traditional Buildings of England*. London: Thames and Hudson.

Riley, Henry T., ed. 1861. *Liber Albus: The White Book of the City of London*. London: Richard Griffin and Co.

Schofield, John. 1995. *Medieval London Houses*. New Haven, CT and London: Yale University Press.

4. London, Transformed

Cavert, William M. 2016. *The Smoke of London: Energy and Environment in the Early Modern City*. Cambridge: Cambridge University Press.

———. 2017. 'Industrial Coal Consumption in Early Modern London'. *Urban History* 44(3): 424–43, doi: 10.1017/S0963926815000991

Chandler, John, ed. 1993. *John Leland's Itinerary: Travels in Tudor England*. Stroud, Glouc.: A. Sutton Publishing.

Court of Orphans, City of London. 1623. Orphans' Inventories, [1600]–1773, CLA/002/02/0003. London: Guildhall.

Gray, Todd. 1996. *Devon Household Accounts, 1627–59, Part II: Henry, Earl of Bath, and Rachel, Countess of Bath, of Tawstock and London, 1639–54*. Exeter: Devon and Cornwall Record Society.

Harrison, William. 1587. *The Description of England*. London: s.n.

Hatcher, John. 1993. *The History of the British Coal Industry: Volume 1 – Before 1700*. Oxford: Oxford University Press.

Herridge, D. M., ed. 2005. *Surrey Probate Inventories 1558–1603*. Woking: Surrey Record Society.

Munby, Lionel, ed. 1986. *Early Stuart Household Accounts*. Hertford: Hertfordshire Record Society.

Reed, Michael, ed. 1988. *Buckinghamshire Probate Inventories 1661–1774*. Aylesbury: Buckinghamshire Record Office.

Richardson, Catherine, and Mark Merry, eds. 2012. *The Household Account Book of Sir Thomas Puckering of Warwick, 1620: Living in London and the Midlands: With His Probate Inventory, 1637*. Stratford upon Avon: Dugdale Society.

Schofield, John, ed. 1987. *The London Surveys of Ralph Treswell*. London: London Topographical Society.

Schofield, John. 1995. *Medieval London Houses*. New Haven and London: Yale University Press.

Vries, Jan de. 2008. *The Industrious Revolution: Consumer Behavior and the Household Economy, 1650 to the Present*. Cambridge: Cambridge University Press.

5. A Spreading Blaze

Agricola, Georgius. 1950 (1556). *De re metallica*, trans. and ed. by Herbert Clark Hoover and Lou Henry Hoover. New York: Dover Publications.

Brinkworth, and J. W. S. Gibson, eds. 1976. *Banbury Wills and Inventories, Part 2, 1621–1650*. Banbury: Banbury Historical Society.

Biringuccio, Vannoccio. 1942 (1540). *De la pirotechnia*, trans. and ed. by Martha Teach Gnudi and Cyril Stanley Smith. Cambridge, MA and London: MIT Press.

Brayshay, Mark. 2014. *Land Travel and Communications in Tudor and Stuart England: Achieving a Joined-up Realm*. Liverpool: Liverpool University Press.

Camden, William. 1600. *Britannia*. London: George Bishop and John Norton.

Chandler, John, ed. 1993. *John Leland's Itinerary: Travels in Tudor England*. Stroud: A. Sutton Publishing.

Clavering, Eric. 1994. 'Coalmills in Tyne and Wear Collieries: The Use of the Waterwheel for Mine Drainage 1600–1750'. *Bulletin of the Peak Mines Historical Society: Mining before Powder* 12(3): 124–32.

Collingwood, W. G., ed. 1987. *Elizabethan Keswick: Extracts from the Original Account Books, 1564–1577, of the German Miners, in the Archives of Augsburg*. Whitehaven, Cumbria: Michael Moon.

Cox, Nancy. 1990. 'Imagination and Innovation of an Industrial Pioneer: The First Abraham Darby'. *Industrial Archaeology Review* 12(2): 127–44, doi: 10.1179/iar.1990.12.2.127

Day, Joan. 1973. *Bristol Brass: A History of the Industry*. Newton Abbot, Devon: David & Charles.

Friel, Ian. 2009. 'Elizabethan Merchant Ships and Shipbuilding'. Museum of London, 29 Sep 2009. Transcript available at: http://www.greshan.ac.uk [accessed 20 Jun 2018].

Gibson, J. W. S., ed. 1977. *Banbury Corporation Records: Tudor and Stuart*. Banbury: Banbury Historical Society.

——. 1985. *Banbury Wills and Inventories, Part 1, 1591–1620*. Banbury: Banbury Historical Society.

Harrison, William. 1587. *The Description of England*. London: s.n.

Hartley, Robert F. 1994. 'The Tudor Miners of Coleorton, Leicestershire'. *Bulletin of the Peak Mines Historical Society: Mining before Powder* 12(3): 91–101.

Hatcher, John. 1993. *The History of the British Coal Industry: Volume 1 – Before 1700*. Oxford: Oxford University Press.

Havinden, M. A., ed. 1965. *Household and Farm Inventories in Oxfordshire 1550–1590*. London: Her Majesty's Stationery Office.

Hollister-Short, Graham. 1994. 'The First Half-Century of the Rod Engine (c.1540–1600)'. *Bulletin of the Peak Mines Historical Society: Mining before Powder* 12(3): 83–90.

Kayll, Robert. 1615. *The Trades Increase*. London: Nicholas Okes.

Moore, John S., ed. 1976. *The Goods and Chattels of Our Forefathers: Frampton Cotterell and District Probate Inventories, 1539–1804.* Chichester: Phillimore and Co.

Nef, John Ulric. 1932. *The Rise of the British Coal Industry.* London: George Routledge & Sons.

Owen, Colin. 1984. *The Leicestershire and South Derbyshire Coalfield 1200–1900.* Ashbourne: Moorland Publishing for Leicestershire Museums.

Reed, Michael A., ed. 1981. *The Ipswich Probate Inventories, 1583–1631.* Suffolk: Boydell Press for the Suffolk Record Society.

Rees, Ronald. 2008. *The Black Mystery: Coal-Mining in South-West Wales.* Talybont, Ceredigion, Wales: Y Lolfa.

Trinder, Barrie. 1974. *The Darbys of Coalbrookdale.* Chichester: Phillimore and Co.

Webb, John, ed. 1966. *Poor Relief in Elizabethan Ipswich.* Suffolk: Suffolk Record Society.

——.1996. *The Town Finances of Elizabethan Ipswich.* Martlesham, Suffolk: Boydell & Brewer.

Williams, Richard. 2015. 'A Question of Grey or White? Why Abraham Darby I Chose to Smelt Iron with Coke'. *Historical Metallurgy* 47(2): 125–37.

6. Cooks' Tools

Bailey, Nathan. 1736. *Dictionarium Domesticum, Being a New and Compleat Household Dictionary, for the Use of City and Country.* London: C. Hitch; C. Davis.

Beeton, Isabella. 1861. *The Book of Household Management.* London: S. O. Beeton.

Byng, John. 1996. *Rides Round Britain,* ed. by Donald Adamson. London: Folio Society.

Davies, Margaret Llewelyn, ed. 1931. *Life as We Have Known It: By Co-operative Working Women.* London: Hogarth Press.

Edmondstone, Eliza. 1856. *Sketches and Tales of the Shetland Islands.* Edinburgh: Sutherland and Knox.

Ellis, William. 1750. *The Country Housewife's Family Companion; or, Profitable Directions for Whatever Relates to the Management of the Domestic Concerns of a Country Life.* London: s.n.

Fiennes, Celia. 1949. *The Journeys of Celia Fiennes,* ed. by Christopher Morris. London: Cresset Press.

Francatelli, Charles Elmé. 1852. *A Plain Cookery Book for the Working Classes.* London: s.n.

Gardiner, Julie, with Michael J. Allen, eds. 2005. *Before the Mast: Life Aboard the* Mary Rose. Portsmouth: The Mary Rose Trust.

Herridge, D. M., ed. 2005. *Surrey Probate Inventories 1558–1603*. Woking: Surrey Record Society.

Hieatt, Constance B., and Sharon Butler, eds. 1985. *Curye on Inglysch: English Culinary Manuscripts of the Fourteenth Century*. Oxford: Oxford University Press.

Jenkins, Robert Thomas. 1972 (1928). *Hanes Cymru yn y Ddeunawfed Ganrif.* Cardiff: Gwasg Prifysgol Cymru.

Leadbetter, Mary. 1811. *Cottage Dialogues among the Irish Peasantry*. London: J. Johnson & Co.

Lehmann, Gilly. 2003. *The British Housewife. Cookery Books, Cooking and Society in Eighteenth-Century Britain*. Totnes: Prospect Books.

MacNeill, F. Marian. 1929. *The Scots Kitchen: Its Traditions and Lore, with Old-Time Recipes*. Glasgow: Blackie & Son Ltd.

Markham, Gervase. 1615. *The English Hus-Wife: Contayning, the Inward and Outward Vertues Which Ought to Be in a Compleat Woman*. London: John Beale.

May, Robert. 1660. *The Accomplisht Cooke; or, The Art and Mystery of Cookery*. London: Nathaniel Brooke.

Moryson, Fynes. 1617. *An Itinerary*. London: s.n.

Royal Commission on Land in Wales and Monmouthshire. 1896. *The Welsh Land Commission: A Digest of Its Report*. London: Whittaker & Co.

Smith, Eliza. 1727. *The Compleat Housewife; or, Accomplished Gentlewoman's Companion*. London: s.n.

——. 1758. *The Compleat Housewife; or, Accomplished Gentlewoman's Companion*, 16th ed. London: s.n.

Swift, Jonathan. 1745. *Directions to Servants*. London: R. Dodsley; M. Cooper.

Varenne de La, François Pierre. 1651. *The French Cook*, trans. by J. D. G. London: s.n.

7. A New Menu

anon. 1500. *The Boke of Cokery*. London: Pynson.

anon. 1545 (1577). *A Proper Newe Booke of Cokerye*. London: s.n.

anon. 1588. *The Good Hous-Wives Treasurie or Book of Cookrye*. London: Edward Allde.

anon. (W. M.). 1655. *The Queen's Closet Opened*. London: Nathaniel Brook.

anon. 1677. *The Compleat Servant-Maid; or, The Young Maidens Tutor*. London: s.n.

Bibliography

anon. 1869. *The Indian Cookery Book: A Practical Handbook to the Kitchen in India*. Calcutta: Wyman & Co.

Barnes, A. R., 1890. *The 'Colonial Household Guide'*. Capetown: Darter Bros. & Walton.

Blackman, M. E., ed. 1977. *Ashley House Building Accounts 1602–7*. Guildford: Surrey Record Society.

J.J. Cartwright, ed. 1888. *The Travels Through England of Dr Richard Pococke* vol.1 Camden Society, Second Series 42.

Cobbett, Anne. 1835. *The English Housekeeper; or, Manual of Domestic Management*, etc. London: s.n.

Craig, Elizabeth. 1936. *Cookery Illustrated and Household Management*. London: Odhams Press.

David, Elizabeth. 1977. *English Bread and Yeast Cookery*. London: Penguin Press.

Dawson, Thomas. 1597. *The Second Part of the Good Hus-Wives Jewell*. London: E. Allde.

Duckitt, Hildagonda J. 1891. *Hilda's 'Where Is It?' of Recipes*. London: Chapman and Hall.

——. 1902. *Hilda's Diary of a Cape Housekeeper*. London: Chapman and Hall.

Ellis, William. 1750. *The Country Housewife's Family Companion; or, Profitable Directions for Whatever Relates to the Management of the Domestic Concerns of a Country Life*. London: s.n.

Everleigh, David J. 2009. 'Cast Iron Progress – The Development of the Kitchen Range'. In Ivan P. Day, ed. *Over a Red-Hot Stove. Essays in Early Cooking Technology*. Totnes: Prospect Books, pp. 19–53.

Farey, John Jr. In *General View of the Agriculture of Derbyshire*, 1813 vol. 2 and also quoted in Everleigh, David J. *'Cast Iron Progress'* within *Over a Red-Hot Stove*, Ivan Day, ed. 2009. London: Prospect Books.

Fettiplace, Elynor. 1999. *The Complete Receipt Book of Ladie Elynor Fetiplace*, vol. 3, ed. by Stuart Peachey. Bristol: Stuart Press.

Francatelli, Charles Elmé. 1852. *A Plain Cookery Book for the Working Classes*. London: s.n.

Loudon, J. C. 1831. *An Encyclopaedia of Agriculture*. London: Longman, Rees, Orme, Brown, and Green.

Markham, Gervase. 1615. *The English Hus-Wife: Contayning, the Inward and Outward Vertues Which Ought to Be in a Compleat Woman*. London: John Beale.

Misson de Valbourg, Henri. 1719. *Memoirs and Observations in His Travels over England*, trans. by Ozell. London: D. Browne; A. Bell; J. Darby; et al.

Murrell, John. 1615. *A New Booke of Cookerie*. London: John Browne.

Orwell, George. 1946. 'British Cookery'. Unpublished essay commissioned by the British Council. Transcript available at: https://www.orwellfoundation.com/the-orwell-foundation/orwell/essays-and-other-works/british-cookery [accessed 30 Oct 2019].

Robinson, Thomas, patent range advertisement in John Johnson Collection of Printed Ephemera, Bodleian Library, University of Oxford

Soyer, Alexis. 1854. *A Shilling Cookery for the People: Embracing an Entirely New System of Plain Cookery, and Domestic Economy*. London: George Routledge & Co.

Spurling, Hilary. 1986. *Elinor Fettiplace's Receipt Book: Elizabethan Country House Cooking*. London: Penguin Books.

Swift, Jonathan. 1745. *Directions to Servants*. London: R. Dodsley; M. Cooper.

Trinder, Barrie, and Jeff Cox, eds. 1980. *Yeomen and Colliers in Telford*. Chichester: Phillimore and Co.

Trinder, Barrie, and Nancy Cox, eds. 2000. *Miners and Mariners of the Severn Gorge*. Chichester: Phillimore and Co.

Woolley, Hannah. 1675. *The Gentlewomans Companion; or, A Guide to the Female Sex*. London: A. Maxwell.

8. Cleaning-Up

anon. 1604. Inventory of Nicholas Wynn, Stockport Probate Records. Record Society of Lancashire and Cheshire, Liverpool.

anon. 1606. Accounts of Ingatestone Hall, D/DP/E2/1-25. Essex Record Office, Chelmsford.

Adams, Simon, ed. 1995. *Household Accounts and Disbursement Books of Robert Dudley, Earl of Leicester*. Cambridge: Press Syndicate of the University of Cambridge.

Batho, G. R., ed. 1962. *The Household Papers of Henry Percy, Ninth Earl of Northumberland*. London: Royal Historical Society.

Beeton, Isabella. 1861. *The Book of Household Management*. London: S. O. Beeton.

Braithwaite, Richard. 1621. *Some Rules and Orders for the Government of the House of an Earle*. London: s.n.

Browne, Anthony-Maria (2nd Viscount Montagu). 1919. 'Household Book'. In: Sir William St. John Hope, ed. *Cowdray and Easebourne Priory in the County of Sussex*. London: *Country Life*, pp. 119–34.

Campbell, Thomas P., 2007. *Henry VIII and the Art of Majesty: Tapestries at the Tudor Court*. New Haven, CT and London: Yale University Press.

Cockayne, Emily. 2007. *Hubbub: Filth, Noise and Stench in England*. New Haven, CT and London: Yale University Press.

Bibliography

Craig, Elizabeth. 1936. *Cookery Illustrated and Household Management*. London: Odhams Press.

Davidson, Caroline. 1982. *A Woman's Work is Never Done: A History of Housework in the British Isles 1650–1950*. London: Chatto & Windus.

Evelyn, John. 1661. *Fumifugium, or The Inconvenience of the Aer and Smoak of London Dissipated*. London: s.n.

Fussell, George Edwin, and Kathleen Rosemary Fussell. 1953. *The English Countrywoman*. London: Andrew Melrose.

Gataker, Thomas. 1638. *A Funerall Sermon on Acts 7 ver. 59 Preached at the Enterrement of the Remaines of Mr's Joice Featly*. London: Elizabeth Purslowe.

Gerard, John. 1597. *The Herball or Generall Historie of Plantes*. London: s.n.

Glasse, Hannah. 1760. *The Servant's Directory; or, House-Keeper's Companion*. London: s.n.

Hamilton, Jean. 1983. *An Introduction to Wallpaper*. London: Her Majesty's Stationery Office.

Hardyment, Christina, ed. 1987. *The Housekeeping Book of Susanna Whatman*. London: Century Hutchinson.

Harrison, William. 1587. *The Description of England*. London: s.n.

Johnson, Mary. 1753. *Madam Johnson's Present; or Every Young Woman's Companion in Useful and Universal Knowledge*. London: H. Jeffery.

Markham, Gervase. 1615. *The English Hus-Wife: Contayning, the Inward and Outward Vertues Which Ought to Be in a Compleat Woman*. London: John Beale.

Matthews, Harold Evan, ed. 1940. *Proceedings, Minutes and Enrolments of the Company of Soapmakers 1562–1642*. Bristol: Bristol Record Society.

Mortimer, Thomas. 1763. *The Universal Director; or, The Nobleman and Gentleman's True Guide to the Masters and Professors, etc.* London: s.n.

Richardson, R. C. 2010. *Household Servants in Early Modern England*. Manchester: Manchester University Press.

Ruscelli, Girolamo [Alexis of Piemont].1560. *The Secretes of Maister Alexis of Piemont*. s.l.: s.n.

Sachs, Hans, with illus. by Jost Amman. 1568. *Das Ständebuch*. Nuremberg: s.n.

Saussure, César de. 1902. *A Foreign View of England in the Reigns of George I and George II: The Letters of Monsieur César de Saussure to His Family*, ed. by van Muyden. London: John Murray.

Scott-Moncrieff, Robert, ed. 1911. *The Household Book of Lady Grisell Baillie 1692–1733*. Edinburgh: Edinburgh University Press for the Scottish History Society.

Smith, Eliza. 1758. *The Compleat Housewife; or, Accomplished Gentlewoman's Companion*, 16th ed. London: s.n.

Smith, John. 1676. *The Art of Painting; Wherein is Included the Whole Art of Vulgar Painting*. London: Samuel Crouch; *et al.*

Steedman, Carolyn. 2009. *Labours Lost: Domestic Service and the Making of Modern England*. Cambridge: Cambridge University Press.

Stow, John. 1598. *A Survey of London*. London: s.n.

———. 1633. *A Survey of the Cities of London and Westminster*, ed. by John Strype. London: A. Churchill; J. Knapton; R. Knaplock; *et al.*

Swift, Jonathan. 1745. *Directions to Servants*. London: R. Dodsley; M. Cooper.

Taylor, Clare. 2018. *The Design, Production and Reception of Eighteenth-Century Wallpaper in Britain*. Oxford: Routledge.

Tusser, Thomas. 1580. *Five Hundred Points of Good Husbandry Together with a Book of Huswifery*. London: s.n.

Vickery, Amanda. 2009. *Behind Closed Doors: At Home in Georgian England*. New Haven, CT and London.: Yale University Press.

Williams, J. D. 1992. 'The Noble Household as a Unit of Consumption: The Audley End Experience 1765–1797'. *Essex Archaeology and History* 23: 67–78.

9. The Domestic Burden

anon. 1869. *The Indian Cookery Book: A Practical Handbook to the Kitchen in India*. Calcutta: Wyman & Co.

anon. 1890. 'The Baptist Manual for Missionaries to the Congo'. s.l.: s.n.

Barnes, A. R. 1890. *The Colonial Household Guide*. Capetown: Darter Bros. & Walton.

Collier, Mary. 1739. *The Woman's Labour: An Epistle to Mr. Stephen Duck; in Answer to His Late Poem, Called The Thresher's Labour*. London: J. Roberts.

Defoe, Daniel. 1722. *The Fortunes and Misfortunes of the Famous Moll Flanders*. London: s.n.

Dietz, Brian, ed. 1972. *The Port and Trade of Early Elizabethan London: Documents*. London: London Record Society.

Duckitt, Hildagonda J. 1891. *Hilda's 'Where Is It?' of Recipes*. London: Chapman and Hall.

Fitzherbert, John [or Sir Anthony]. 1523. *Boke of Husbandrie*. London: s.n.

Harrison, William. 1587. *The Description of England*. London: s.n.

Haywood, Eliza Fowler. 1743. *A Present for a Servant-Maid; or, The Sure Means of Gaining Love and Esteem*. Dublin: George Faulkner.

Johnson, Mary. 1753. *Madam Johnson's Present; or Every Young Woman's Companion in Useful and Universal Knowledge*. London: H. Jeffery.

Kil, Hye Ryoung. 2010. 'Soap Advertisements and *Ulysses*: The Brooke's

Monkey Brand Ad and the Capital Couple'. *James Joyce Quarterly* 47(3): 417–26.

Mackenzie, Murdoch. *c.* 1913. *Twenty-Five Years in Honan.* Toronto: Board of Foreign Missions, Presbyterian Church in Canada.

Magubane, Zine. 2004. *Bringing the Empire Home: Race, Class, and Gender in Britain and Colonial South Africa.* Chicago: University of Chicago.

Martin, Robert Montgomery. 1833–4. *Taxation of the British Empire.* London: E. Wilson.

Mascall, Leonard. 1583. *A Profitable Boke Declaring Divers Approved Remedies, to Take Out Spottes and Staines.* London: s.n.

Miller, David Philip. 2004. 'True Myths: James Watt's Kettle, His Condenser, and His Chemistry'. *History of Science* 42: 333–60.

Misson de Valbourg, Francis Maximilian [or Henri]. 1719. *Memoirs and Observations in His Travels over England,* trans. by Ozell. London: D. Browne; A. Bell; J. Darby; *et al.*

Nightingale, Florence. 1859. *Notes on Nursing: What It Is and What It Is Not.* London: Harrison.

Penny, Norman, ed. 2014. *The Household Account Book of Sarah Fell of Swarthmoor Hall.* Cambridge: Cambridge University Press.

Ramamurthy, Anandi. 2003. *Imperial Persuaders: Images of Africa and Asia in British Advertising.* Manchester: Manchester University Press.

Richardson, Samuel. 1740. *Pamela; or, Virtue Rewarded.* London: C. Rivington; J. Osborn.

Sarasua, Carmen. 2007. 'The "Hardest and Most Unpleasant" Profession: The Work of Laundresses in Eighteenth-, Nineteenth- and Twentieth-Century Spain'. In: José A. Piqueras and Vicent Sanz Rozalén. *A Social History of Spanish Labour: New Perspectives on Class, Politics and Gender,* trans. by Paul Edgar. New York: Berghahn Books, pp. 64–91.

Shakespeare, William. 1602. *The Merry Wives of Windsor.* s.l.: s.n.

Smith, Arthur H. 1918. *A Manual for Young Missionaries to China.* Shanghai: Christian Literature Publishing House.

Stanley, Liz, ed. 1984. *The Diaries of Hannah Cullwick: Victorian Maidservant.* Tiptree, Essex: Anchor Brendon Ltd.

Taylor, Joseph. 2009 (1703). *A Journey to Edenborough in Scotland.* s.l.: Dabney Press.

Tucker, Josiah. 1749. *A Brief Essay on the Advantages and Disadvantages, Which Respectively Attend France and Great Britain, With Regard to Trade.* London: s.n.

Vanes, Jane, ed. 1979. *Documents Illustrating the Overseas Trade of Bristol in the Sixteenth Century.* Bristol: Bristol Record Society.

Woolley, Hannah. 1675. *The Gentlewomans Companion; or, A Guide to the Female Sex.* London: A. Maxwell.

INDEX

Page numbers in *italic* refer to illustrations.